Becoming a
LEARNING
SYSTEM

Becoming a LEARNING SYSTEM

BY
Stephanie Hirsh,
Kay Psencik, and
Frederick Brown

learningforward

Printed in the United States of America
Item #B576
ISBN: 978-0-9903158-0-3

Reference citation:
Hirsh, S., Psencik, K., & Brown, F. (2014). *Becoming a learning system*. Oxford, OH: Learning Forward.

This publication was produced by Learning Forward with support from the MetLife Foundation.

Learning Forward
504 S. Locust St.
Oxford, OH 45056
513-523-6029
800-727-7288
Fax: 513-523-0638
Email: office@learningforward.org
www.learningforward.org

About MetLife Foundation
MetLife Foundation is committed to building a secure future for individuals and communities worldwide through a focus on empowering older adults, preparing young people, and building livable communities. In education, MetLife Foundation seeks to strengthen public schools through effective teaching and collaborative leadership, and to prepare students for access to and success in higher education, particularly during the crucial first year. The foundation's grant making is informed by findings from the annual *MetLife Survey of the American Teacher*. More information is available at www.metlife.org.

Becoming a Learning System
Developmental editor: Valerie von Frank
Project manager: Valerie von Frank
Cover & design: Kate Hawley
Production: Three Pages Publishing Services
Vignettes in Chapters 5-24 are as told to Valerie von Frank

"As the world becomes more interconnected and business becomes more complex and dynamic, work must become more 'learningful.' It is no longer sufficient to have one person learning for the organization, a Ford or a Sloan or a Watson. It's just not possible any longer to 'figure it out' from the top, and have everyone else following the orders of the 'grand strategist.' The organizations that will truly excel in the future will be the organizations that discover how to tap people's commitment and capacity to learn at all levels in an organization."

—Peter Senge, *The Fifth Discipline: The Art & Practice of the Learning Organization* (2000, p. 4)

Contents

SECTION I: **BELIEFS AND VISION**

SECTION II: **ROLES AND RESPONSIBILITIES**

SECTION III: **BUILDING THE LEARNING SYSTEM**

Tools online

Tools online

Tools online

All tools can be found online at http://learningforward.org/publications/learning-system-tools
For access, use password SystemHPB14.

Acknowledgments

Learning Forward's position is that school-based professional learning is the most effective process for ensuring that adult learning affects student learning positively. As Joellen Killion states in *Becoming a Learning School*, "The concept of school-based professional development recognizes that the school is the primary center of learning and that teachers can often learn best with and from one another" (2009, p. 8).

Becoming a Learning School inspired many educators to develop learning schools and systems. This remarkable work, written by Killion and Patricia Roy, was a joint effort between the Office of Academic and Professional Standards at the New Jersey Department of Education and Learning Forward. The book, inspired by Victoria Duff and Eileen Aviss-Spedding, former New Jersey Department of Education staff members, has been used successfully throughout the country and internationally to help schools develop purposeful, effective learning organizations.

Becoming a Learning School's success, and the knowledge that schools exist within systems and that systems play a fundamental role in promoting learning at the school, inspired us to write *Becoming a Learning System*. In addition, research

by Robert J. Marzano and Timothy Waters (2009) affirms the role of district-level leaders in school success and student achievement. Research supported by The Wallace Foundation and conducted by the University of Washington's Center for Educational Leadership and Meredith I. Honig resulted in recommendations that district leaders transform themselves into the kind of models of service and support that teachers need (2013). Learning Forward's vision of a learning system and district leaders' roles in such systems is developed in *Becoming a Learning System*.

We believe that if appropriately applied, the ideas and strategies promoted in *Becoming a Learning System* will result in an organization that is experiencing and modeling high-quality professional learning—professional learning that is long term, sustained, and standards driven; grounded in a cycle of continuous improvement; and capable of inspiring all to take responsibility for the learning of every adult and student in the organization.

We are most grateful to A. Richardson Love, with the MetLife Foundation, for his understanding of the importance of professional learning and his support for this book. MetLife Foundation is a valued partner and we are grateful for its sustained commitment to Learning Forward's learning school agenda.

We have been so honored to partner in this work with Fort Wayne (Ind.) Community Schools. Fort Wayne is the largest school district in Indiana, serving 30,980 students, of whom more than 70% are eligible for free and reduced-price lunch. Fort Wayne educators are convinced that professional learning is central to their continued success. The system includes many who are models of true learning leaders.

Fort Wayne Superintendent Wendy Robinson, chief learner, is deeply respected for her advocacy and leadership. She is a model superintendent and one from whom others who are or aspire to be superintendents can learn much.

We are also grateful to members of the district leadership team, who are working collaboratively to develop a learning system and who courageously take what they are learning and apply it to the work they are doing with principals and school leadership teams. Laura Cain, Ramona Coleman, and Todd Cummings have been particularly integral to leading learning in the district and modeling a learning community. We are grateful to them for the partnership we have developed together and for allowing us to tell their story. They are learners who work collaboratively with other district leaders and never lose sight of their moral purpose to educate every child to high standards.

We want to acknowledge Security Innovation Network for producing a moving video about Fort Wayne Community Schools and its journey toward becoming a learning system. The video offers a perspective of what leaders say and do in learning communities and learning systems.

We are indebted to Valerie von Frank, who had the monumental task of taking the writings of three different writers, making sense out of our work, and producing this book. She is amazing, patient, and kind, as well as a highly skilled editor. Without her intensive work and care for this project, *Becoming a Learning System* would still be a dream. The production team at Three Pages Publishing Services deserves praise for their careful consideration of every aspect of production, their flexibility, and their constant attention to the smallest details, all of which are critical to creating a quality final product.

We also want to thank Terry Morganti Fisher and Victoria Duff for their brilliant expertise and contribution to the learning tools that support the work outlined in this book.

The three of us acknowledge that the work we do could not be accomplished without the loving support of our families. Thanks to their cheerleading, forgoing time with us, and taking the lead with home responsibilities, we have been able to concentrate on the challenging task of writing. We love them and thank them for partnering with us in this endeavor.

Foreword

Nothing will change unless everything changes. In the arena of school improvement, this statement rings especially true.

As school districts have faced increasingly high expectations and heard ever louder demands for improvements that will lead to higher student achievement, the responsibility for improvement has fallen squarely on teachers' shoulders. State and school district officials have planned what teachers must do to implement reform initiatives, yet seldom have they looked to themselves for needed change.

If schools are expected to produce better results for students, the school district as a whole and its leaders—school board members, superintendents, central office administrators, principals, and teacher leaders—must heed lessons from systems change research that remind practitioners they must change the component systems in order to change the system as a whole. School districts, regardless of size, are complex, with multiple interrelated component systems: human capital, data, curriculum, instruction, assessment, support services, parents and community members, governance, and budget and finance. The success of any change depends on leaders' ability to examine, analyze, and orchestrate changes within components of the whole system to achieve different results.

Leaders must be ready to thoughtfully, critically, and analytically examine their current practices and make essential modifications that support deep and sustained implementation of learning initiatives. Only when district leaders commit to this level of work will schools be able to meet the expectation that they will increase educator effectiveness and, in turn, improve student learning.

In other words, schools are able to succeed only when they have support from the central office. When educators strive to refine their efforts to improve student achievement, their efforts must be embedded in a culture of continuous improvement and supported by systems and structures that afford them the resources, tools, and learning needed to meet their goals.

Sustainable organizational change requires building a shared vision and values among partners; developing skillful and committed leaders; engaging stakeholders in planning, making decisions about, implementing, and adapting new practices; understanding the landscape within which the change is occurring; building staff members' capacity; and strengthening the organizational infrastructure.

Authors Stephanie Hirsh, Kay Psencik, and Frederick Brown have applied their wisdom and expertise—and Learning Forward's wealth of resources related to achieving educator effectiveness and student success—to writing this book. They offer strategies educators can use to leverage professional learning to create meaningful change.

Becoming a Learning System is a companion to *Becoming a Learning School* (NSDC, 2009) and focuses on the critical dimension of a school district's role in improving teaching so that more students learn at higher levels. It is based on the same principles as those featured in the earlier book:

- Learning is at the heart of every change.
- Leaders and leadership matter.
- Continuous improvement requires focused action.
- Student success is a collective responsibility.

The authors strategically build on the premise that leaders must strengthen adult learning in order to succeed with any change initiative. They examine the role of district leaders in creating and carrying out a vision of continuous improvement for the entire system. They ground their writing in research and practice to create a useful resource that will allow leaders to plan, implement, and evaluate professional learning.

As this book demonstrates, when teacher change is accompanied by changes in principals' practices and support from central offices and state agencies, students are more likely to succeed.

Introduction

We have many good schools throughout North America. In too many cases, however, children go each day to a school that is not very good. Even more unfortunate is the fact that two students who are very alike can attend different schools within the *same school district* and achieve very different outcomes.

Every child deserves to graduate high school ready for a career or college. Every child needs the knowledge and skills to pursue his or her goals and reach his or her potential. Every child should be prepared to participate in a democratic and civil society. To accomplish this vision, we need to ensure that every child attends an excellent school.

For all students to attend great schools, we need school districts that are *learning systems*. At Learning Forward, we believe this goal is attainable; however, reaching it requires that all school districts, as well as all schools, focus more intently on learning. We need both learning schools *and* learning systems.

In learning systems, all educators commit to continuous learning and to applying that learning to their own and others' performance. Educators at the district and school levels share responsibility for their own learning and for ensuring great teaching for every student every day.

In learning systems, individuals understand their role in and responsibility for helping the district achieve its vision, mission, goals, and objectives. In learning systems, educators at every level of the organization share responsibility for student and adult learning, dedicate themselves to continuous improvement, use data to drive decisions, and monitor and adjust their practices based on feedback.

Learning Forward has dedicated the last 20 years to thinking about and studying great teaching, and to designing and creating resources and tools to help and support district leaders in their role as learning leaders. The clearest examples of the organization's efforts to support learning systems are Learning Forward's Standards for Professional Learning, definition of professional learning, and Innovation Configuration maps for district employees.

This book is based on Learning Forward's definition of professional learning and Standards for Professional Learning, which together offer district leaders a framework to guide daily decisions that promote continuous improvement. The book outlines the knowledge, skills, attitudes, dispositions, and behaviors district leaders need in order to lead, facilitate, and coach school leaders and leadership teams to embed the definition and standards into educators' daily routines.

The tools and strategies that accompany the definition and Standards can guide district staff in establishing principal learning communities, monitoring implementation of new initiatives, determining the meaning and implications of data, coaching principals to higher levels of performance, providing feedback to colleagues and principals, and much more.

Definitions

System: A system is a group of interrelated components essential to achieving a common purpose. For example, the human circulatory system includes the heart, blood vessels, and blood supply (interrelated components); it circulates blood throughout the body, delivers nutrients and other essential materials to cells, and removes waste products. Every system

- Has a purpose larger than itself;
- Includes components that must work effectively for the system to achieve its purpose;
- Includes parts that must be arranged in a specific way for the system to carry out its purpose; and
- Changes in response to precise feedback.

Learning system: A learning system is one in which all members of an organization are continuously involved in the learning process, and in which learning and working are seamlessly intertwined.

District leaders: School district leaders have been called many things: central support, central office, district-level staff, central office staff. Here, the term *district leaders* is used to mean school board members, superintendents, assistant superintendents, and directors—anyone responsible for the system achieving its vision, goals, and moral purpose.

How to use *Becoming a Learning System*

This resource guide is designed to help multiple audiences.

AUDIENCE	USE
Superintendents so that they can . . .	• Ensure the district's vision and goals align with Learning Forward's definition of and Standards for Professional Learning. • Model standards-driven professional learning in their work with other district and school leaders. • Ensure that district-level professional learning is well-designed.
School boards so that members can . . .	• Financially and systematically support professional learning as the central strategy used to increase staff and student achievement. • Educate the public about the power of professional learning and how it affects student achievement. • Ensure all policies align with the definition of and Standards for Professional Learning.
District leadership teams so that members can . . .	• Design, lead, and facilitate standards-driven learning aligned with the definition of and Standards for Professional Learning. • Understand their role in helping adults in the district have a greater effect on student learning.

AUDIENCE	USE
Area/assistant superintendents so that they can . . .	• Model for principals what standards-driven professional learning looks like. • Support and facilitate learning, and coach principals and school leadership teams to high levels of effectiveness. • Establish clear learning designs grounded in the principles of adult learning and a theory of change. • Give school leaders precise feedback about their progress toward developing a highly skilled community of learners.
District curriculum and instructional leaders so that they can . . .	• Lead and facilitate content-specific professional learning aligned with the Standards for Professional Learning. • Lead and coach school leadership teams in developing results-driven theories of change and logic models. • Model powerful designs for learning that can be embedded in the school day at all schools.
District professional learning leaders so that they can . . .	• Design, facilitate, model, and lead professional learning grounded in the principles of and aligned with the definition of and Standards for Professional Learning. • Help district and school leadership teams understand which results-driven, standards-based, job-embedded professional learning protocols and designs would be most effective at the school level. • Coach and support district and school leadership teams in establishing educator effectiveness systems and assessing the effect of professional learning.

Readers can approach *Becoming a Learning System* in various ways. Not every school district will be at the same point in the learning journey, and so one way to begin is to review chapter titles to consider areas for attention.

Chapters 1–4 detail what we mean by a *learning system*, including the assumptions and beliefs, vision, definition of professional learning, and standards needed to create it. Readers who begin here will have the foundation for launching a learning agenda.

Chapters 5–9 help district leaders understand their roles and responsibilities, as well as the essential behaviors and skills needed to lead the organization toward greater learning and improvement.

Chapters 10–15 address the challenges district leaders encounter in facilitating, supporting, and maintaining a learning organization.

Chapters 16–23 discuss strategies that create opportunities for leaders to improve upon learning systems.

Finally, Chapter 24 envisions an effective system of adult learning.

Although the book's material is presented sequentially, readers might review the questions in the following chart, determine which address the specific issues that are most relevant to their district's needs, and then organize a learning agenda around those questions.

What is our vision for a learning system? What is the role of professional learning in our district? How do we build understanding and support for it?	Chapters 1, 2, 18
How do Learning Forward's definition of and Standards for Professional Learning contribute to our district's vision for improvement and learning?	Chapters 1, 2, 4
How do Learning Forward's definition of and Standards for Professional Learning define our district employees' work?	Chapters 4, 5, 6, 7, 8
What are our assumptions and beliefs about professional learning and continuous improvement? How do we leverage these assumptions and beliefs to improve practice and performance?	Chapter 1
How do we develop capacity for leading and learning? How might we improve our advocacy for professional learning? What supports do we provide?	Chapters 5, 18, 19
In what ways might our leadership team assume collective responsibility for a group of students? How do team members assume collective responsibility for a school leadership team?	Chapters 2, 10, 11, 12
How do individuals in learning systems think and act differently from those in traditional districts?	Chapters 2, 3, 5, 6, 7, 8
What is a cycle of continuous improvement? What strategies promote understanding and application of such a cycle? Is the cycle grounded in a thoughtful theory of change that makes sense to all in the district?	Chapters 2, 14, Appendix
How do we define, develop, and support principal and teacher leadership in a learning system?	Chapter 8
How do we define, leverage, and manage relationships with external assistance providers and other partners to ensure productive and positive outcomes?	Chapter 9
What can we do to build more effective and trusting relationships between the central office and school leadership teams?	Chapter 10
What essential roles do school boards and superintendents play in ensuring that all students succeed?	Chapters 5, 6
How do we work with school board members to advocate for and identify changes needed to become a learning system?	Chapters 5, 18
How do we ensure that assistant superintendents, directors, and central office staff model and support school-based professional learning?	Chapter 7
How do we create a system that prepares leaders at all levels to create high-performing schools where all students succeed?	Chapters 1, 2, 6, 7, 8, 22

How do we prepare and support principals to be effective instructional leaders in a learning system?	Chapters 8, 10, 11, 12, 13, 14, 15
How do we leverage relationships with parents to promote school improvement and professional learning?	Chapter 17
What strategies do we use to build shared vision around professional learning in a school district? In a school?	Chapters 1, 2, 11
What strategies increase our leadership team's effectiveness in using data?	Chapters 12, 13
What does it mean to be an instructional leader? How do we create a system to ensure that all principals become instructional leaders?	Chapters 10, 11, 12, 13, 14, 15, 20, 22
How does a district leadership team more effectively support school leaders?	Chapters 7, 10, 11, 12, 13, 20
How do we ensure that professional learning is designed to achieve its intended results?	Chapters 2, 4, 14
How do we consistently and thoughtfully support schools and school teams working through the challenges of second-order change?	Chapter 15
How do our instructional framework, teaching and leadership standards, and student achievement standards influence our improvement agenda?	Chapters 12, 13, 14, 15
How well are we using performance appraisals to balance individuals' needs with those of the district and schools?	Chapter 16
How effective is our feedback? How can it be improved?	Chapter 16
How well do our leadership and career advancement opportunities align with our appraisal processes?	Chapters 16, 20
How do we create and maximize our use of a leadership network to support and coach leaders and to share powerful ideas that affect the district's professional learning?	Chapter 21
How do we develop results-oriented approaches to leaders' learning?	Chapters 20, 21, 22
How can coaching increase leaders' effectiveness? How do we include coaching as a component of leadership development?	Chapter 22
In what ways do we honor work, energize teams, build confidence, and keep the focus on the district's mission and goals?	Chapter 23

How do we partner with teacher organizations to support policies and practices that advance a shared vision of professional learning?	Chapter 19
How might we use coaching and other differentiated support to more fully implement new practices?	Chapter 22
How do we leverage innovation to achieve our vision and goals?	Chapter 24

Structure of the chapters

Becoming a Learning System has the same structure and format as *Becoming a Learning School* (NSDC, 2009). The two books are meant to be companion resources, and each addresses topics through the use of resources, case studies, and tools. Chapters begin and end with guiding questions to promote pre- and post-assessments of users' commitment to deepening learning.

Readers will find these elements in each chapter:

Where we are. These statements allow readers to think about their school district's status and the chapter's key ideas. The statements may be used for pre- and post-assessments.

Narrative. The narrative builds foundational knowledge of the topic, offering ideas, practical examples, and research to promote deeper understanding, thoughtful actions, and ongoing reflection.

Reflections. The questions in this section encourage readers to examine their commitment to creating learning schools and learning systems. By recording and reviewing readers' responses, leaders can examine their thinking, analyze progress, redirect actions, and celebrate successes.

Tools Index. The Tools Index directs readers to accompanying online resources that will help district leadership teams initiate their work. These resources offer a starting point for designing district transformation and a professional learning agenda.

Resources. Each chapter lists resources that teams can use to develop conceptual understanding, discover new protocols and practices, and stimulate creativity and innovation as leaders build the learning system.

System leadership is complex and challenging. Ensuring great teaching and high levels of student performance across all classrooms and schools requires exceptional district-level leadership and professional learning. Effective system leaders establish professional learning as an expectation for the leadership team and work to ensure that team members share both an intense moral belief in that expectation and a strong commitment to creating a learning system. They courageously implement the recommended strategies and continuously reflect on their progress toward their goal.

Becoming a Learning System sets out the expectations, standards, content, and strategies that define a high-performing system. It can be a resource to help leaders better understand the definition and Standards for Professional Learning, review key roles and responsibilities, study essential structures, build cultures conducive to change and improvement, and find strategies and tools that will allow leaders to achieve the district's vision and goals.

The power of beliefs and assumptions

WHERE ARE WE NOW?

We can articulate our beliefs and assumptions about the central office's role in professional learning and student success.

| STRONGLY AGREE | AGREE | NO OPINION | DISAGREE | STRONGLY DISAGREE |

We can articulate the values and principles that define who we are as an organization and the work we do together.

| STRONGLY AGREE | AGREE | NO OPINION | DISAGREE | STRONGLY DISAGREE |

We identify learning as the core of our work.

| STRONGLY AGREE | AGREE | NO OPINION | DISAGREE | STRONGLY DISAGREE |

We examine our assumptions before executing a new plan of action.

| STRONGLY AGREE | AGREE | NO OPINION | DISAGREE | STRONGLY DISAGRE |

We ensure that any changes are consistent with our core values.

| STRONGLY AGREE | AGREE | NO OPINION | DISAGREE | STRONGLY DISAGREE |

Every school district is responsible for creating schools that ensure all students receive an excellent education. This statement is a key assumption underlying the work of becoming a learning system.

A second, perhaps more controversial statement, is: Creating schools that ensure an excellent education for all students requires transformation.

District leadership teams seldom are organized in a way that produces consistently high-performing schools across the district. Too few school districts leverage learning to produce that outcome. To achieve improved outcomes, school districts need to transform their central offices.

While most readers likely agree that the central office is fundamentally responsible for creating a system of good schools, some may disagree that the central office must be transformed. They believe that their central office staffs already operate with structures and strategies to produce great schools. A few may think it is not the

> District leadership teams seldom are organized in a way that produces consistently high-performing schools across the district.

central office's responsibility to produce great schools. Others may believe it is fundamentally impossible to have every school in a district be a great school.

In a learning system, leaders recognize the need to discuss these underlying beliefs and assumptions in order to promote change. For deep change to occur, those engaged in change must understand the existing, unspoken beliefs and assumptions that may help or hinder transformation.

To transform a district into a learning system is hard work. The first piece of that work is clearly identifying beliefs and assumptions that exist within the staff, examining contradictions that may impede change, and confronting the challenge of transformation.

Identify beliefs and assumptions

Acquiring new behaviors requires understanding and examining the beliefs and assumptions that drive new actions. Others term these ideas *core values* (beliefs) and *principles* (assumptions).

"Without understanding the principles of a given task," says Stephen Covey (1990), "people become incapacitated when the situation changes and different practices are required to be successful. . . . When we teach practices without principles, we tend to make people dependent on us or others" (p. 25).

Beliefs are what we hold to be true. They endure over time. They drive what we say, think, and do. Our words and actions convey how deeply held our beliefs are. What we say, think, and do are symbolic indicators to others who share our beliefs. Beliefs can be the source of deep conflict and strong alliances among people (Hirsh & Killion, 2007).

Assumptions are the logic behind our beliefs and signal the reasons for those beliefs. Assumptions guide how we behave, what we plan, and what we execute. They provide the rationale for our intended outcomes, our best-laid plans, and our expectations for success. Assumptions are deemed accurate when we achieve our intended outcomes; they are questioned when results differ from expectations. Assumptions are the basis for our beliefs, behaviors, theories of action, and change strategy.

"Transformational learning is based on the view that an individual's beliefs influence his or her actions in powerful ways that may or may not be evident to the person," Dennis Sparks writes. "While an educator's belief system may be called by different names—mental model, paradigm, worldview—that belief system exerts considerable influence on teaching and leadership" (2003, p. 29).

Many educational change initiatives fail because leaders focus too much on actions and not enough on their underlying assumptions. New behaviors often are not sustained over time because people's beliefs have not been transformed, and the principles and assumptions needed to sustain the effort are not deeply embedded in the individuals and organization.

In *Good to Great,* Jim Collins recommends that businesses preserve a set of core values while stimulating progress and change. "Enduring, great companies preserve their core values and purpose while their business strategies and operating practices endlessly adapt to a changing world," he writes. "There is the magical combination of 'preserve the core and stimulate progress'" (2001, p. 195). Core beliefs keep the organization grounded even amid rapid change.

"What separates a learning community from an ordinary school is its collective commitment to guiding principles that articulate what the people in the school believe and what they seek to create," state Richard DuFour and Robert Eaker. "Furthermore, these guiding principles are not just articulated by those in positions of leadership; even more important, they are embedded in the hearts and minds of people throughout the school" (1998, p. 25).

Becoming a Learning System is based on numerous assumptions, the most foundational of which is that learning is essential to change and change is essential to improvement. Several beliefs and assumptions about high-achieving school districts guide this book:

- Every school district is responsible for creating schools that ensure all students receive an excellent education.
- Creating schools that ensure an excellent education for all students requires transformation.
- Becoming a learning system requires that all school staff commit to continuous improvement and ongoing learning.
- Central office staff ensure that every school and teacher performs at a high level.
- Leaders of high-performing learning systems set and reinforce expectations through their thoughts, actions, and the ways they engage others in learning.
- Leaders recognize learning as central to all change and improvement efforts.
- Leaders of high-performing learning systems assume responsibility for their own learning, model that commitment, and develop a sense of collective responsibility for others' learning throughout the organization.
- When educators continuously learn, students achieve more.
- Learning Forward's definition of professional learning and Standards for Professional Learning are essential components of a high-performing learning system, and educators must understand and know how to apply them.

Every great accomplishment is undergirded by its architects' set of beliefs and assumptions about their vision and their process for achieving it. These underlying beliefs and assumptions affect outcomes for the educators and students within school districts.

Beliefs and principles influence our decisions and guide us in solving problems. They are touchstones that we return to when we face conflict, dilemmas, or challenges. They set a common foundation that members of a community share.

Members of the community also are challenged to uphold and protect the principles because these beliefs and assumptions shape what the community stands for. Developing that common understanding is essential to transformation. The first step toward creating a common foundation is examining existing contradictions.

Examine the contradictions

Regularly discussing our beliefs and assumptions opens up deeper understanding of ourselves and our colleagues. Examining our beliefs and assumptions allows us to test our theories, weigh our comfort levels, openly discuss our concerns, and change our plans. It promotes understanding of different points of view—often grounded in very different experiences—and as a result may increase empathy, respect, and collegiality. Examining and discussing our beliefs and assumptions may explain the reasons behind something that puzzled us.

People sometimes say they believe one thing and yet behave in a way that is incongruent with

Regularly discussing our beliefs and assumptions opens up deeper understanding of ourselves and our colleagues.

that stated belief. A disconnect appears between their espoused beliefs and their behaviors. These instances are not hard to identify. For example, some people say they believe in the value of exercise and commit to friends and family to exercise five times a week. Then they offer many reasons why they are not successfully meeting

their commitment. Their explanations represent the disconnect between an espoused belief and commitment to action. When they recognize this disconnect, they may be more open to examining their beliefs and reevaluating their actions.

We see similar disconnect in our schools. When a principal says she supports parental involvement in her school (espoused principle) and yet creates a complicated system for registering parent volunteers (principle in action), her espoused principle and her principle in action contradict one another. It may be difficult for her to see this contradiction, yet it is relatively easy for others to spot (Hirsh & Killion, 2007). Figure 1.1 examines the differences between what is said, what is evident, and what others see.

Margaret Wheatley writes that, "as humans, we often contradict ourselves—we say one thing and do another. We state who we are, but then act contrary to that. We say we're open-minded, but then judge someone for their appearance. We say we're a team, but then gossip about a colleague" (2009, p. 22).

We experience dissonance if we act and speak in a way that is incongruent with our beliefs and assumptions. Learning system leaders believe that all schools must be great schools with great leaders; however, in some cases, they do not see this happening. Acknowledging the disconnect may lead them to examine existing beliefs and actions and determine what changes are needed in order to behave in a way consistent with their beliefs.

As Stephanie Hirsh and Joellen Killion write, "When practices change without deep exploration of the principles that guide them, people will be pulled back to their old ways" (2007, p. 21).

Figure 1.1 Principles and evidence

ESPOUSED PRINCIPLES (What is said)	PRINCIPLES IN ACTION (What is evident)	EVIDENCE IN PRACTICE (What others see)
Training without follow-up is malpractice.	Educators are held accountable for implementing practices that they learned in training without support or assistance.	Limited or no follow-up opportunities are embedded into professional learning designs.
Professional learning is integral to school improvement.	Professional development workshops are planned and delivered in isolation from school improvement planning and goal setting.	Professional development occurs sporadically throughout the school year or outside the contract day.
Teachers are professionals.	Teachers are technicians, carefully implementing programs of prescriptive curriculum.	Professional development trains all teachers to implement prescriptive behavior with limited variation.
Effective professional learning is measured in terms of its effect on student learning.	Seat time, not application of learning, is rewarded.	States and local school districts have policies that recognize or reward participation based on hours attended rather than evidence of learning.
Professional learning respects and adheres to principles of adult learning.	All adults are expected to comply with the same professional development requirements.	Educators experience one-size-fits-all learning.

Honest, constructive feedback can help us recognize dissonance and ultimately transform our beliefs, principles, and practices. When we examine our espoused principles and align them with our principles in action, we resolve discrepancies and are able to function at a higher level—the level of transformational change.

Confront the challenges of transformational change

Lasting change requires more than a quick fix. Transforming practice requires transforming learning. For professional learning to refine and improve professional practice so that educators affect student achievement, individuals' underlying principles must be consistent with their purposes.

Working to establish and clarify a common set of beliefs and assumptions guides system transformation and leads to success. The process takes time and dialogue, because members of the organization bring their own sets of beliefs based on their experiences.

While it is easiest to work with colleagues who share our beliefs and assumptions, it is also valuable to work with those who offer other beliefs and assumptions. By analyzing and discussing

By analyzing and discussing different views, leaders

can design an action plan based on a common set

of assumptions to which everyone can commit.

different views, leaders can design an action plan based on a common set of assumptions to which everyone can commit.

Covey suggests that when we think about change, even if the desire for change is generated from within, "we usually think in terms of learning new skills rather than showing more integrity to basic principles. But significant breakthroughs often represent internal breaks with traditional ways of thinking" (1992, pp. 17-18).

According to Wheatley, we must be willing to have others challenge our beliefs and ideas and to be curious about what others believe. She identifies the essence of transformation as a willingness to allow ourselves to undertake the difficult work of being challenged.

"As we work together to restore hope to the future, we need to include a new and strange ally—our willingness to be disturbed," she writes. "No one person or perspective can give us the answers we need to the problems of today. Paradoxically, we can only find those answers by admitting we don't know. We have to be willing to let go of our certainty and expect ourselves to be confused for a time" (2009, p. 38).

Working to clarify underlying beliefs and assumptions can be difficult but ultimately contributes to vision, inspiration, and accountability.

Reflection
questions

- What purpose does declaring beliefs and assumptions serve in ensuring our central office achieves its mission?

- How necessary for transformation is it for us to examine our beliefs and assumptions?

- How is transformation different from continuous improvement? What beliefs and assumptions distinguish each?

- How does Jim Collins' combination of "preserve the core and stimulate progress" (2001, p. 195) manifest itself in our work?

- What contradictions can we identify between our "espoused principles" and "principles in action?"

- How would we define for others the terms *beliefs*, *principles*, and *assumptions*?

RESOURCES

Argryis, C. (1982). *Reasoning, learning, and action.* San Francisco, CA: Jossey-Bass.

Pasi, R. (2003). Introduction to the special issue: Leadership with vision and purpose. *NASSP Bulletin, 87*(637), 1.

Schon, D. (1983). *The reflective practitioner: How professionals think in action.* New York, NY: Basic Books.

Senge, P. (1990). *The fifth discipline.* New York, NY: Doubleday.

Sparks, D. (2004). A call to creativity. *JSD, 25*(1), 54–62.

Sparks, D. (2007). *Leading for results: Transforming teaching, learning and relationships in schools* (2nd ed.). Thousand Oaks, CA: Corwin Press and National Staff Development Council.

Tichey, N. (2002). *The cycle of leadership: How great leaders teach their companies to win.* New York, NY: Harper Business.

Von Frank, V. (2009). Talking the walk renews schools: The transformational leader links values to actions. *The Learning Principal, 4*(6), 1, 6–7.

TOOLS INDEX

TOOL	TITLE	PURPOSE
1.1	Examining beliefs and assumptions	Begin a conversation to clarify beliefs and assumptions about professional learning and change.
1.2	Uncovering assumptions	Identify and write assumptions that undergird individuals' beliefs and actions.
1.3	Clarifying beliefs and assumptions in Learning Forward's Standards for Professional Learning	Consider the underlying beliefs and assumptions regarding change associated with the Standards for Professional Learning.
1.4	Writing beliefs and assumptions	Clarify a district's or school's principles about professional learning or other topics.
1.5	Writing a teachable point of view	Write a teachable point of view that helps individuals uncover their beliefs and assumptions.
1.6	Article: Navigation	Assist district leaders in looking at data through new lenses.

CHAPTER 2

Vision of a
learning system

WHERE ARE WE NOW?

Our school district has embraced a vision and mission for professional learning.

STRONGLY AGREE AGREE NO OPINION DISAGREE STRONGLY DISAGREE

Our school district has adopted a formal definition of professional learning.

STRONGLY AGREE AGREE NO OPINION DISAGREE STRONGLY DISAGREE

Our school district leaders align their advocacy and practice to the district vision, mission, and definition of professional learning.

STRONGLY AGREE AGREE NO OPINION DISAGREE STRONGLY DISAGREE

Every educator in our district engages in effective professional learning every day so that every student achieves.

STRONGLY AGREE AGREE NO OPINION DISAGREE STRONGLY DISAGREE

Professional learning in our schools occurs primarily within learning communities committed to continuous improvement.

STRONGLY AGREE AGREE NO OPINION DISAGREE STRONGLY DISAGREE

Despite the fact that learning is schools' core business, school districts are not naturally inclined to be learning organizations. For school districts to remain viable entities, they need to be flexible enough to respond and adapt to the rapidly changing conditions around them. Districts must "learn" quickly while simultaneously encouraging principals, school-based teams, and individual classroom teachers to shift their practices. Districts must develop procedures and practices that thoughtfully incorporate changes, such as career- and college-ready student standards, ever-developing technologies, and revised federal guidelines. School districts must see themselves as "learning systems."

Learning systems
- Value adult learning as much as student learning;
- Align their practices to student learning outcomes;
- Have a collective commitment to continuous improvement of people and processes throughout the organization;
- Thrive on precise feedback;
- Provide conditions that scale and sustain effective teaching and leading;
- Are committed to innovating; and
- Celebrate and honor success.

The concept of schools as learning organizations is not new. For decades, researchers including Shirley Hord, Learning Forward's scholar laureate, and Susan Loucks-Horsley, former executive director of Biological Sciences and Curriculum Study, studied learning organizations and described their attributes to guide research and application in schools.

Reports are clear about what academically successful learning systems look like and act like.

Learning systems require
- Collegial and facilitative participation of the superintendent and principal, who share leadership—and thus, power and authority—through engaging staff in decision making, problem solving, and designing the work of learning together;
- A shared vision that is developed from unswerving staff commitment to student learning and that is consistently articulated and referenced for the staff's work;
- Collective learning among staff, and application of that learning to solutions that address student needs; and
- The visitation and review of each school and teacher's classroom behavior by peers as a feedback and assistance activity to support individual and community improvement.

(Hord, 1997)

This body of work, along with findings in the field of professional learning and student achievement, contributed to Learning Forward's shift from viewing professional development as a set of workshops or disjointed activities to defining professional learning as the key strategy for increasing organization and educator effectiveness in order to improve student outcomes. The shift in definition has prompted educators to think more deeply about systemic change, the role of learning communities, and the responsibility of district and school leaders to ensure that learning occurs every day for both students and educators. Learning Forward's positions on, definition of, and Standards for Professional Learning help districts and school leaders link professional learning to increasing the effectiveness of adults in the organization in order to accelerate and deepen student learning.

Professional learning today calls for long-term, sustained focus on embedding the practice of learning into the system so that those who have the greatest impact on student learning are continuously developing precision in their work to produce better outcomes for all.

Learning systems do not occur without strong district leadership. In a learning system, the central office is a place where trust exists across departments. District leaders partner with school leaders rather than trying to control them. Because adult learning is valued throughout the district, learning communities are the norm in the central office and in schools. Professional learning systems are in place, and resources are allocated to support them. Those who work at the district level are not simply part of the background noise related to school improvement, but exercise essential leadership—in partnership with school leaders—to build capacity throughout the district for high-quality teaching and learning (Honig & Copland, 2008, 2011).

Leverage a new vision

Robert Fritz (1989) proposes that structures are powerful forces for preserving the status quo and preventing systemic change; however, he suggests that it is not impossible to free ourselves from the pull of traditional structures.

To release from traditional structures requires a morally compelling vision, ruthless assessment of reality, and two or three powerful strategies. A learning system vision for professional learning focuses on its dual moral obligations to educators and students. Learning system leaders ensure that all educators have the knowledge and skills they need to teach at a level that improves student learning. School districts fulfill these dual responsibilities by embracing a vision of education that engages every educator in effective professional learning every day.

Too few school districts today succeed in achieving this vision. A ruthless assessment will help determine barriers to the vision as well as opportunities for achieving it. Learning system leaders examine the processes that support districtwide and individual learning. They ask questions about leaders' capacity to guide the essential work needed to reach the district's goals. They examine how learning and support are organized

A learning system vision for professional learning focuses on its dual moral obligations to educators and students.

and differentiated for individuals and groups. They seek clear expectations and accountability for implementation. They ensure that data are leveraged to guide necessary change.

In many districts, professional development is treated as an end, rather than a means to accomplish important goals. School districts spend considerable effort figuring out what counts rather than what matters. Too much of the professional development conversation focuses on credits, licenses, and salaries. Too little focuses on what educators need to improve their performance and that of their students.

Learning systems assess their resources. They are able to account for all expenditures and are not reluctant to deploy them in ways that make a significant difference. Learning system leaders are prepared to ask tough questions regarding the purpose, process, and impact of investments in professional learning.

Learning systems take a hard look at their expectations for professional learning. They build school capacity and support school leaders in leveraging professional learning to produce intended results. Central office staff embrace new roles to ensure the cycle of improvement is effectively implemented in all schools.

System leaders turn their vision into reality by

- Adopting a local professional development policy that offers a vision, recognizes Learning Forward's Standards for Professional Learning, and uses its definition of quality professional learning to create educators' learning;

Learning systems organize professional learning within communities to advance continuous improvement, promote collective responsibility, and support alignment of individual, team, school, and school district goals.

- Shifting district requirements related to school improvement to focus on a cycle of continuous learning and the lessons and results achieved through implementation;
- Establishing and supporting demonstration sites where early adopters can demonstrate the power of the vision of a professional learning system and motivate all constituencies to move toward the vision; and
- Using early adopters' results to provide the additional leverage and support necessary to sustain any successful change effort.

Engage in continuous improvement

The first standard of Learning Forward's Standards for Professional Learning addresses learning communities and offers a clear, concise, and compelling description of adult actions in a learning system:

Professional learning that increases educator effectiveness and results for all students occurs within learning communities committed to continuous improvement, collective responsibility, and goal alignment.

Learning systems organize professional learning within communities to advance continuous improvement, promote collective responsibility, and support alignment of individual, team, school, and school district goals. Learning systems ensure that learning communities convene regularly and frequently during the workday to strengthen teacher practice and boost student achievement. Learning community members are accountable to one another for achieving school and district goals and supporting continuous improvement.

Learning communities follow a cycle of continuous improvement, engaging in inquiry, action research, data analysis, planning, implementation, reflection, and evaluation. The cycle of continuous improvement is characterized by these actions:

- Using data to determine student and educator learning needs
- Identifying shared goals for student and educator learning
- Extending educators' knowledge of content, content-specific pedagogy, student learning patterns, and classroom management strategies
- Selecting and implementing appropriate, evidence-based strategies to achieve student and educator learning goals

- Applying learning with job-embedded support
- Using evidence to monitor and refine implementation and to evaluate results

Create alignment and accountability

Professional learning provides ongoing support for continuous improvement and implementation of school and districtwide initiatives. School district leaders create policies that establish formal accountability for results along with the support needed to avoid fragmentation and silo building, and achieve results. To be effective, these policies and supports align with an explicit vision and goals for the district.

Members of learning communities align their goals with those of the school and school district, engage in continuous professional learning, and hold all members collectively accountable for results. The professional learning that occurs within learning communities supports and is supported by policy and governance, curriculum and instruction, human resources, and other functions within a school district. Learning community members bridge the knowing-doing gap by transforming macro-level learning (knowledge and skill development) into micro-level learning (the practices and refinements necessary for full implementation in the classroom or workplace). When professional learning occurs within a district driven by high expectations, shared goals, professionalism, and peer accountability, the outcome is deep change for individuals and districts (Learning Forward, 2011).

Develop collective responsibility

Learning system leaders promote responsibility for the learning of all students within the school or school district. Collective responsibility brings together members of the education

workforce—teachers, support staff, school district staff, administrators, families, policymakers, and other stakeholders—to increase effective teaching in every classroom. Within learning systems, peer accountability—rather than formal or administrative accountability—ignites a commitment to professional learning. Collective participation advances the goals of a whole school or team, as well as those of individuals. Communities of caring, analytic, reflective, and inquiring educators

Collective participation advances the goals of a whole school or team, as well as those of individuals.

collaborate to learn what is necessary to increase student learning. Every student benefits from the strengths and expertise of every educator when communities of educators learn together.

Within learning systems and communities, members exchange feedback about their practices, visit one another's classrooms or work settings, and share resources. Colleagues strive to refine their collaboration, communication, and relationship skills to work within and across both internal and external systems to support student learning. They develop norms of collaboration and relational trust and use processes and structures that unleash expertise and strengthen capacity to analyze, plan, implement, support, and evaluate their practices.

Although some professional learning—such as learning designed to address individual development goals—occurs individually, the more educators share and support each other's learning, the more quickly a culture of continuous improvement, collective responsibility, and high expectations for students and educators grows. Collective responsibility and participation foster peer-to-peer support for learning and maintain learners' consistent focus on shared goals within and across communities. Technology facilitates and expands community interaction, learning, resource archiving and sharing, and knowledge construction and sharing. Some educators may meet with peers virtually in

Professional learning that increases educator effectiveness for all students must occur at all levels in the district to ensure high levels of practice.

local or global communities to focus on individual, team, school, or school district improvement goals. Technology improves cross-community communication within schools, among schools, and among school districts; reinforces shared goals; promotes information sharing; strengthens coherence; taps into educators' expertise; and increases access to and use of resources.

Communities of learners may vary in size; include members with similar or different roles and responsibilities; and meet face-to-face, virtually, or in a blended format. Educators may be members of multiple learning communities. Some communities may include members who share common students, areas of responsibility, roles, interests, or goals. Because the education system reaches out to include students, their families, community members, the education workforce, and public officials who share responsibility for

student achievement, some learning communities may include representatives of these groups.

Commit to change

Professional learning that increases educator effectiveness for all students must occur at all levels in the district to ensure high levels of practice. True learning systems fully implement the definition of quality professional learning. Learning system leaders must recognize that scaled and sustained learning for all will not happen by chance; they must create a culture that values learning and develop conditions that enable such learning to occur.

Each year, parents approach school or district administrators to get their children assigned to the "best teachers" or transferred to the "best schools." As educators strive to implement strategies that transition their district to a learning system, they hold on to the moral imperative that no matter where students are assigned, those students will

- Have the benefit of the thinking, expertise, and dedication of all teachers in that grade level or subject area;
- Be part of a school system that requires all teachers to participate in learning teams that are given regular time to plan, study, and solve problems together; and
- Benefit from collaboration ensuring that best practices and high expectations spread across classrooms and grade levels.

Given that these same expectations are held for principals, best practices and support also spread from school to school. Through a commitment to systemic change, learning system leaders ensure that every student experiences quality teaching every day.

Reflection
questions

- Why is having a vision for professional learning important?

- How do leaders in learning systems ensure that all staff throughout the system share a common vision and understanding of quality professional learning?

- How does a learning system maintain progress toward achieving its vision?

- What are the most critical attributes of a vision for professional learning in our district?

- What is the relationship between having a detailed description of a learning community and a vision for professional learning?

- How can district and school leaders develop a culture of collective responsibility for student learning?

RESOURCES

Darling-Hammond, L. et al. (2009). *Professional learning in the learning profession: A status report on teacher development in the United States and beyond.* Oxford OH: NSDC.

Elmore, R. (2000). *Building a new structure for school leadership.* Washington, DC: Albert Shanker Institute.

Hargreaves, A. & Fullan, M. (2012). *Professional capital: Transforming teaching in every school.* New York, NY: Teachers College Press.

Killion, J. & Hirsh, S. (2007). *The learning educator: A new era for professional learning.* Oxford, OH: NSDC.

Senge, P., Ross, R., Smith, B., Roberts, C., & Kleiner, A. (1994). *The fifth discipline fieldbook: Strategies and tools for building a learning organization.* New York, NY: Broadway Books.

TOOLS INDEX

TOOL	TITLE	PURPOSE
2.1	Understanding shared vision	Study the theory and practice of learning organizations.
2.2	Blue sky scenario	Stimulate district leaders' thinking about what a successful educational system for all students might look like.
2.3	Forecasting scenario	Help district leadership teams consider alternatives to the current reality and challenge the way the district functions in order to create a more successful system.
2.4	Diagnosing your district culture	Assess the relationship between the central office and building leaders.
2.5	Ensure effective district and school leadership	Complete a self-evaluation of your school or district's progress toward practices and policies that support becoming a learning system.
2.6	Learning Communities Standard	Articulate key elements of learning communities in order to create a vision and mission for a learning system.

CHAPTER 3

Components of a
comprehensive
learning system

WHERE ARE WE NOW?

Our school district is developing a plan that addresses all the components of a comprehensive learning system, as well as the fundamental purposes of professional learning.

STRONGLY AGREE   AGREE   NO OPINION   DISAGREE   STRONGLY DISAGREE

We have clearly defined central office roles and responsibilities as they relate to professional learning.

STRONGLY AGREE   AGREE   NO OPINION   DISAGREE   STRONGLY DISAGREE

Our school district has systems in place to monitor and continuously improve professional learning.

STRONGLY AGREE   AGREE   NO OPINION   DISAGREE   STRONGLY DISAGREE

We regularly and systematically evaluate professional learning's effect on educator practice and student results.

STRONGLY AGREE   AGREE   NO OPINION   DISAGREE   STRONGLY DISAGREE

We have redefined district leaders' roles and responsibilities to ensure great schools throughout the school district.

STRONGLY AGREE   AGREE   NO OPINION   DISAGREE   STRONGLY DISAGREE

A professional learning system "is like the engine in an automobile," writes Joellen Killion (2013) in an *Education Week* blog. "Just as an engine propels a vehicle, professional learning drives an education system. Indeed, one might say that learning drives change."

Schools and school districts, state and federal education agencies, initiatives such as the Common Core State Standards, and new assessments for students and approaches to measuring educator effectiveness all have created a new imperative for a different type of professional learning—a different engine that will drive teaching for deeper learning.

Changes as significant as those that educators face require examining, tuning, or rebuilding the learning engine. While most districts and states have created systems for professional learning, few are comprehensive under the definition of

While most districts and states have created systems for professional learning, few are comprehensive under the definition of a learning system.

a learning system. They were created by opportunity and happenstance as districts and schools added courses and programs in response to initiatives. Rather than add on yet again, district and state leaders remodel professional learning so that it is purposeful, finely tuned, and provides every educator with continual learning opportunities. Then, they must periodically maintain and replace options so that professional learning, the engine of education systems, can increase educators' efficiency, effectiveness, and reliability. When they

create a new infrastructure and support it, leaders ensure professional learning achieves its purposes.

Create the infrastructure

The learning system's infrastructure comprises six core components (Learning Forward, 2013) that drive educator and student learning. How the components interact varies according to the context in which they operate. Learning system leaders guide the continuous improvement process, as well as plans for professional learning, by assessing how applicable the components are to their context and determining where to focus attention.

1. Vision and mission statements

Most educators recognize the value of adopting vision and mission statements. Many districts and schools have adopted a short statement as well as a longer version documenting educators' commitment to the educational experience and to the outcomes they seek for their students. In some cases, they develop a narrative describing the role that educators, parents, and other stakeholders will play in achieving the vision.

Learning system leaders are deliberate about stating how educator learning helps achieve the vision. They formally adopt vision and mission statements for professional learning. The statements may be extracted from the longer district vision statement or written as a corollary to the vision statement. They may expand the district vision with a vision of professional learning. The professional learning statement may include the aspiration (vision) and function (mission) of professional learning.

Learning Forward adopted a vision statement:
- "Every educator engages in effective professional learning every day so every student achieves."

Other examples:

- "Every educator commits to continuous learning and collaborative problem solving so that all students succeed."
- "Every educator shares collective responsibility for continuous improvement and success for every student."

A mission statement identifies the learning system's purpose and function. Learning Forward created a mission statement:

- "Advancing educator effectiveness and results for all students through standards-based professional learning."

Other examples:

- "To ensure educators' effectiveness through standards-based professional learning."
- "To improve instruction every day for every student through continuous learning for educators."

Vision and mission statements direct professional learning toward a fundamental purpose: Improve educator effectiveness so that students achieve success.

2. Standards for Professional Learning

Professional learning standards define the essential elements of quality professional learning that produce its intended effect on educators and students. District leaders use the standards to guide planning, implementation, and evaluation of professional learning. Adopting and using standards promotes equity, excellence, and effectiveness of professional learning and demonstrates the district's commitment to quality learning for all employees. Standards are not just a checklist; they are the foundation for supporting continuous improvement in a learning system. All standards have equal weight and are essential to achieving intended goals for professional learning.

3. A definition of quality professional learning

Definitions help learning systems promote common understandings and expectations. Although standards define conditions and elements, definitions offer detail and direction. A definition of professional learning translates standards into learning practices for educators. The definition operationalizes the standards into educators' day-to-day work and answers the question of

Adopting and using standards promotes equity, excellence, and effectiveness of professional learning and demonstrates the district's commitment to quality learning for all employees.

what standards-based professional learning looks like in practice. The definition offers insight into what kinds of experiences the school district wants educators to have and can provide exemplars for effective learning experiences. It helps staff members see how the standards integrate into a cohesive and powerful system of learning and support.

4. New roles and responsibilities

Learning system leaders declare new roles and responsibilities for each stakeholder group and detail new responsibilities in job descriptions. They use Innovation Configurations to document the continuum of practices that those in various departments and roles use to advance and implement high-quality professional learning. Through job descriptions and Innovation Configuration maps, learning system leaders articulate, support, assess, and refine staff responsibilities related to professional learning.

Definition of Professional Development

Working with our allies and advocates, Learning Forward created this formal definition of professional development for use in the reauthorized version of the No Child Left Behind Act. Learn more about the definition at http://learningforward.org/who-we-are/professional-learning-definition.

Proposed Amendments to Section 9101 (34) of the Elementary and Secondary Education Act as reauthorized by the No Child Left Behind Act of 2001.

(34) PROFESSIONAL DEVELOPMENT—The term "professional development" means a comprehensive, sustained, and intensive approach to improving teachers' and principals' effectiveness in raising student achievement.

(A) Professional development fosters collective responsibility for improved student performance and must be comprised of professional learning that

(1) is aligned with rigorous state student academic achievement standards, as well as related local educational agency and school improvement goals;

(2) is conducted among educators at the school and facilitated by well-prepared school principals and/or school-based professional development coaches, mentors, master teachers, or other teacher leaders; and

(3) primarily occurs several times per week among established teams of teachers, principals, and other instructional staff members where the teams of educators engage in a continuous cycle of improvement that —

   (i)   evaluates student, teacher, and school learning needs through a thorough review of data on teacher and student performance;

   (ii) defines a clear set of educator learning goals based on the rigorous analysis of the data;

   (iii) achieves the educator learning goals identified in subsection (A)(3)(ii) by implementing coherent, sustained, and evidenced-based learning strategies, such as lesson study and the development of formative assessments, that improve instructional effectiveness and student achievement;

   (iv) provides job-embedded coaching or other forms of assistance to support the transfer of new knowledge and skills to the classroom;

   (v)   regularly assesses the effectiveness of the professional development in achieving identified learning goals, improving teaching, and assisting all students in meeting challenging state academic achievement standards;

   (vi) informs ongoing improvements in teaching and student learning; and

   (vii) that may be supported by external assistance.

(B) The process outlined in (A) may be supported by activities such as courses, workshops, institutes, networks, and conferences that

(1) must address the learning goals and objectives established for professional development by educators at the school level;

(2) advance the ongoing school-based professional development; and

(3) are provided by for-profit and nonprofit entities outside the school such as universities, education service agencies, technical assistance providers, networks of content-area specialists, and other education organizations and associations.

When learning is placed at the center of educators' work, school district leaders discover opportunities to reduce fragmentation and increase integration. Department staffs and individuals find new reasons to collaborate. Cross-department teams break down traditional silos, and the organization is restructured as operating systems evolve.

5. Ongoing assessments and evaluation

Assessment tools and evaluation plans are essential for monitoring professional learning's effects and for making improvements in order to generate better results. Comprehensive learning systems collect data, create clear and accepted goals and outcomes, monitor implementation, ensure formative and summative measures, and schedule final reports.

6. Resources to support professional learning

Professional learning cannot happen without critical resources, including personnel, funding, time, and facilities. Learning systems use external and internal audits to identify existing resources and allocate them in ways that achieve the highest-quality outcomes.

Address the three purposes of professional learning

Professional learning exists to advance educator practice in order to improve student achievement. To plan professional learning to achieve these outcomes, educators consider three fundamental purposes of professional learning:

- Individual development
- Team and school improvement
- Program implementation

To ensure that educator practice and student learning improve *systemwide*, comprehensive learning systems address all three purposes.

Individual development. Learning system leaders recognize that pathways to individual improvement are the foundation for ensuring each educator has the opportunity to succeed. They align individuals' development with educator evaluations, using evaluations and observation feedback to inform professional learning on pedagogy, and data on student outcomes to help identify what content knowledge teachers may need to learn. Districts create systems to help individuals identify strengths and weaknesses, make available professional learning opportunities to address areas of need, and then monitor individual performance to determine if expected improvements occur.

Many districts create teaching and learning frameworks and evaluation rubrics to define educator performance expectations. Teaching and learning frameworks and rubrics give teachers clear targets for quality teaching, allow for explicit feedback, and can help the district align professional development with individual improvement. Teacher learning frameworks prompt teachers to develop individual growth plans that are tied to performance and student outcomes. Supervisors, coaches, and peers guide individuals through developing a personal growth plan that honors that individual's strengths and addresses areas that require attention.

Supervisors, coaches, and peers participate in the growth plan cycle by examining student and educator performance data, selecting learning targets, setting growth goals, identifying strategies for achieving the targets and goals, and then monitoring results and using feedback to ensure the plan is followed and goals are achieved. In learning systems, the development plan cycle typically occurs within learning team and school leadership team improvement cycles. Educators share goals, learn, and implement new practices together in order to learn from one another and create better results for all students.

Individual growth plans allow teachers to target their specific needs and get the support they need to make necessary improvements; however, individual growth plans alone will not allow the learning system to achieve its vision.

Team and school improvement. Learning systems also require team and school improvement plans that follow the same cyclical process outlined for individuals but which require teachers to collaborate with their peers, a move that results in increased support and, sometimes, accountability. Schools typically organize learning teams by grade level or subject.

Grade-level or subject learning teams engage in a cycle of continuous improvement that requires team members to assess student performance data on an ongoing basis, identify student and adult learning needs, select learning strategies, implement what they have learned in classrooms, offer feedback and follow up, and assess results. The group may repeat the cycle several times a year as members achieve one set of outcomes and move on to their next challenges.

Team and school improvement stresses building capacity at the school level for educators to use data to identify strengths and determine areas of weakness. Teachers need dedicated time within the school day to work in teams on the cycle of continuous improvement, professional learning that often is referred to as *job embedded*. Teachers work in professional learning communities to improve the whole school and use formative and summative student achievement data to drive their learning.

Learning system leaders ensure that school-based educators have the support they need to implement what they learn in ways that produce the desired outcomes. Leaders responsible for guiding such processes are well-prepared and skilled, undertaking tasks such as monitoring school data to indicate where school-based educators need additional help.

Program implementation. In most school districts, the central office is responsible for developing programs to ensure all students reach college- and career-ready standards. Learning systems ensure that teachers and schools consistently implement the desired programs.

Learning systems recognize that educators deserve support through quality professional learning to implement curricula, instructional strategies, or technology the district has adopted. They determine the professional learning educators need in order to implement a program well by gathering observational data on key practices and methods.

The learning system may develop programs for a particular grade level, subject, or selected schools. Central office leaders are responsible for ensuring that these programs are implemented with fidelity, and are charged with planning, implementing, and evaluating professional development.

Ultimately, individual, team, school, and program plans all must be part of a comprehensive strategy ensuring that no individual tries to learn and implement too much in one year. The learning system must have a clear purpose and goals, along with plans and processes to support them. Without a clear purpose, educators will either ignore plans or touch upon them lightly, and little improvement will occur.

Developing or redesigning a school district into a learning system is accomplished in many ways. The work is complex, yet the result is a broad-based understanding of research and an appreciation of and advocacy for the contribution professional learning must make to achieving the district vision and mission.

Reflection questions

- Which aspects of a learning system are new to us?

- What are some benefits of the six components recommended for a learning system?

- Which components are well-developed in our district? How do we know?

- Which components could benefit from our attention?

- How does our school district address the three purposes for professional learning?

- What district systems might change if all educators in our district identified learning as our core work?

RESOURCES

Killion, J. (2013). *Professional learning plans: A workbook for states, districts, and schools.* Oxford, OH: Learning Forward. Available at http://learningforward.org/docs/default-source/commoncore/professional-learning-plans.pdf?sfvrsn=4

Killion, J. (2013). *Comprehensive professional learning system: A workbook for states and districts.* Oxford, OH: Learning Forward. Available at http://learningforward.org/docs/default-source/commoncore/comprehensive-professional-learning-system.pdf?sfvrsn=10

Killion, J. & Roy, P. (2008). *Becoming a learning school.* Oxford, OH: NSDC.

Von Frank, V. (2009, August/September). Leadership teams create lasting change. *Tools for Schools, 13*(1), 1–4.

Von Frank, V. (2010, April). State policy is key to building strong leaders: An interview with Gene Wilhoit. *JSD, 31*(2), 19–22.

TOOLS INDEX

TOOL	TITLE	PURPOSE
3.1	Designing a learning system	Help task force members make critical operational decisions related to designing a professional learning system.
3.2	Policy attributes rubric	Rate current policies according to key policy attributes.
3.3	Linking systems for success	Examine how a learning system connects with other systems.
3.4	Leadership for a learning system	Conduct a periodic review of leadership responsibilities for the learning system.
3.5	Three purposes of professional learning	Clarify the three major purposes of professional learning in order to develop shared understanding.
3.6	Continuous improvement of a comprehensive professional learning system	Prioritize continuous improvements to the comprehensive professional learning system.

CHAPTER 4

The Standards
for Professional
Learning

WHERE ARE WE NOW?

Our school board has adopted Learning Forward's Standards for Professional Learning.

STRONGLY AGREE   AGREE   NO OPINION   DISAGREE   STRONGLY DISAGREE

Our district and school leaders are able to articulate the Standards' purpose, meaning, and importance to staff and student success.

STRONGLY AGREE   AGREE   NO OPINION   DISAGREE   STRONGLY DISAGREE

All district and school leaders use the Standards to plan and evaluate professional learning.

STRONGLY AGREE   AGREE   NO OPINION   DISAGREE   STRONGLY DISAGREE

District and school leaders use the Standards for Professional Learning as a framework to ensure that every day educators and students are learning.

STRONGLY AGREE   AGREE   NO OPINION   DISAGREE   STRONGLY DISAGREE

District and school leaders use Learning Forward's Innovation Configuration maps and Standards Assessment Inventory to determine progress and set goals for becoming a learning system.

STRONGLY AGREE   AGREE   NO OPINION   DISAGREE   STRONGLY DISAGREE

In a learning system, district and school leaders use Learning Forward's Standards for Professional Learning as a framework for learning and change. A framework is a set of assumptions, concepts, values, and practices that helps practitioners examine and understand ideas. A framework adds value to an organization by giving seemingly discrepant practices, policies, and protocols meaning and showing how they fit together to achieve the organization's moral purpose.

Learning Forward's Standards for Professional Learning make clear that professional learning helps educators develop their own knowledge, skills, practices, and dispositions so they can help students perform at higher levels. Research studies over the last 20 years confirm a strong relationship between teacher practices and student learning (Loucks-Horsley, Hewson, Love, & Stiles, 1998; Wang, Frechtling, & Sanders, 1999). Since professional learning improves teacher effectiveness (Yoon, Duncan, Lee, Scarloss, & Shapley, 2007), students benefit from adults' professional learning.

Additional studies indicate a dynamic relationship between district and school leader effectiveness and teacher effectiveness (Marzano, Waters, & McNulty, 2005).

Learning system leaders use the Standards in their own learning, accept collective responsibility for success, design staff learning systems that shift practice, employ a cycle of continuous improvement (see Appendix), and hold themselves accountable for learning. When leaders assimilate the indicators of effectiveness defined in the Standards, educators' effectiveness and student learning improve.

The Standards are only useful, however, when they are fully understood. The Standards work in concert with each other; all are equally important. They do not form a linear or sequential framework. Each Standard has a clear set of descriptors and exemplars, and leaders can use the Standards to evaluate their efforts in establishing a learning system. If a Standard is disregarded, any intended result from professional learning likely will be minimized.

The full value of using the Standards as a framework becomes evident when they are used as a foundation for professional conversations among practitioners seeking to enhance complex teaching skills.

The framework may be used as the foundation of a school or district's mentoring, coaching, professional development, and teacher evaluation processes, linking those activities and helping teachers become more thoughtful practitioners.

In learning systems, leaders leverage the Standards to ensure that every day everyone is learning. They make intentional, purposeful use of the Standards to personalize learning.

District and school leaders in learning systems

- Make sure everyone in the organization understands the Standards and their implications for all aspects of the organization;
- Publicize adoption of the Standards and the rationale for adopting them;
- Apply the Standards in planning and executing decisions about professional learning;
- Evaluate professional learning annually with adherence to the Standards and results of educator and student learning;
- Build a community of learning leaders at the district and school levels who collaborate to apply Standards to their work supporting school improvement and educator effectiveness; and
- Advocate for school-based professional learning for teaching teams, and call attention to practices that contradict it.

The relationship between professional learning and student results

This cycle works in two ways:

- If educators are not achieving the results they want, they determine what changes in practice they need to make and what knowledge, skills, and dispositions they need to acquire to make those changes.
- They consider how to apply Learning Forward's Standards for Professional Learning so that they can learn what they need to strengthen their practice.

1. When professional learning is standards based, it has a greater potential to change what educators know, do, and believe.
2. When educators' knowledge, skills, and dispositions change, they have a broader repertoire of effective strategies to use to adapt their practices to meet performance expectations and student learning needs.
3. When educator practice improves, students have a greater likelihood of achieving results.
4. When student results improve, the cycle repeats, leading to continuous improvement.

Source: *Standards Quick Guide* (Learning Forward, 2012, p. 16).

Learning Forward's Standards for Professional Learning

Learning communities: Professional learning that increases educator effectiveness and results for all students occurs within learning communities committed to continuous improvement, collective responsibility, and goal alignment.

Leadership: Professional learning that increases educator effectiveness and results for all students requires skillful leaders who develop capacity, advocate, and create support systems for professional learning.

Resources: Professional learning that increases educator effectiveness and results for all students requires prioritizing, monitoring, and coordinating resources for educator learning.

Data: Professional learning that increases educator effectiveness and results for all students uses a variety of sources and types of student, educator, and system data to plan, assess, and evaluate professional learning.

Learning designs: Professional learning that increases educator effectiveness and results for all students integrates theories, research, and models of human learning to achieve its intended outcomes.

Implementation: Professional learning that increases educator effectiveness and results for all students applies research on change and sustains support for implementation of professional learning for long-term change.

Outcomes: Professional learning that increases educator effectiveness and results for all students aligns its outcomes with educator performance and student curriculum standards.

Establish goals and assess progress

To identify and describe the major components of the Standards in operation, learning systems use Innovation Configuration (IC) maps. Learning Forward developed the IC maps to describe evidence that shows staff developing greater competence as they work toward precision. The maps help those in various roles understand what actions to take to implement a change systemwide. Learning system leaders use IC maps to create a clear picture of the Standards in practice and to guide others in increasing the quality and results of professional learning.

An IC map defines quality and measures fidelity. As users identify the level of their practice using the maps, they can look toward higher levels of implementation to define their next actions.

Table 4.1 is a sample IC map for district leaders working on the Learning Communities standard. The first desired outcome (1.1.1) is that district leaders develop the capacity to apply the cycle of continuous improvement. The highest level of proficiency is Level 1. Effective district leaders continuously refocus their efforts by reflecting on their progress and setting goals to move to the next highest level.

Table 4.1 Engage in continuous improvement

Level 1	Level 2	Level 3	Level 4	Level 5	Level 6
Desired outcome 1.1.1: Develops the capacity to apply the seven-step cycle of continuous improvement					
• Develops own knowledge and skills about the seven-step cycle of continuous improvement • Develops staff and participant knowledge and skills about the seven-step cycle of continuous improvement	• Develops own knowledge and skills about the seven-step cycle of continuous improvement • Develops participant knowledge and skills about the seven-step cycle of continuous improvement	• Develops own knowledge and skills about the seven-step cycle of continuous improvement • Recommends that participants learn about the seven-step cycle of continuous improvement	• Develops own knowledge and skills about the seven-step cycle of continuous improvement	• Fails to develop own and others' knowledge and skills about the seven-step cycle of continuous improvement	

Source: Learning Forward. (2013). *Standards into practice: School system roles Innovation Configuration maps for Standards for Professional Learning.* Oxford, OH: Author.

Outline effective professional learning

The Standards Assessment Inventory 2, revised to align with the new Standards, outlines the characteristics of professional learning that leads to effective teaching practices, supportive leadership, and improved student results. Teachers take an online survey about their perceptions of their school's progress in becoming a learning school.

Successfully applying any major change in schools requires deep study and commitment to a shared vision of what that change will look like once implemented.

The results give decision makers data on
- The quality of the district's professional learning, as defined by Learning Forward's Standards for Professional Learning;
- How a system's professional learning aligns with the Standards;
- The degree of success or challenge the district is encountering with respect to implementing professional learning and new practices; and
- Ways to strengthen the district's use of the Standards to improve educator effectiveness and student achievement.

District and school leaders use the data to set each school's professional learning goals. Studies of implementation of innovations have shown that successful implementation strategies vary.

Each organization has its own challenges, as well as staff and student needs. "Just because authorities mandate, experts request, or colleagues agree to adopt innovations does not guarantee fidelity of implementation" (Learning Forward, 2012, p. 7).

Successfully applying any major change in schools requires deep study and commitment to a shared vision of what that change will look like once implemented. Central office staff coordinate districtwide programs, professional learning, and the resources needed to help each educator achieve the goals for student achievement.

The Standards provide a clear vision of high-quality, results-oriented professional learning. "The Standards seek to eliminate the gap between what we know about quality, effective adult learning and what many experience in their daily professional lives," write Stephanie Hirsh and Shirley Hord (2012, p. 1).

Reflection
questions

- How do Learning Forward's Standards for Professional Learning help staff shift practices to positively affect student learning?

- How well does our professional learning align with the Standards?

- How might we use the Standards as a framework to make decisions about district- and school-level professional learning?

- What tools and strategies would help us understand where we are in developing as a learning system?

- How have district and school leaders helped others deepen their understanding of the Standards?

- What could central office administrators do to ensure educators throughout the district appreciate and apply the Standards?

RESOURCES

Armstrong, A. (2012, Fall). Where do I start? *Tools for Learning Schools, 16*(1), 1–3.

Hirsh, S. & Hord, S. (2012). *A playbook for professional learning: Putting the standards into action.* Oxford, OH: Learning Forward.

Learning Forward. (n.d.). Overview information and videos on each Standard are available at www.learningforward.org/standards-for-professional-learning.

Learning Forward. (2011, October). *JSD: Learning Designs, 32*(5).

Learning Forward. (2012, February). *JSD: Resources, 33*(1).

Learning Forward. (2012, April). *JSD: Implementation, 33*(2).

Learning Forward. (2012, June). *JSD: Learning Communities, 33*(3).

Learning Forward. (2012, August). *JSD: Data, 33*(4).

Learning Forward. (2012, October). *JSD: Outcomes, 33*(5).

Learning Forward. (2012, December). *JSD: Leadership, 33*(6).

Reach the highest standards in professional learning. A series by various authors based on the Standards. Thousand Oaks, CA: Corwin Press.

TOOLS INDEX

TOOL	TITLE	PURPOSE
4.1	Understanding the Standards for Professional Learning	Guide individuals, teams, system, and school leaders to think deeply about the Standards and their application to learning in their organizations.
4.2	*A Playbook for Professional Learning* activities	Expand understanding and capacity to use the Standards in everyday work.
4.3	Scenarios	Consider these scenarios to improve understanding of the Standards.
4.4	Connecting the Standards	Discover the standards' coherence and connections by discussing questions about each.
4.5	How my standard connects	Demonstrate the connection and coherence among the Standards for Professional Learning.
4.6	Managing changes in practice	Understand the breakdown when a Standard is missing.
4.7	Moving standards into practice	Consider the effects of implementing the Standards in an organization and barriers to doing so.

CHAPTER 5

The role of the
school board

WHERE ARE WE NOW?

Our school board has adopted and adheres to Learning Forward's Standards for Professional Learning.

STRONGLY AGREE	AGREE	NO OPINION	DISAGREE	STRONGLY DISAGREE

Our school board has adopted a vision and mission that embrace the tenets of continuous professional learning for educators and students.

STRONGLY AGREE	AGREE	NO OPINION	DISAGREE	STRONGLY DISAGREE

Our school board emphasizes professional learning to develop leaders at all levels.

STRONGLY AGREE	AGREE	NO OPINION	DISAGREE	STRONGLY DISAGREE

Our school board prioritizes resources for professional learning over competing issues.

STRONGLY AGREE	AGREE	NO OPINION	DISAGREE	STRONGLY DISAGREE

Our school board includes the quality and effectiveness of the system's professional learning in the superintendent's evaluation.

STRONGLY AGREE	AGREE	NO OPINION	DISAGREE	STRONGLY DISAGREE

Our school board members work with district administrators to examine the implications for professional learning when they consider whether to adopt a new program or service.

STRONGLY AGREE	AGREE	NO OPINION	DISAGREE	STRONGLY DISAGREE

School boards play a vital role in transforming a school district into a learning system. In partnership with the superintendent and in collaboration with district leaders, teacher leaders, and administrators, school board members ensure that conditions and structures are in place to support change. As trustees of the schools, school board members may influence district transformation. They help build the district vision and mission, develop leaders, allocate resources, approve programs, hire and evaluate the superintendent, engage families, and support professional learning.

Build the vision and mission

School boards are responsible for school and student results. This commitment is translated into a vision that emphasizes student and educator learning. Board members collaborate with the superintendent, district staff, and the broader community to develop a vision and mission that sets clear expectations for all students and educators in the district. The board communicates the vision by identifying the district's short-term, intermediate, and long-range goals; associated objectives; and supporting tasks (National School Boards Association, n.d.).

School board members' roles and responsibilities

Board members in learning systems

- Hire and support superintendents who value professional learning as a strategic way to increase student and staff success;
- Take seriously their role in ensuring all children's success by establishing a clearly articulated mission and vision and setting challenging goals;
- Understand the definition of professional learning and Learning Forward's Standards for Professional Learning, and advocate for professional learning to ensure every teacher in every classroom is learning what he or she needs to know to positively affect student learning;
- Explain the cycle of improvement to staff and community;
- Invest in staff by allocating sufficient resources to ensure professional learning throughout the district is adequately funded;
- Advance collective responsibility by examining policies and practices that contradict shared principles;
- Model collective responsibility by participating in learning communities;
- Adopt board agreements and model collaboration in all interactions with colleagues, superintendent, staff, and community members;
- Advocate with families and community for professional learning time, and communicate the effect of professional learning on student learning;
- Evaluate the superintendent based on his or her skill and expertise in advancing a learning system;
- Stay in continual dialogue with families and community members to ensure they deeply understand the power of professional learning and its effect on student learning; and
- Recognize learning leaders, progress toward achievement of goals, and success stories.

Source: Learning Forward. (2013). *Standards into practice: School system roles Innovation Configuration maps for Standards for Professional Learning.* Oxford, OH: Author.

The foundation for becoming a learning system is a vision grounded in a commitment to ensuring that everyone within the district is continuously learning. School board members are frequently the only citizens interested in the success of all of the district's students rather than students in just one school or classroom. Board members do everything necessary to ensure each student has an opportunity for the same quality education. As community representatives, board members adopt policies that hold educators accountable for results, allocate resources, and then support the learning that staff need in order to achieve those results.

Develop leaders

School board members set the expectation that the district will identify and support leaders, and that those leaders will be learning leaders. To develop learning leaders, learning systems support programs and strategies that allow aspiring leaders to continue learning. Administrators in learning systems plan ongoing, job-embedded learning and coaching not only for teachers, but also for district and school leaders. Research has documented that an effective school leader is second only to an effective teacher in ensuring student achievement (Leithwood, Seashore Louis, Anderson, & Wahlstrom, 2004).

Board members also set expectations that system and school leaders develop the knowledge and skills they need in order to lead professional learning. School boards commit to results-oriented learning for leaders, ask them to publicly share their professional learning goals, and ensure that leaders continue to learn until they attain their desired outcomes. They participate in professional learning consistent with the Standards for Professional Learning (Learning Forward, 2011).

Allocate resources

The board creates the framework for the school district's operations by approving and adopting a budget. All of the system's operations occur within that framework. One study found the national average of districts' spending on professional learning may be as low as 1.5% of the district's operating budget (Odden, 2011). Research also has found that successful school districts invest significantly in professional learning. The board is responsible for ensuring that the superintendent and district leaders create a budget that adequately funds professional learning at district and school levels to achieve the district's intended outcomes.

In learning systems, board members ask questions and insist on a budget that reflects the system's goals and vision. They base priorities on the system's vision, strategic plan, mission statement, and goals. While professional learning resources may not be clearly identified as a budget line item, these resources include nonduty time set aside for professional learning and collaboration; instructional coaches for teachers; leadership coaches for principals; technology; external assistance provider support; money for materials, supplies, and travel; and personnel who coordinate, deliver, evaluate, and manage professional learning.

School boards regularly ensure that the learning system's administration conducts time and financial audits to ensure professional learning resources are being used as intended and are having a positive effect on student achievement and staff learning.

Approve programs

School board members consider and approve new programs, from math and literacy curricula to technology initiatives, that may help improve student achievement. In a learning system, district leaders present the board with as much information as possible about a proposed program, including a clear theory of change and logic model that outlines essential professional learning. Board members ask pertinent questions before approving the program. Helping students achieve requires that those planning and implementing the program discuss data, personnel, financial requirements, need for communication with and input from appropriate groups, evaluation, and professional learning. Planning around these issues will lead to success.

In a learning system, board members understand how the proposed program complements the district's existing efforts. They consider such questions as, How does the program align with and add value to existing programs? How does the program support district goals? Does the proposed program duplicate existing efforts? They consider how many students are affected and the program's cost: Is it a relatively inexpensive pilot program to be tested with a small number of participants and then, if successful, extended to more students?

They also may ask about the kind of professional learning needed to support the program:

- What will it take for educators to successfully prepare for, implement, and sustain the program?
- Are there specific plans for how that professional learning will take place?
- How is the professional learning for the new program structured? Is it ongoing within schools?
- Will it provide the knowledge and skills that educators need in order to implement the program?
- Will it be consistent with established professional learning practices?

Board members may ask whether the program has been implemented in school districts they can visit or seek information about the program's results in other locations. They discuss proposed programs with stakeholders to gain each stakeholder's input and garner valuable data before making any decision. Involving stakeholders makes it more likely that the program will succeed (SREB, 2010).

Evaluate the superintendent

Through the evaluation process the school board makes public its commitment to continuous improvement and high expectations for students and educators. "If you want to see *continuous improvement* in your school," writes Del Stover (2012), "then take your annual board and superintendent's evaluations seriously."

Effective evaluations are part of the board and superintendent's ongoing relationship. The evaluation's quality and integrity affect how the superintendent sees his or her role as the district leader, as well as how the superintendent and school board function as a team and as community leaders in public education. Learning systems develop an evaluation process that is collaborative, open, and ongoing.

School board members use the superintendent evaluation to understand the superintendent's contribution to developing a learning system. Board members look for evidence that improving educators' practice has improved student results and ask the superintendent to document practices that demonstrate the improvement. They use benchmarks to identify progress, discuss the professional learning that will support the superintendent and staff in attaining agreed-upon goals, and set dates for regular feedback. At the end of each evaluation cycle, all are on the same page because of the continuous flow of information and dialogue around progress.

The school board can look to national and state associations for examples of evaluation processes. The superintendent evaluation process should model the employee evaluation process and advance individual and collective responsibility, continuous growth, and professional learning.

Engage families

In a learning system, school boards recognize the importance of parent engagement and expect to see district leaders make professional learning for families a priority. Learning systems extend interaction with families beyond one-way communication to include gatherings that promote dialogue about and understanding of how families can support schools and their children's education.

School board members can encourage schools to use various methods to engage families:

- Parent leadership academies that provide information about how schools work, their academic structure, discipline policies, and board members' roles

- Education sessions to offer information about curriculum, testing, and accountability measures

- Districtwide leadership programs that expose parents to school finance, facilities, assessments, accountability, curriculum, school board governance, and other topics in year-long courses

- Decision-making groups, including school councils, site councils, and communications groups, where family input is sought, welcomed, and considered

Families also need information as to why professional learning is important for educators. They may complain when schools release students early or for an entire day while teachers take part in professional learning. Many districts have not explained how teacher professional learning benefits children. Learning systems share information with a core group of families who can then translate the rationale for others, building support (Hoover-Dempsey et al., 2005).

When families have the information and knowledge they need to partner with schools for student achievement and continuous improvement, students have the best chance to succeed.

Support professional learning

School board members, as representatives of what the community wants for its schools, can light the fire of learning and set parameters for continuous improvement. To support continuous learning, board members enrich their own knowledge and advocate for, lead, and support professional learning. School board members serve many constituents—schools, students, teachers, administrators, paraprofessionals, support staff, community members, families, and fellow board members. Modeling and ensuring effective professional learning may be the most important thing a board member can do to effectively serve the community.

Board members spend time learning together, demonstrating that they value learning, and study Learning Forward's Standards for Professional Learning to become knowledgeable about what effective learning looks like for the district. The Standards include concepts board members need to understand—about learning communities, leadership, resources, data, learning designs, implementation, and outcomes (Learning Forward, 2011). School board members' understanding of these concepts and how each standard contributes to continuous improvement helps them understand the outcomes they are holding the district accountable for achieving.

Once members have studied and committed to the Standards, the board adopts them in order to create a system of continuous learning and improvement that fully develops personnel. The Standards define the kind of support to be provided to staff members and how that support should occur. School boards can ask for annual reports on how well professional learning measures up to the Standards.

School boards that adopt and treat the Standards seriously give educators the most influential tool possible: the opportunity to grow and learn in order to do the job they are asked to do. The school board is responsible for ensuring that all students learn, and each student's access to a high-quality education improves through every educator's access to ongoing professional learning.

Board's role is to advocate, support, suggest

What has been most evident in the change in our school district is the acknowledgment that we as a district can improve. The board is in the best position to be that voice saying, "We can do better." The board has to—in a constructive, appropriate way—be the group that reminds the administration that we can *always* improve.

Fort Wayne Community Schools is blessed with responsible, professional educators who elected responsible folks to lead them, and we have a very good school board. A good school board doesn't meddle in administrative matters, but is interested in overall goals for the district and in supporting the district and superintendent.

It's our role to hold the administration, the teachers, and ourselves accountable to objective standards. When the district lost a key referendum, we used the loss to change what we were doing. As a board, we rolled up our sleeves and articulated districtwide goals. We decided to use a balanced scorecard to open up everything we were doing to the public, and we set real districtwide objectives that we could measure. We evaluate the superintendent based on agreed upon standards and goals that can be objectively measured.

We want our professional educators to understand that we support them; however, we had to accept the fact that until we arrived at a critical mass of teachers who accept change, we were going nowhere. Once you reach critical mass and the majority of teachers understand that they can learn new ways of doing things, then change can occur. Professional learning was part of that. Without a full understanding of the need for professional learning, we would've been stuck saying, "We're doing everything just fine. It's not our problem."

But you only get to real change if teachers believe the board is supporting them. If as a board and administration, you support your professional educators and they sense you believe in them, you begin winning them over to change. You start to build excitement, enthusiasm, and camaraderie.

We have to treat educators as colleagues, not employees, and stand with them against attacks on public education. The administration needs to know the board is behind them and that we all speak with one voice.

As board members, we have to stay informed. We study, learn, read, and understand the issues in education today so we can provide strategic feedback. Every time a new board member is elected, we bring in a facilitator to lead a retreat on what is appropriate action by the board.

It takes understanding the current political obstacles to become a learning system. Our board has become very aware of the political landscape in which we are operating, and that is critical. Board members study educational issues, and we are advocates for public education.

What has happened to move this district forward wouldn't have happened without all of us—the administrative team, quality professional educators, and definitely not without the support of the school board. It took a three-legged stool to support the changes we've made.

— Mark GiaQuinta, school board president
Fort Wayne (Ind.) Community Schools

Reflection
questions

- How do we, as school board members, advocate for the changes needed for the district to become a learning system?

- How can we, as school board members, have more influence on the district's learning agenda?

- What actions have we taken to fulfill the roles and responsibilities identified in this chapter? How well prepared are we to take such actions? What do we need to learn to do so?

- How might we reallocate resources to better support learning?

- How do we engage stakeholders in understanding the relevance and importance of professional learning?

RESOURCES

Banks, P. A. & Maloney, R. J. (2007). Changing the subject of your evaluation. *School Administrator, 64*(6), 10–12, 14, 17.

Borba, A. L. (2010). The superintendent's evaluation: Bridging the gap from theory to practice. Available at www.aasa.org/content.aspx?id=12766&terms=the+superintendent's+evaluation%3a+bridging+the+gap

Carver, J. (2006). *Boards that make a difference: A new design for leadership in nonprofit and public organizations* (3rd ed.). San Francisco, CA: Jossey-Bass.

Dervarics, C. & O'Brien, E. (2011). Eight characteristics of effective school boards. Alexandria, VA: Center for Public Education and National School Boards Association.

Marquardt, M. J. (2011). *Building the learning organization: Achieving strategic advantage through a commitment to learning* (3rd ed.). Boston, MA: Nicholas Brealey Publishing.

Mizell, H. (2008). School board leadership is critical to put new definition into practice. *The Learning System, 4*(2), 2.

Mizell, H. (2010). *Why professional development matters.* Oxford, OH: Learning Forward.

Odden, A. (2011). Resources: The dollars and sense of comprehensive professional learning. *JSD, 32*(4), 26–27, 29–32.

TOOLS INDEX

TOOL	TITLE	PURPOSE
5.1	When policy joins practice	Gain deeper understanding of school board members' role in relation to effective professional learning and develop an action plan to ensure effective professional learning within the school system.
5.2	Assessing board actions as professional development leaders	Assess the school board's effectiveness in advancing effective professional learning.
5.3	Examining investments in professional learning	Gain new perspectives on the status of various aspects of professional learning and determine whether to consider new actions.
5.4	Establishing a learning agenda	Help school board members model and increase their effectiveness through intentional professional learning.
5.5	What's your professional development IQ?	Generate a productive conversation regarding research, perceptions, and misperceptions about professional learning and determine questions school board members might want to have answered about their district.
5.6	Adopting Standards	Discuss formally adopting the Standards.
5.7	Reflecting on practice	Identify actions to reinforce and add to the school board action and learning agenda.

CHAPTER 6

The role of the
superintendent

WHERE ARE WE NOW?

Our superintendent ensures that professional learning meets Learning Forward's Standards for Professional Learning.

STRONGLY AGREE   AGREE   NO OPINION   DISAGREE   STRONGLY DISAGREE

Our superintendent has led the district to adopt a vision and mission that embraces the tenets of continuous professional learning for educators and students.

STRONGLY AGREE   AGREE   NO OPINION   DISAGREE   STRONGLY DISAGREE

Our superintendent ensures that professional learning is a priority in developing leaders at all levels of the district.

STRONGLY AGREE   AGREE   NO OPINION   DISAGREE   STRONGLY DISAGREE

Our superintendent prioritizes resources for professional learning over competing issues.

STRONGLY AGREE   AGREE   NO OPINION   DISAGREE   STRONGLY DISAGREE

Our superintendent emphasizes professional learning for parents, business partners, and community volunteers.

STRONGLY AGREE   AGREE   NO OPINION   DISAGREE   STRONGLY DISAGREE

Superintendents play a leading role in transforming a school system into a learning system. Superintendents, in partnership with the school board and in collaboration with the central office, teacher leaders, and administrators, focus on improving student and educator performance outcomes. They align resources to meet the district vision and goals. They build leadership and encourage learning communities. They oversee the transformation of the central office by routinely using data, investing only in the most powerful strategies to support educator practice, and focusing deeply on a few priorities. They continually advance Learning Forward's Standards for Professional Learning.

According to Gene Bottoms and Jon Schmidt-Davis, "In all the talk about building principals'

key role in producing 'turnaround' high schools, one critical factor often gets lost in the policy shuffle. *Districts matter.* The vision and action of system leaders and school board members frequently determine whether principals can be effective in leading school improvement" (2010, p. ii).

Focus on performance outcomes

In a learning system, superintendents ensure that performance standards are defined for all employees and students and use those standards to identify employees' professional learning needs. To improve educator and student performance, writes Hayes Mizell, districts

- "Clearly and consistently articulate to educators and the community at large the purpose of professional learning;

Superintendents' roles and responsibilities

Superintendents in learning systems

- Use the cycle of continuous improvement (see Appendix) to lead professional learning;
- Advance collective responsibility for all students' achievement;
- Set high expectations for all;
- Focus on performance outcomes;
- Model learning by actively participating in individual, team, school, and district professional learning;
- Lead school boards to value, support, adopt, and advocate for professional learning by applying Learning Forward's Standards for Professional Learning to their work;
- Foster learning communities in all schools;
- Develop the capacity to give and receive feedback;
- Build leadership throughout the organization;
- Develop a support system for school leaders that includes coaching;
- Align resources to ensure adequate support for professional learning;
- Use data effectively to assess the effect of professional learning on changing educator practice and increasing student learning;
- Expect learning and advance the Standards for Professional Learning; and
- Inspire others and advocate for children, education, and professional learning.

Source: Learning Forward. (2013). *Standards into practice: School system roles Innovation Configuration maps for Standards for Professional Learning.* Oxford, OH: Author.

- Hold educators accountable for organizing and engaging in professional development that causes teachers to become more effective;
- Support educators' application and refinement of their new learning; and
- Collect and report data that document the extent to which professional development is raising the performance levels of teachers and their students" (2011, p. 2).

Effective superintendents use district goals, along with the standards set by the board, to self-assess their performance and define their own learning priorities. They engage in coaching, feedback, and reflection to analyze and improve the effects of their leadership on student learning outcomes.

They build congruence between professional learning and district and school priorities. They explain to the board, staff, and other stakeholders the connections between district and school goals, individual performance evaluations, and professional learning. They engage district and

"Keeping the instructional core at the center of our work also supports stronger alignment and coherence between and among classrooms, schools, and central office," writes Kenneth Salim, Learning Forward's 2012 president and superintendent of the Waymouth (Mass.) Public Schools. "Professional learning should build on what educators have learned and also align with local and national curriculum and assessments." (2012, p. 69).

school leaders in integrating professional learning with district operations, including finance, assessment, curriculum, and human resources.

Align resources to the vision and goals

Superintendents in learning systems ensure that sufficient resources are available for the district to achieve intended adult and student learning outcomes. Allan Odden suggests that for districts to become a learning system, they take the following actions:

- Eliminate all professional development, program improvement, and training programs not focused on school or district curriculum and instruction.
- Use the majority of teachers' pupil-free days and any others provided for training for curriculum-based professional development that is central to district and school goals.
- Organize schools into multiple, appropriate collaborative teams so that all teachers have time to incorporate new instructional practices into their classroom practice.

(Odden, 2011)

Odden recommends a cost structure that gives districts a way to examine and deploy resources to get the best return on investment: "(T)he costs of a comprehensive, effective, and ongoing professional development program for all teachers is . . . about $590 per pupil or 5.4% of a district's operating expenditure per pupil. And that figure includes 10 pupil-free days for training, instructional coaches at a rate of one for every 200 students (eight teachers), and sufficient funds for trainers and miscellaneous costs" (2011, p. 31).

Effective professional development leads to improved instructional practice that boosts student learning and helps close achievement gaps, according to research. "Low-performing schools are unlikely to turn around unless educators who work in schools have extensive opportunities to learn and implement more effective practices to engage students in learning challenging materials," write Bottoms and Schmidt-Davis. "Effective districts invest in the learning not only of students, but also of teachers, principals, district staff, superintendents and school board members" (2010, pp. iv-v).

Barbara Nakaoka, superintendent of Hacienda La Puenta Unified School District in City of Industry, California, said superintendents' budgets make explicit their values. In a system that serves more than 20,000 students, 70% of whom are eligible for free- and reduced-price lunch, Nakaoka prioritized funding time and staff for professional learning aligned with district, school, and individual goals. To ensure resources were not wasted, she used data to monitor implementation and effects (Von Frank, 2011).

Build leadership

A six-year study on the effects of successful school leadership found that leaders provided direction and exercised influence over student learning. The study states that in order to transform districts into organizations that consistently graduate students who meet higher standards, district leaders need to design professional learning for district administrators and principals and a framework for individual and collective growth to realize leaders' potential (Seashore Louis, Leithwood, Wahlstrom, & Anderson, 2010).

According to Gene Spanneut and Mike Ford, "Superintendents who champion the development of their principals as instructional leaders begin by establishing common understandings with them about why principals' instructional leadership is necessary for school success. They reinforce this by actively providing support for their principals to develop and refine their effectiveness as instructional leaders" (2008, p. 28).

Superintendents in learning systems develop their own and others' capacity for leading professional learning. They set expectations that aspiring leaders prepare for those roles. They develop leadership throughout the system, not just at the school leader level.

The most successful school districts have comprehensive systems to support and use principal *and* teacher leadership. Karen Seashore Louis, Kenneth Leithwood, Kyla Wahlstrom, and Stephen E. Anderson report, "When principals and teachers share leadership, teachers' working relationships with one another are stronger and student achievement is higher. District support for shared leadership fosters the development of professional communities. Where teachers feel attached to a professional community, they are more likely to use instructional practices that are linked to improved student learning" (2010, p. 282).

Encourage learning communities

"Superintendents provide the daily vision and oversight necessary to turn around their districts' battleship of traditional staff development," Mizell writes. "Only superintendents have the authority to organize and deploy school districts' resources so a new approach to professional learning becomes an operational reality at the school level in all schools" (2008, p. 2).

Superintendents in learning systems understand that to continuously improve as an organization, the district must leverage best practices.

Learning communities offer a powerful structure for educators to use to build collective responsibility and for teachers to use to transfer educational expertise from classroom to classroom and school to school. Superintendents ensure that learning teamwork aligns with district and school priorities and that leaders monitor implementation for fidelity. Superintendents establish a consistent process to define learning communities' work, ensuring that staff and students achieve their intended goals.

Learning system superintendents participate in their own district learning communities and in communities outside the system. They model the application of the district-adopted definition of quality professional learning in meetings and in formal and informal learning conversations.

Use data

Superintendents in learning systems routinely use data to drive action. They establish a plan to review district and school progress toward achieving professional learning goals, and evaluate how professional learning prompts changes in educator practice, student learning, and district and school culture, structures, and processes. There is a difference, however, between valuing data and using data appropriately.

When district leaders use data appropriately, they engage all those affected by the data in analyzing the data. Superintendents in learning systems develop their own and staff members' capacity to analyze and interpret data. They ensure that all staff have the knowledge and skills needed to access, organize, display, analyze, and interpret system and school data, as well as use data to establish professional learning goals.

They ensure that multiple sources of data are used to make district and school decisions about professional learning. They use formative and summative student, educator, and district data

to monitor progress on goals; decipher trends, patterns, outliers, and root causes; and make inferences and predictions. They consider trends over time and possible causal factors before initiating an innovation or research-based remedy. They also ensure that the data analysis pinpoints strengths in teaching and professional learning needs. This ongoing analysis of data at all levels of the organization lets everyone in the district answer the question, "How well are we doing?" and guides more effective decision making.

Chris Steinhauser, superintendent of the Long Beach (Calif.) Unified School District, says professional development played a key role in the large school district's success. "When you have highly trained individuals," he said, "you're able to really push looking at student data, finding out what your holes are and aligning your professional development to whatever those proficiencies are. You can then attack whatever the issue is and use the data to see if whatever you identified as the problem and the solution are working" (in Crow, 2009 p. 56.)

Go deep on few priorities

A national study of urban school districts that transformed the relationship between the central office and schools found that they built staff members' capacity by radically changing central office administrators' daily work so that the work focused directly on improving teaching and learning. "Deep, sustainable changes in practice, furthermore, are not likely to occur spontaneously, or without concentrated attention to building capacity," write Meredith I. Honig, Michael A. Copland, Lydia Rainey, Julie Anna Lorton, and Morena Newton (2010, p. xi).

Superintendents in learning systems are driven by a vision, mission, and goals. They set high standards and explicit educator and student performance outcomes. They know and understand adult learning theories, research, and models.

They ensure that support for reaching expectations is differentiated according to needs or learning styles. Superintendents in learning systems advocate for appropriate learning designs, including in-person, blended, and online professional learning. They model their own active engagement throughout these processes.

They support research-based tools that help staff implement what is expected of them instructionally.

Effective superintendents also understand the change process and patiently support staff through changes. They receive and review regular reports on implementation in order to respond to concerns. They stay focused during the challenge of long-term change and remind constituents that substantive change requires three to five years. They take time to celebrate with the school board and staff any progress toward system, school, and individual goals, and to recognize how professional learning contributes to achieving those goals.

Superintendents in learning systems advocate for appropriate learning designs, including in-person, blended, and online professional learning.

In the West Valley School District in Spokane, Washington, Superintendent Polly Crowley created structures and support systems to ensure that professional learning is routine for all staff in the 4,000-student district. All use a cycle of inquiry to guide their learning. The superintendent's 2012 problems of practice were

- Making all principal meetings learning-centered by incorporating new knowledge, research, and relevancy into district and building leaders' problems of practice;

- Conducting goal-setting conferences with each district leader twice a year;

- Providing required resources, such as data and time; and

- Visiting classrooms, followed by data conversations with the principal and teacher.

(Rasmussen & Karschney, 2012)

Advance the standards

In learning systems, the superintendent becomes the leading advocate using Learning Forward's Standards for Professional Learning to achieve effective professional learning districtwide. The superintendent recommends that the school board members adopt and commit to the Standards. The superintendent becomes the district expert on the Standards, helping staff, public officials, and community members understand all that is expected as a result of adopting the Standards by explaining the connection between professional learning and student learning. The superintendent expects that all educators throughout the district will use the Standards to make decisions about professional learning. The superintendent uses the Standards to define actions and respond to criticism. Adopting and adhering to the Standards gives the superintendent confidence that professional learning in the district will achieve its intended outcomes.

Superintendents in learning systems acknowledge their own accountability for the quality and results of professional learning. They establish the district and school conditions required for effective professional learning, including allocating resources, setting policies, establishing calendars, maintaining schedules, and putting in place procedures. They ensure that staff understand and use a cycle of improvement grounded in research. (See Appendix.)

In 2011, McLouth (Kansas) Unified School District 342, a small rural district, became the first school system to adopt Learning Forward's Standards for Professional Learning. Sherry Thomas, a teacher, and Superintendent Steve Splichal led discussion and learning sessions with the school board, and board members then adopted the Standards, reallocated the resources to put them in place, and determined exactly what data the board expected to receive to ensure the district met the Standards and did all it could to support teachers.

Chief learner gets everyone singing from the same book

What sparked so much of our concept of district improvement was that we had reached a plateau for student achievement. We were trying to figure out why we weren't going faster or hadn't moved—and in some cases, why we'd gone backward. And it was because we weren't really learning from each other. We were isolated in terms of sharing practices and being a professional learning community.

At around the same time that I became superintendent, elections brought in a new wave of board members. The new board members came in wanting to improve the district and hold it more accountable, and as they developed what they stood for, they gave me the backing to make these ideas part of our conversation. The board set a direction and policies, and I had to take the board's direction and vision and operationalize it. It was almost this perfect marriage of having a very active public board talking about accountability and me as the superintendent having to find a vehicle that made it all make sense.

My role as superintendent is to be the district's chief learner and to model that. As a part of my work with the cabinet, we are developing what professional learning means in the district. We are taking a series of courses to explore what it means to be a learning community at a districtwide level. We talk a lot about the district office being a resource for schools, and how that idea has to be more than just lip service. Our role at the district office is to know our schools well.

Twice each month, my academic team meets to talk about cross-department projects. These are folks from Title 1, the English language learner department, curriculum, special education, response to intervention, guidance. They coordinate their work, and now that core group is attending principal meetings. The result is that principals have an opportunity to talk about academic, curriculum, or special education issues with their supervisor, their assistant superintendent, and the directors and coordinators from the academic team. They're solving problems looking at each other rather than through emails or memos.

That's professional learning. That's a professional learning community.

It's not my role to set up that kind of collaboration. It should happen naturally because people know that central office is a resource and they're there to make sure that we stay on point. I'm informed, and I just want to hear about the result when we meet in cabinet.

At the same time, all of our goals have to be within the frame of the board's goals. Then I have to communicate with the board about what the issues are and what the data say, but we can't settle matters with them before including all of the people in the classrooms and in the departments.

The combination of the board setting a direction and being extremely transparent about the need for accountability, and then the superintendent, cabinet, administrators, and teachers coming together as professional learners really operationalizes our vision. And the message is clear about our goals and our vision, about our moral purpose for educating all students. If we're all still not on the exact same page, at least we're in the same book. Because how can anyone argue with educating more students to higher standards?

— Wendy Robinson, superintendent
Fort Wayne (Ind.) Community Schools

Reflection
questions

- How might our superintendent's role change based on this guidance for leading a learning system?

- Which of the superintendent's roles and responsibilities in a learning system seem most important and relevant to our school district?

- What kind of professional learning might help a superintendent fulfill those roles and responsibilities?

- What role will Learning Forward's Standards for Professional Learning play in transforming our district?

- What ideas from the chapter can we identify that demand immediate attention? What ideas can we identify as needing long-term attention?

RESOURCES

Armstrong, A. (2012, Fall). Where do I start? *Tools for Learning Schools, 16*(1), 1–3.

Armstrong, A. (2012, Fall). Advocacy can be the avenue for change. *The Leading Teacher, 8*(1), 1, 4–5.

Hirsh, S. A. (2008, Fall). Let stakeholders know what you intend to accomplish. *JSD, 29*(4), 53–54.

Hirsh, S. & Hord, S. (2012, August). A playbook for data. *JSD, 33*(4), 10–14.

Learning Forward. (2013). *Standards into practice: School system roles Innovation Configuration maps for Standards for Professional Learning.* Oxford, OH: Author.

Marzano, R. J., Waters, T., & McNulty, B. A. (2005). *School leadership that works: From research to results.* Alexandria, VA: ASCD.

Wells, C., & Keane, W. G. (2008, Winter). Building capacity for professional learning communities through a systems approach: A toolbox for superintendents. *AASA Journal of Scholarship & Practice, 4*(4), 24–32.

TOOLS INDEX

TOOL	TITLE	PURPOSE
6.1	Introducing the Standards for Professional Learning	Introduce a leadership team to the Standards for Professional Learning.
6.2	Adopting standards	Guide a discussion with the school board about adopting the Standards for Professional Learning.
6.3	Aligning actions with the Standards	Determine the superintendent's effectiveness for advancing quality professional learning.
6.4	Reflecting on leadership	Assess current practice and determine potential new directions.
6.5	Linking research to practice	Use this protocol to guide discussion of foundational research that can connect direct actions to student achievement.
6.6	Using data to guide the learning system	Consider the superintendent's role in using data to advance the learning systems agenda by studying an excerpt from *A Playbook for Professional Learning* by Stephanie Hirsh and Shirley Hord.
6.7	Building a case for professional learning	Conduct an internal analysis of current professional learning expenditures using this article and chart and determine how to reallocate or justify additional investments.
6.8	Funding professional learning	Conduct an internal analysis of current professional learning expenditures using this article and chart and determine how to reallocate or justify additional investments.

CHAPTER 7

The role of
district leaders

WHERE ARE WE NOW?

All district leaders practice professional learning consistent with Learning Forward's Standards for Professional Learning.

STRONGLY AGREE	AGREE	NO OPINION	DISAGREE	STRONGLY DISAGREE

All district leaders model continuous learning.

STRONGLY AGREE	AGREE	NO OPINION	DISAGREE	STRONGLY DISAGREE

District leaders design learning experiences that are systematic, ongoing, job embedded, sustained, and results oriented.

STRONGLY AGREE	AGREE	NO OPINION	DISAGREE	STRONGLY DISAGREE

All district leaders serve and support site-based staff with knowledge, research, and best practices about professional learning.

STRONGLY AGREE	AGREE	NO OPINION	DISAGREE	STRONGLY DISAGREE

All district leaders are experts in their area of responsibility so that staff have the knowledge they need in order to ensure all students are engaged in high-quality instruction.

STRONGLY AGREE	AGREE	NO OPINION	DISAGREE	STRONGLY DISAGREE

District leaders build trusting, respectful relationships with school leaders and engage them in a process of discovery and inquiry before making decisions that affect teaching and learning.

STRONGLY AGREE	AGREE	NO OPINION	DISAGREE	STRONGLY DISAGREE

Over the last decade, central office personnel have been on the front line of managing the changes associated with new accountability requirements, state content standards, student assessments, and principal and teacher evaluation systems. These massive shifts have required district leaders to develop new skills and lead in new ways.

In traditional central offices, "units were organized with staff assigned to deliver particular services to all or large groups of schools, and to deliver those services in a relatively one-size-fits-all manner"(Honig et al., 2010, p. 8). Leaders of those units had resources for which they were

> When district administrators regularly and actively engage with site-based staff, they eliminate any mystery about how district leaders are facilitating, coaching, and supporting schools' work.

responsible and over which they held authority. School personnel in need of the resources often had to approach these gatekeepers individually, which was both inefficient and ineffective.

In districts that have transformed their structures and practices, "individual central office staff members specialized in particular schools, not services, and were assigned to address whatever needs arose in those schools across their department; likewise, staff were assigned to cross-unit project teams that addressed particular problems or challenges related to school support that did not fit neatly within any one central office unit" (Honig et al., 2010, p. 71).

In a learning system, central office personnel assume collective responsibility for schools and go about their work very differently. They are responsible not for departments and programs only, but for student learning. They demonstrate that responsibility by engaging in data-informed conversations about student achievement. These conversations model a culture of collective responsibility for schools. When district administrators regularly and actively engage with site-based staff, they eliminate any mystery about how district leaders are facilitating, coaching, and supporting schools' work.

Effective central offices have transitioned from a commanding and controlling management style to one focused on support and solutions. As professional learning has moved from a centralized to a school-based function, central office staff members' work has changed from determining content and delivering the learning to assisting school staff. In a learning system, leaders collaborate rather than compete, build systems rather than silos, and exchange rather than hoard information. As Margaret Wheatley notes (1992), control is not the connective tissue; dynamic interconnectedness matters.

Central office personnel in a learning system set expectations, build capacity, provide resources that help schools achieve goals, monitor results, hold educators accountable when outcomes are not met, and meet the challenge of complex work.

Set expectations

People have a strong emotional attachment to compelling goals and visions that align with their belief systems. They fully engage in those things they care deeply about. How district leaders engage others in conversations about the district's moral purpose, how they structure learning approaches to share stories with one another, and what they do to deepen the organization's culture around its moral purpose all matter. When staff sense they are a dynamic part of a larger system held together by an inspiring moral purpose they are energized, and that energy becomes the fuel that transforms the organization (Loehr & Schwartz, 2003).

Effective district leaders help develop a shared vision and set of values, and they establish a compelling moral purpose everyone in the organization owns. District leaders work with communities throughout the system to establish goals so that the goals become nonnegotiable. The collaborative community, not just district leaders, monitors progress toward achieving the district's goals, shifting practices and professional learning when anyone encounters a barrier.

With effective collaboration, district leaders create trusting relationships. Employees know they can count on district leaders to be reliable,

District leaders' roles and responsibilities

District leaders in learning systems

- View leadership as a shared responsibility among all district- and school-level staff;
- Create a collaborative culture among district and school leaders, believing all to be self-motivated;
- See professional learning as fundamental to student performance;
- Apply the cycle of continuous improvement (see Appendix) with fidelity to lead professional learning;
- Model collaboration and a culture of high expectations, collective responsibility, mutual respect, and trust;
- Establish program evaluations, including evaluations of professional learning, to gather data about program effectiveness and adjust as needed;
- Engage in professional learning in order to develop expertise in specific areas of responsibility and ensure that the best research, practices and protocols, and systems for learning are made available to students and staff;
- Are deeply knowledgeable about Learning Forward's Standards for Professional Learning and experts in adult learning and its design;
- Guarantee parents and students a rigorous, relevant, viable curriculum;
- Differentiate support and service systems based on school needs;
- Hold school communities accountable for results while ensuring adequate service and support that allow schools to achieve their goals;
- Share authority for decisions with school leaders, expecting the best from everyone, presuming positive intent, and using inquiry and problems of practice to overcome issues and barriers schools face; and
- Inspire others, encourage innovation, highlight positive deviance, and recognize and celebrate progress and achievement.

Source: Learning Forward. (2013). *Standards into practice: School system roles Innovation Configuration maps for Standards for Professional Learning.* Oxford, OH: Author.

sincere, and competent. Trust and shared vision cannot come from a directive or mandate; they come from hours of conversation about what is important to the learning community, from goals that stakeholders set, and as the result of actions and learning undertaken to achieve those goals.

Build capacity

In a learning system, learning is the core work of all district staff members. Effective district leaders are assertive learners. Central office administrators in learning systems develop their knowledge and skills about continuous improvement and model a cycle of continuous improvement (see Appendix) to school-based staff. Central office personnel work through the cycle of continuous improvement, determine their own learning goals, and engage in learning experiences that close their knowledge and skill gaps. Everyone at the district and building levels agrees to use the same continuous improvement model. Doing so allows for common language and increases the likelihood of common practice.

District staff may seek outside expertise or coaching support. They gauge the effect of their own learning and determine what additional learning experiences they need—from experts, colleagues, or other sources. Administrators pay careful attention to modeling their own growth and learning, which should be transparent and aligned to schools' work.

District leaders use their expertise in curriculum design to plan thoughtful, districtwide professional learning based on a clear theory of change and a logic model. These learning experiences are systematic, ongoing, job embedded, sustained, and results oriented. Leaders understand pedagogical and content knowledge related to the content areas they support, and they reflect with those they serve about the best strategies for increasing student success in those areas.

District leaders align systems and structures to secure, develop, and support principals by improving pre-service training, establishing hiring procedures that identify promising future leaders, and ensuring that hard-to-staff schools have top-quality leaders. They value school leaders' contributions and ensure that building leaders have access to professional learning that develops their proficiency in the skills, attitudes, and behaviors needed to create effective learning environments and align their practices and those of their leadership team members to district goals (Center for Educational Leadership & Honig, 2013).

Central office leaders in a learning system work collaboratively with site-based leaders to ensure that together they achieve results. In *Multipliers: How the Best Leaders Make Everyone Smarter*, authors Michelle Wiseman and Greg McKeown (2010) state that "multipliers extract all of the capability from people" (p. 11). Multipliers value others' genius and capitalize on the intelligence of all those in the organization. They help others to extend and grow their intelligence. "Our research confirms that Multipliers not only access people's current capability, they stretch it," the authors write. "They get more from people than they knew they had to give. People reported actually getting smarter around Multipliers. The implication is that intelligence itself can grow" (p. 12). (See Table 7.1.)

Becoming a multiplier requires courage, confidence, and belief in collective wisdom. In a learning system, central office administrators believe that together, all are smarter, and so they make sure each voice is not only heard, but valued.

Provide resources

In learning systems, central office staff serve and support site-based staff with knowledge, research, and professional learning based on best practices. Central office staff structure departments to meet

Table 7.1 Five disciplines of multipliers

DIMINISHER		MULTIPLIER	
The Empire Builder	Hoards resources and underutilizes talent	**The Talent Magnet**	Attracts talented people and uses them at their highest point of contribution
The Tyrant	Creates a tense environment that suppresses people's thinking and capabilities	**The Liberator**	Creates an intense environment that requires people's best thinking and work
The Know-It-All	Gives directives that showcase how much they know	**The Challenger**	Defines opportunity that causes people to stretch
The Decision Maker	Makes centralized, abrupt decisions that confuse the organization	**The Debate Maker**	Drives sound decisions through rigorous debate and learning
The Micromanager	Drives results through personal involvementt	**The Investor**	Gives people ownership for results and invests in their success

Source: Wiseman, L. with McKeown, G. (2010). *The 5 Disciplines of Multipliers.* New York, NY: Harper Business. p. 23

school needs rather than adhering to structures outlined in traditional flow charts that are organized by role (superintendent, director, consultant, coordinator) or function (human resources, maintenance and operations, school administration, finance, technology, curriculum and instruction, legal).

Working collaboratively and focusing on a shared vision of districtwide priorities, central office staff advocate for building-level staff, helping them access district resources in ways that transform teacher practice and increase student learning. School district budgeting often masks intradistrict disparities, allowing administrators and policymakers to ignore inequities and putting students who live below the poverty level at a significant disadvantage (Luebchow, 2009).

District leaders must work to meet the needs of low-achieving schools, especially when district funding disparities cause these schools to be disproportionally staffed with teachers and principals with the least experience and fewest credentials.

To avoid such problems, teams of district and school leaders use data to decide how to allocate resources based on student and adult needs. District leaders also recognize the specific needs of each school's leader, staff, and students. They do

Learning system leaders see each person on the team as essential to achieving the district's goals for all students.

not play favorites. One principal does not receive more services than another simply by calling in and requesting aid.

Learning system leaders see each person on the team as essential to achieving the district's goals for all students. "These leaders gush with enthusiasm when describing their staff and students. They view those with whom they work as the solution to the challenges they face and not the cause of those challenges, and they demonstrate their regard for and commitment to others by creating the conditions to help them succeed" (DuFour & Marzano, 2011, p. 197).

Monitor results

Ensuring that educators have the knowledge and skills to implement a program with fidelity requires setting clear expectations for the knowledge and skills they are expected to gain, and being clear about interim benchmarks and final assessments.

In a learning system, district leaders ensure programs—including professional learning—that are vital to student success are continually evaluated. They use a variety of sources and types of student, educator, and system data to plan, assess, and evaluate professional learning. They use multiple data collection tools to diagnose, plan, monitor, assess, and celebrate results. Tools include: Innovation Configuration maps, Levels of Use inventories, snapshots, walk-throughs, classroom observations, observations of professional learning, teacher surveys, and student focus groups. They gather the data needed, share it with school leaders, and initiate shifts in practice (Killion, 2008; Marzano & Waters, 2009). In some cases, district offices contract with external evaluators to independently evaluate a program or initiative.

Although they have well-planned evaluation systems in place, learning system leaders do not rely on evaluations alone to change adult practices. They also take steps to ensure that system priorities and initiatives are aligned.

Hold educators accountable

To support implementation of new innovations in a learning system, district leaders use Learning Forward's definition of quality professional learning, the principles behind the definition, and the Standards for Professional Learning. District leaders also know how adults learn, understand career stages, respect the stages of concern adults experience as they implement innovations, and are adept at observing and tracking teachers' levels of implementation. They work with school leaders to develop standards-driven lessons and analyze those lessons with others to ensure instructional strategies are effective and research-based.

Learning system leaders ensure that the district has the capacity to promote learning for all students and create a culture in which learning is the norm. They model, encourage, and support collective responsibility based on the belief that learning in a community has the greatest impact on staff and student outcomes. They establish structures that encourage staff to share their best ideas. They reward educators for collective or team, rather than individual, performance.

All district leaders need highly developed expertise in their area of responsibility to ensure all students are exposed to high-quality instruction. District leaders must stay current in their field in order to understand quality teaching and learning. They must engage in continuous improvement through thoughtful, reflective conversations that lead to quality decisions about strategies to increase student success.

Meet the challenge of complex work

School districts are complex organizations not only because of the challenge of ensuring all students and staff are learning, but because the work must be done by many different people. The heart of this work, its moral purpose, is ensuring all students are successful—another reason the work is so complex.

A study by Stephen Fink, Anneke Markholt, John Bransford, and Michael A. Copland (2011) found that few district and school leaders are ready to do the complex work needed to create high-achieving learning systems. The study reached the following conclusions:

- Too few leaders charged with leading instructional improvement have developed sufficient expertise to identify high-quality teaching and explain what makes that teaching high quality.
- With limited instructional expertise, school leaders are more likely to have difficulty identifying and envisioning an improvement trajectory for specific teachers.

> All district leaders need highly developed expertise in their area of responsibility to ensure all students are exposed to high-quality instruction.

- With limited instructional expertise, school and district leaders are more likely to have difficulty envisioning broader strategic improvement initiatives aimed at deepening the professional learning of all teachers within a system.

Effective district leaders meet these challenges and inspire courage and high levels of performance by building a shared vision around a strong, uplifting, moral purpose; learning from the best; inspiring others to commit to innovation and risk taking; challenging assumptions that hold districts back; and designing and engaging in systematic, ongoing, results-oriented professional learning.

Tearing down central office silos

One of our aha moments as district leaders came when we realized that the old notion of working in silos at the central office doesn't work. It fails to provide the support people need and want when we're looking for long-term change.

The role of central office in the past was that if a principal brought forward a problem, the central office would provide information; however, the professional learning component wasn't really addressed. As a principal, if I had a concern, I would call the director in the central office and she might say, "Call the curriculum department. They'll work you through it." Currently, if someone comes with a concern, we as central office leaders ask, "What is the issue?" and "What do the data show?" And then we work with the school team on site to come up with a resolution and the necessary professional learning for the staff. As district administrators, we try to provide whatever supports school-based leaders need.

In the past, when we analyzed data, that's where it ended. We struggled with next steps. Now when we work with schools based on data to identify a need, I can gather the necessary resources across departments—curriculum, special education, English language learners, and others. We work together to go through our theory of change and problem solve. We collectively put our heads together to increase teacher effectiveness and student achievement. We're now gathering everyone around the table to consider, overall, how we can support our schools for the greater good.

In our office, we're a learning team of five administrators—the assistant superintendent for elementary education, two directors of elementary education, and two technology coordinators.

We have weekly team meetings to look at individual schools and analyze data to identify schools of concern and schools to celebrate. We use the state standardized test and also district common assessment data, looking at results school by school and, at times, at the level of individual teachers. We participate periodically with teacher leadership teams at the schools so they see what analysis looks like—it's a "practice what you preach" approach. We figure out barriers to student learning and commit to doing something rather than just mandating change, giving schools edicts, and calling it a day.

Central office administrators really want to collaborate with schools. Two years ago, we held a principals' institute at which central administrators and principals learned together. We used tuning protocols and discussed our district's theory of change.

Central office staff yearn for that kind of partnership. We're disconnected from children, and yet the children are why we come to work every day. It's important to get into schools so that we continue to feel connected to our purpose.

We still have a ways to go to become a learning system top to bottom. We recognize that it takes some people longer than others to get there, but we've already seen the benefits in improved student achievement as a result of the changes we've made. Our big push is to stay the course. We recognize that there will be distractions, but we always go back to our moral purpose—educating *all* students to high standards.

— John Key, director of elementary education
Fort Wayne (Ind.) Community Schools

Reflection
questions

- What are district leaders' most important roles and responsibilities?

- How will the relationship between our district's central office staff and schools change as the district becomes a learning system?

- What knowledge and skills might our district leaders need in order to operate effectively in a learning system?

- What are our district leaders doing to build capacity?

- How is our central office structured to support schools?

- How do district leaders monitor the results of innovations in our schools?

RESOURCES

Fullan, M. (2009). *The challenge of change: Start school improvement now* (2nd ed.). Thousand Oaks, CA: Corwin Press.

Leithwood, K., Seashore Louis, K., Anderson, S., & Wahlstrom, K. (2004). *How leadership influences student learning.* St. Paul, MN: University of Minnesota, Center for Applied Research and Educational Improvement, and University of Toronto, Ontario Institute for Studies in Education.

Mizell, H. (June, 2010). Whether a building or a state of mind, the central office must evolve. *JSD, 31*(3), 46–48.

Von Frank, V. (2009, December/January.). District-level professional learning builds a framework of support. *The Learning System, 4*(4), 1, 6–7.

Von Frank, V. (2010, June). Central office plants the seeds, schools cultivate their own learning. *JSD, 31*(3), 38–41.

TOOLS INDEX

TOOL	TITLE	PURPOSE
7.1	Understanding the principles, definition, and Standards for Professional Learning	Identify the critical attributes of a learning system and the effectiveness of the cycle of continuous.
7.2	Declare roles and responsibilities using KASAB	Describe the roles and responsibilities of district level leaders in a learning system.
7.3	Support the elements of learning and leadership	Assess district leadership support for professional learning, a distinguishing characteristic of learning systems.
7.4	Designing professional learning	Ensure that district leaders engage principals and school leadership teams in effective professional learning that leads to practices aligned with new expectations.
7.5	Assessing professional learning's effect	Learn to evaluate professional learning to ensure that outcomes are reached.

CHAPTER 8

The role of principals and teacher leaders

WHERE ARE WE NOW?

Our district has leadership standards and an evaluation system that clearly define the principal's role in supporting effective teaching and learning.

STRONGLY AGREE   AGREE   NO OPINION   DISAGREE   STRONGLY DISAGREE

Our principals are effective in creating shared vision and values within their schools.

STRONGLY AGREE   AGREE   NO OPINION   DISAGREE   STRONGLY DISAGREE

Our principals develop and distribute leadership within their schools.

STRONGLY AGREE   AGREE   NO OPINION   DISAGREE   STRONGLY DISAGREE

Principals and teacher leaders in our district understand the relationship between adult learning and student success.

STRONGLY AGREE   AGREE   NO OPINION   DISAGREE   STRONGLY DISAGREE

All of our principals and teacher leaders see themselves as leaders of learning in their schools and use data to monitor results.

STRONGLY AGREE   AGREE   NO OPINION   DISAGREE   STRONGLY DISAGREE

Our principals and teacher leaders advocate for effective professional learning and understand how to create the systems and structures necessary to support it.

STRONGLY AGREE   AGREE   NO OPINION   DISAGREE   STRONGLY DISAGREE

Principals and teacher leaders in learning systems keep instruction at the forefront, understand Learning Forward's Standards for Professional Learning, and advocate for quality professional learning. They clearly articulate the link between educators' learning and improved student outcomes, and they set clear expectations for others in their schools. They educate parents and students about the power and value of adult learning and the impact that learning has on student learning. They provide staff with opportunities to develop leadership skills and knowledge, and they nurture and coach them as they develop their own capacity to learn about, lead, and advocate for professional learning. They create the support systems and structures that will ensure effective learning occurs for educators and students into the 21st century.

Few jobs present as many challenges to an individual's intelligence, problem-solving ability, and emotions as school leadership. Principals deal with literally hundreds of brief tasks each day, sometimes 50 to 60 separate interactions in an hour (Peterson & Deal, 1998; Peterson & Cosner, 2005). In addition, over the last few decades as the principal's role has changed from that of a building manager to an instructional leader, many principals have had to learn new skills.

An effective principal masters a broad spectrum of educational and management challenges. To improve student learning, leaders motivate teachers and encourage professional community (The Wallace Foundation, 2012). Essentially, leaders support teacher and student learning by creating an effective system of professional learning.

Principals' and teacher leaders' roles and responsibilities

Principals and teacher leaders
- Model and cultivate courageous leadership;
- Have an intense, zealous, and persistent focus on student learning;
- Develop systems that support students and adults;
- Build a sense of collective responsibility for the learning of all students;
- Use a compelling moral purpose to build shared vision and values that pave the way for accelerating staff and student learning;
- Know the importance of skillful, precise work on curriculum, assessment, and instructional design and implementation;
- Value professional learning as the means to increase teacher effectiveness and student learning;
- Develop others' leadership skills;
- Advocate for profession learning;
- Lead change processes and create support systems;
- Distribute responsibility for people, data, and processes that nurture a culture of continuous improvement and empowerment; and
- Regularly monitor, recognize, and highlight progress, and celebrate successes.

Source: Learning Forward. (2013). *Standards into practice: School system roles Innovation Configuration maps for Standards for Professional Learning.* Oxford, OH: Author.

Create a shared vision and values

Highly effective principals inspire others to own the district's moral purpose. They guide school staff through processes and protocols for figuring out what the moral purpose really means and what it looks like when they are achieving it.

Principals regularly ask, If we are honestly living our moral purpose, how would we handle this situation? What would we be doing? What would our students be doing? What would parents be doing?

Effective principals also gently confront long-held assumptions that prevent a school community from achieving desired student outcomes. They ask, Is that belief really getting us what we want? If we believed. . . , what results might we have?

Teacher leaders inspire colleagues by modeling the district's moral purpose. They contribute to discussions of barriers and, by unearthing their own assumptions, help others recognize their own.

Develop capacity and share decision making

In a learning system, district and school leader have a clear understanding of what effective leadership looks like and of the need for leadership standards, the foundation on which everything rests. Clear expectations for leaders affect recruitment, hiring, induction, mentoring, ongoing professional learning, and evaluation (Rowan, 2013).

The learning leader builds capacity in others by making a public commitment to professional learning and then modeling his or her own learning. Learning system leaders continually seek feedback from supervisors, peers, and staff. They persevere until they master their goals.

Because effective leaders understand the importance of developing others' leadership, they create opportunities for staff to serve in leadership roles—as mentors, learning team facilitators, and members of the school leadership team. They

coach school-based facilitators and coaches, providing materials, guidance, and feedback, and helping them solve problems. Leaders also monitor and supervise school-based professional learning facilitators and coaches.

In learning systems, leadership is distributed among key stakeholders, often through a school leadership team. Effective district and school leaders invite leadership team members to share in making critical decisions. School leadership team members, like the principal, develop knowledge and skills that they, in turn, share with colleagues whom they mentor and coach, colleagues who may be future members of the leadership team.

The leadership team members model their own learning and growth, publicly sharing their professional learning goals and engaging in a cycle of continuous improvement that includes support and follow-up.

Team members use Learning Forward's Standards for Professional Learning to make decisions about professional learning in the school and have staff members study the standards as they plan professional learning in their teams, basing decisions on research and the latest information about effective adult learning.

As they take on leadership roles for professional learning and make decisions, deepening their understanding of the Standards and research about effective professional learning, team members are able to take an active role in planning, implementing, and evaluating individual, team, and school-wide professional learning. Although the principal retains full responsibility for the quality and results of professional learning at the school, leadership team members are able to clearly explain their role and responsibilities as they help guide the process.

Use resources wisely

Effective principals identify professional learning needs and ensure that these needs are addressed with appropriate learning opportunities aligned with school improvement priorities. They monitor human, fiscal, material, technological, and other resources, and solve problems to make sure that professional learning is effective.

They realize and value time as a powerful resource and work with the building leadership team to find time during the school day for team-

Skilled principals understand that energy in the organization is essential for its success and recognize that when people are passionate about and fully engaged in their work, they have more energy for it.

based, job-embedded professional learning. They are eager to systematically free teachers to observe each other, conduct walk-throughs, plan lessons together, engage in analyzing student work, and plan school-based curriculum. They ensure not only that time for learning is available, but also that the professional learning achieves the intended outcomes. They monitor the work to make sure that professional learning time is focused, planned, and results oriented.

Most important, school leaders see resources used for professional learning as an investment, not a cost. Technology and material resources for professional learning create opportunities to access information that enriches practice. Using high-speed broadband, web-based and other technologies, professional journals and books, software, and a comprehensive learning management system supports individual and collaborative professional learning. Access to just-in-time learning resources

and participation in local or global communities or networks available to individuals or teams of educators during their workday expand opportunities for job-embedded professional learning.

Emphasize results and use data

Effective principals focus intently on student outcomes throughout the school year. They regularly monitor student performance data—not just to uncover findings, but also to determine what factors might have led to those results, what research the learning community should undertake to address any shortcomings, and what the collective community might do to help all students achieve their potential.

They not only value student performance data, but with the leadership team, they also carefully examine the effect professional learning is having on teacher practice. Under the leadership of a focused principal, the leadership team conducts regular walk-throughs and classroom observations, hosts student focus groups to garner student feedback, and takes steps to ensure that professional learning is intensive and targets student needs.

Skilled principals understand that energy in the organization is essential for its success and recognize that when people are passionate about and fully engaged in their work, they have more energy for it.

One of the highest and most challenging expectations of principals is facilitating curriculum development. Principals know that standards- and concepts-driven curriculum maps are essential for all school teams. They understand the importance of assessments *of* and *for* learning, and they are skilled at helping teams develop high-quality assessments that give them the information they need to redesign their instructional plans.

They coach teachers to discover and use high-yield instructional strategies to engage students. They are not willing to settle for low-level instructional practices or "follow the text" instructional approaches. They recognize that analyzing data is not just about remediating students, but also about adjusting adult practice (Psencik, 2009).

These principals also know that their job and the job of the leadership team is to celebrate and honor progress. They take seriously the need to monitor their goals on a regular basis and to recognize progress. They host regular celebrations to honor those who are putting out great effort to achieve the goals everyone has established, and they celebrate small successes along the way. These celebrations keep people focused and help them realize the difference they are making.

Create support systems and structures

In learning systems, principals and teacher leaders establish systems and structures for effective professional learning. A report from The Wallace Foundation states, "Education research shows that most school variables, considered separately, have at most small effects on learning. The real payoff comes when individual variables combine to reach critical mass. Creating the conditions under which that can occur is the job of the principal" (2013, p. 4).

Skillful principals create the policies and procedures, calendar, and schedules that support staff understanding of high-quality, standards-driven professional learning, which in turn contributes to implementation. Principals identify and address assumptions about and barriers to collaboration, and create opportunities for collaboration at least three times a week during the school day. They provide ongoing support for individual, team, and schoolwide professional learning goals, including using faculty meeting time to examine the progress and results of collaborative professional learning.

Kathy Larson, principal of Heritage Elementary School in Woodburn, Oregon, made celebrations a priority. She began the school year by starting a mural on the media center wall to depict staff members' progress toward their goals. In the beginning, the mural featured only a statement of goals and pictures of summer professional learning sessions. As the year progressed, Larson took and posted additional photos of teachers learning together and trying new strategies in their classrooms. She posted student performance data and charts showing student progress. She also posted exemplary student work. Seeing the growth in student achievement and progress in student work inspired the staff, especially in April when energy was flagging. By the end of the year, everyone in the school stopped in to admire the wall, including parents and visiting district leaders. The mural celebrating successes motivated teachers to continue to push for progress.

The school leadership team establishes, with colleagues and the principal, schoolwide conditions for effective professional learning, such as helping colleagues understand what effective professional learning looks like.

Working together, teacher leaders and principals help and support staff in learning to collaborate effectively to achieve individual, team, and school goals. They model collaboration in their own interactions with colleagues, students, parents, community members, and system leaders. They contribute to a collaborative culture by developing and applying their own research-based knowledge and skills about collaboration to support colleagues' learning and collaborative work. They further their own knowledge and skills to more effectively facilitate and resolve conflict. They assess the school culture to gauge the quality of individual, team, and schoolwide interactions; level of expectations; sense of collective responsibility; mutual respect; and relational trust.

Principals also advocate for coaches for themselves and seek out peer principals with whom they form their own learning community. They know that not only are teachers smarter and faster learners when they work with each other, but that they, as leaders, are smarter and learn faster when working with a peer group as a learning team.

They advocate for coaches to support teachers, knowing that coaching is a professional learning design that results in desired practices. They set guidelines to ensure that instructional coaches distribute their time equitably among learning teams or team members.

Principals also advocate for coaches for themselves and seek out peer principals with whom they form their own learning community. They know that not only are teachers smarter and faster learners when they work with each other, but that they, as leaders, are smarter and learn faster when working with a peer group as a learning team.

Advocate for professional learning.

In a learning system, school leaders clearly articulate the link between professional learning and student learning, explaining and offering clear examples of that connection. They also help staff members learn to articulate how their own professional learning affects student outcomes.

Principals and school leaders develop a succinct message about the value of professional learning to discuss with other staff, students, parents, system leaders, public officials, and community members and partners. They support collaborative professional learning even when they are challenged.

With their school leadership team, they study and promote the standards for high-quality professional learning in order to become strong advocates for school and districtwide educator learning. They work to create the necessary conditions to support individual, team, and schoolwide professional learning by finding time to collaborate and by using effective designs—including peer observations, action research, and analysis of student work—to deepen the learning practices of the community. They challenge ineffective practices, experiences, and designs, and seek improvements.

Effective principals address staff learning

Research shows that effective principals anchor their work on the central issues of teaching, learning, and continuous school improvement. Effective principals ensure that staff learning needs are appropriately addressed and that professional learning aligns with school improvement priorities (Schmoker, 1999).

Timothy Waters, Robert J. Marzano, and Brian A. McNulty identified 21 Leadership Responsibilities (2004) and established a framework for principals of the traits that affect student achievement. McREL's 21 Leadership Responsibilities are significant because they represent researched practices and confirm school leaders' effect on student achievement.

In 2007, the National Association of Secondary School Principals established these recommendations for the highly effective principal or assistant principal:

- Demonstrates awareness of and has experiences with the knowledge, skills, and attitudes needed to effectively lead teaching and learning appropriate to the needs of all students in the school

- Has successfully completed a state-approved principal licensure program that builds the knowledge, skills, and attitudes to effectively lead people, lead learning, and manage school operations

- Engages in continual professional development, using a combination of academic study, developmental simulation exercises, self-reflection, mentorship, and internships

- Demonstrates the capacity to establish and maintain a professional learning community that effectively extracts information from data to improve the school culture and personalize instruction for all students to result in improved student achievement

- Demonstrates knowledge of youth development appropriate to the age level served by the school

- Demonstrates the capacity to create and maintain a learning culture within the school that provides a climate conducive to the development of all members of the school community

Educators do 'whatever it takes' to create superhighways of learning

One year we had a child named Sam, and he was a handful. I made it a point to match students with teachers, and his teacher came to me in tears one day asking me why I assigned Sam to her. I told her she was going to turn this child around. She had a structured classroom, and I knew he couldn't push her around.

I had to help staff understand we had to customize learning. We sat down regularly during team meetings to talk about our students' learning styles, their needs and personalities. We had to understand that whatever a kid needed to get through the school day, we would do. We did lots of professional learning to make our school a learning community. We had weekly team meetings that were mandatory to look at data and understand where students weren't secure in a standard.

I was the cheerleader for everybody. I was involved with each individual child and knew each one's progress. We created data walls in the hallways and teacher lounge. Every nine weeks, we moved the individuals represented by colors. So we could see that four students moved from red to yellow, six moved to blue. We became data fanatics, and the kids were getting involved and excited about growth.

We were very goal-oriented. Everybody posted goals on their doors or in the hallways or in their rooms. It could be improvement on the state standardized test, our reading assessment, or books read. One of the smartest things we did was teaching teachers to include kids in learning.

Every nine weeks we had an assembly to recognize kids' learning. We had a system in which they received a little colored plastic book to put on a keychain representing their Lexile reading score. Our goal was that by the time they left 5th grade, they would be at 1,000 and have the blue book. I tried to have daily conversation with kids to connect learning and growth.

Kids became alive with connections. It changed the pathways in their brains, making those connections go from dirt paths to superhighways.

Once the kids are enthused, it's easier for teachers to teach. I told the teachers I would take care of discipline and they were here to teach, and we worked together. I was involved in their learning day, and they thought of me as another teacher. I wasn't a prima donna. I didn't have a parking spot. I made it a point to let them know I was one of them. At the same time, I tried to get them to lead our professional learning.

I also regularly let them know I appreciated them through small gestures, like bringing in cookies, decorating the lounge on Valentine's Day with banners about how sweet it was to work with all of them, having an egg hunt before spring break, a white elephant exchange in the winter. I initiated breakfasts before each of our faculty meetings.

We changed our faculty meetings so we worked in teams during that time. I let teachers know they had my support, and they became more relaxed, more confident that if something fell apart, we were going to work together to handle it. Our teachers became teacher leaders.

Our school became a learning environment.

— Stephany Bourne, former principal
Indian Village Elementary School

Reflection
questions

- How does school leadership in a learning system look different from school leadership in a traditional system?

- What resources and support do our principals and teacher leaders need so that they can improve their learning? How might they go about getting needed support?

- In what ways do principals and teacher leaders demonstrate an understanding of the link between professional learning and student learning?

- How do principals advocate for effective professional learning?

- How do highly effective principals create systems and structures to support effective professional learning?

RESOURCES

Fink, S. (2012, October). *School and district leaders as instructional experts: What we are learning.* Washington, DC: Center for Educational Leadership and University of Washington.

Leithwood, K., Seashore Louis, K., Anderson, S., & Wahlstrom, K. (2004). *How leadership influences student learning.* St. Paul, MN: University of Minnesota, Center for Applied Research and Educational Improvement, and University of Toronto, Ontario Institute for Studies in Education.

Marzano, R. J., Waters, T., & McNulty, B. A. (2005). *School leadership that works: From research to results,* Alexandria, VA: ASCD.

National Association of Secondary School Principals. (2013, November 7). Highly effective principals. Reston, VA: Author. Available at www.nassp.org/Content.aspx?topic=55879

Psencik, K. (2011). *The coach's craft: Powerful practices to support school leaders.* Oxford, OH: Learning Forward.

Von Frank, V. (2009, May). Principal-coaches transform teachers and schools. *The Learning System, 4*(8), 1, 6–7.

TOOLS INDEX

TOOL	TITLE	PURPOSE
8.1	Principal self-assessment and goal setting	Give principals an opportunity to reflect on their skills and set meaningful professional learning goals for themselves.
8.2	Analyzing the Innovation Configuration maps for principals and setting goals	Understand the desired outcomes for principals essential for them to lead learning communities.
8.3	Building shared vision around professional learning	Ensure everyone in the school is clear about what effective, standards-driven professional learning looks like in the school.
8.4	Building collective responsibility for student learning	Help teams value collective responsibility for student and staff learning.
8.5	Leading a community of learners	Lead groups of principals to develop skills to build a shared vision and understand their role in leading a community of learners.

CHAPTER 9

The role of external assistance providers

WHERE ARE WE NOW?

Our school district has positive relationships with external assistance providers.

STRONGLY AGREE   AGREE   NO OPINION   DISAGREE   STRONGLY DISAGREE

Our school district introduces external assistance providers at appropriate phases in our continuous improvement cycle.

STRONGLY AGREE   AGREE   NO OPINION   DISAGREE   STRONGLY DISAGREE

Our school district has established productive procedures and protocols for building successful relationships with third-party providers.

STRONGLY AGREE   AGREE   NO OPINION   DISAGREE   STRONGLY DISAGREE

Our school district sees external assistance providers as valued partners who contribute significantly to district improvements.

STRONGLY AGREE   AGREE   NO OPINION   DISAGREE   STRONGLY DISAGREE

Our school district evaluates external assistance providers using Learning Forward's Standards for Professional Learning.

STRONGLY AGREE   AGREE   NO OPINION   DISAGREE   STRONGLY DISAGREE

Learning Forward once held the assumption that a person doing a job should know the job better than anyone else. After considerable debate, the organization added caveats: The person doing the job knows it best, assuming that the individual is *well-prepared, well-supported, well-supervised,* and *recognizes the value that other perspectives can add.* However, the ultimate goal remains that those charged with a job should know best what is required to succeed at the job.

Partnerships with external assistance providers can help districts achieve that success. Effective partnerships increase staff effectiveness and outcomes for all students. Effective partners help districts build internal capacity while accelerating progress toward agreed-upon goals. Partners can help school systems with expertise, funding, and services that they otherwise might not be able to access.

> Partners can help school systems with expertise, funding, and services that they otherwise might not be able to access.

Partners bring to the table expertise that helps districts grow beyond what they are capable of on their own. When the external assistance providers leave, the districts are changed in fundamental ways, and educators are able to carry on with the work as the result of the new skills, attitudes, behaviors, and knowledge they have gained.

In a learning system, district leaders look for external assistance providers who demonstrate an understanding and appreciation for the district's context and expectations, and who are committed to Learning Forward's Standards for Professional Learning. In that case, the provider becomes a seamless extension of the learning system. The provider is respected for his or her expertise and adds capacity to the district. Finding the right partner with whom to combine expertise distinguishes a learning system from struggling districts. With the right partner, the learning system builds capacity and expertise, gaining from the partner's knowledge. The learning system integrates external expertise, verifies the value of potential partnerships, negotiates deliverables with clear outcomes, builds positive ongoing relationships, and aligns work to the Standards.

Integrate external expertise

Learning Forward's definition of professional learning calls for all educators to engage in a cycle of continuous improvement (see Appendix) that defines when a district, school, department, or grade-level team may need external assistance. The improvement cycle begins when learning teams analyze data to clarify the goal, problem, or need. After analyzing the data, the team determines what members need to learn or do to produce different results and what expertise is needed. When the team or organization does not have that expertise, the team looks outside for assistance. By engaging external assistance at this point, all parties are clear about the reason and staff have greater buy in.

External providers offer on-the-job support and ongoing assessment of results. Each stage of the process can last several months or move more quickly depending on the initial data analysis and problem, and may be repeated several times in a school year. A district may be involved in multiple, simultaneous cycles with different providers.

Partners offer different levels of expertise. Their interests and services vary according to their goals. A consumer-oriented company interested in attracting young customers may want to partner with a school district interested in increasing external funding sources. Effective partnerships improve educator and student performance through professional learning. Potential partners to support school system learning goals can include any of the following:

- Universities
- Community colleges
- Federal- and state-funded technical assistance organizations
- Small, private consulting firms
- Foundations
- Not-for-profit associations
- Not-for-profit technical assistance organizations
- For-profit technical assistance organizations

Most partners offer a variety of services: in person, one-to-one, and small- and large-group training; consultation; planning; audits; curriculum development; technology infrastructure and support; face-to-face and virtual coaching; materials and resources; networks; site-visit coordination; program evaluation; and the ability to serve as critical friend.

Effective partnerships become a seamless component of the district's learning and improvement agenda. The district and the provider are equally invested in the outcomes, and the external provider is a valued member of the learning team. When the relationship is poor, district teams may view external assistance as distractions to be ignored.

Verify the value of potential partnerships

Learning systems establish procedures and protocols to select from the array of external partners. External partners assist in the early "discovery" process by making available information to help ensure that both parties will succeed. The best external assistance providers offer a variety of information:

The Southwest Educational Development Laboratory (SEDL), an education research and service agency based in Austin, Texas, formed a relationship with Georgetown County (S.C.) School District. A team of SEDL facilitators worked with the district's learning teams, providing expertise and resources, modeling quality practices, and evaluating progress. The district valued that SEDL took time to understand district culture, provided an experienced team to coordinate and facilitate district learning, developed a flexible plan, and took steps to ensure the district was able to carry on with the work once the partnership was over. SEDL appreciated that the district designated a staff member to coordinate work with the school system, the superintendent's and school board's commitment to the partnership, and the districtwide—rather than piecemeal—approach to improvement. SEDL noted that the district invested in coaches, and district leaders met regularly with the provider (Tobia, Chauvin, Lewis, & Hammel, 2011).

The Connecticut Center for School Change approaches partnerships by clearly stating beliefs. Working with six geographically and demographically diverse school districts, the center develops districts' leadership and organizational capacity. Its mission is based on foundational beliefs:

- Partnering and collaboration are essential skills for success in the 21st century.

- The work of instructional improvement at scale requires collaboration and teaming across all levels of the organization, and with stakeholders and external partners.

- Schools and districts must work collaboratively in order to become high-performing systems that improve student achievement.

- Organizations must continue to learn in order to improve and sustain improvements in practice.

(Lachman & Wlodarczyk, 2011).

- *References.* The quality of relationships, work, and outcomes with previous contractors can indicate what service districts may expect.
- *Research base for work.* The research that providers use to guide their work points to credibility and how relevant the work is to the district's goal or need.
- *Evidence of expertise.* Prior experiences ensure the provider has expertise in the area of focus.
- *Explanation of value to be added.* The partner's value is expertise that is unavailable within the district. Clarifying that expertise and the value the provider sees in working with the district benefits both parties.
- *Learning design.* The proposed work should align with Learning Forward's Standards for Professional Learning.
- *Qualifications of on-site workers.* Those negotiating the contract indicate which consultants, if not themselves, will provide the service, and they describe the qualifications of those who will be on site.
- *Alignment to prescribed needs and priorities.* The service offering should clearly align to the district's needs as established by the data.

Negotiate deliverables with clear outcomes

Learning system leaders negotiate contracts that result in clear expectations and shared commitments to the goals.

In a well-executed contract, both parties have a stake in the partnership's success. A well-executed contract addresses the following issues:

- *Clear outcomes.* External assistance providers state outcomes in the format district employees use. They specify frequent, early indicators of success and agreed-upon times to discuss the indicators.

- *Time span.* Most major change efforts require three to five years to institutionalize. Both parties need to commit to and have the capacity to steer the effort through all phases.
- *How the work will be delivered and by whom.* Establishing the work team and clarifying roles and expectations are essential. It is important to agree on the theory of action, strategies, and deliverables. In addition, learning systems require evidence that the work aligns with Learning Forward's Standards for Professional Learning.
- *Expected effort.* A high-quality work plan details how many hours the effort is expected to take and the anticipated compensation.
- *Who will supervise the external assistance provider.* Clear lines of authority and procedures for resolving problems in the partnership can prevent difficulties in the relationship.

Build a positive, ongoing relationship

Partnerships require trust and commitment. Those entering a long-term partnership explore several fundamental questions. Conversations on these topics begin in the exploratory phases but continue and evolve throughout the relationship as partners invest time in getting to know each other, understanding their beliefs and assumptions, becoming comfortable with their views, and developing respect for one another's expertise. Conversations answer the following questions:

- What are our goals and vision?
- What principles guide our work?
- What values do we seek in a partner?
- How will we each contribute to the shared outcomes?
- How will we overcome barriers and conflicts that arise along the way?
- What evidence will we accept to show we are making progress and achieving our goals?

- How often will we reflect on our work and the quality of our partnership?
- How will we hold each other accountable?

Because partnerships seldom are binding in the long term, goals and vision hold partners together and help build greater passion for the outcomes. Without checking back in, reflecting on the work, and celebrating progress, partners may lose interest and revert back to their own priorities.

Align work to Learning Forward's Standards for Professional Learning

Learning systems ensure that their work with external providers aligns with Learning Forward's Standards for Professional Learning. The Standards detail the essential conditions, processes, and outcomes for professional learning that advances educator and student performance. Innovation Configuration (IC) maps describe in more detail how the practices of those in different roles contribute to outcomes. Educators can use the IC maps as a guide to selecting, negotiating, planning, executing, and evaluating an external assistance partner's work.

External providers' work aligns with the Standards in these ways::

Learning Communities. External partners may coach members of learning communities, help organize their work and provide them with needed resources, guide group conversations, and ask probing questions (Horwitz, Hoy, & Bradley, 2011). External partners' work is built into and clearly aligned with the district's cycle of continuous improvement, and the provider develops individuals' capacity to implement the steps in the cycle (see Appendix).

The provider also can help develop a districtwide definition of collective responsibility. As a result, the external partner should be able to document and

External assistance providers' roles and responsibilities

External assistance providers

- Develop others' capacity to lead professional learning;
- Understand and use Learning Forward's Standards for Professional Learning to make decisions about professional learning;
- Coach designated participants on programming;
- Help district leaders articulate the link between student learning and professional learning;
- Advocate for high-quality professional learning;
- Influence systems and structures essential for effective professional learning;
- Cultivate and support a collaborative culture;
- Prepare others to become more skillful collaborators; and
- Promote expectations for collaborative professional learning within the school day.

Source: Learning Forward. (2013). *Standards into practice: School system roles Innovation Configuration maps for Standards for Professional Learning.* Oxford, OH: Author.

showcase exemplars and demonstrate the effects of collective responsibility emerging from the services provided. The partner is equally responsible for ensuring that services align with school system goals and is accountable to the district.

> The partner is equally responsible for ensuring that services align with school system goals and is accountable to the district.

Leadership. External assistance providers may demonstrate continuous professional learning by publicly sharing their own professional learning goals and persisting with their own learning until they achieve mastery. They participate in follow-up and coaching, and they ask for constructive feedback from their supervisors, staff, peers, and partners.

Resources. External assistance providers partner with learning system leaders to leverage professional development resources to achieve the intended outcomes. Partners may help districts identify or reallocate resources based on an audit. For example, they may support district leaders in considering ways to allocate time for professional learning. They may work with the district to seek outside funding sources. External assistance providers monitor how they use resources to achieve mutually agreed-upon goals and report when resources are not being used as stipulated. They carefully use resources to fully and deeply implement district priorities.

Data. Clearly defining goals that can be evaluated benefits both partners (Koch & Borg, 2011). External assistance providers take the following actions:

- Ensure their staff and district staff have the skills to interpret and use data.
- Identify and describe sources of student, educator, and organization data that can be used to assess the district's needs.
- Analyze on their own and with district staff what the data show.

- Distinguish and use formative data to monitor progress of improvement efforts.
- Use formative data to make improvements in programming and support.
- Develop the capacity of their own staff and district staff to plan and conduct an evaluation of professional learning.
- Build understanding of and commitment to formative. and summative evaluation of professional learning.

Learning Designs. External assistance providers typically fill a gap in the district's expertise and build district staff members' capacity to meet an identified need. The provider considers the district's characteristics and setting to ensure learning translates to the desired, improved practices. The provider and district work together to develop a shared vision of the learning, select learning strategies, develop a theory of change or action and logic model to make it happen, and determine who is responsible for what.

Implementation. External assistance providers apply change research to their efforts and develop in district staff the capacity to do the same. They cite explicit research to support their actions and recommendations. They demonstrate patience and perseverance as they support staff through the change process. They use appropriate tools and strategies to address challenges that surface during implementation of new programs and processes. With district staff, they develop tools for gathering data on implementation of practices resulting from professional learning. They build differentiated support and may use a variety of job-embedded, in-person, technology-enhanced, and blended support strategies to achieve fidelity of implementation. They use data to determine actions to refine implementation. And they establish routines and skills for providing support and receiving ongoing, critical feedback.

> External assistance providers typically fill a gap in the district's expertise and build district staff members' capacity to meet an identified need.

Outcomes. Although an external assistance provider's value to a district may be measured in multiple ways, the ultimate measure is the degree to which the service contributes to the district's intended outcomes for staff and students. Aligning outcomes to educator and student performance standards, as well as to district goals and priorities, is key.

Learning system leaders collaborate with external assistance providers to deconstruct educator and student performance standards to determine the knowledge, skills, and practices educators need to achieve professional learning goals and student growth. They monitor professional learning content and related services for alignment with the Standards and intended outcomes.

External assistance providers work with district leaders to build coherence between the scope of their work and professional learning and other system and school initiatives. They know that without coherence, implementation is unlikely to be sustained over time, resources will dwindle, and commitment will implode.

External relationships help district soar

When Duval County Public Schools began to restructure its professional development to make learning a district priority, we looked for organizations that might help us understand more of what we needed.

We wanted an emphasis on implementation and program evaluation—the impact of professional development. We had done a lot of planning and delivering, as many districts do, but we were not as strong on looking at teacher implementation and assessing what we were doing with our learning.

We started by going out in the marketplace to see what was available. At one time, the district had a formal vetting process in place for external service providers. Each service provider was required to complete an application with items such as purpose, resources, implementation model, cost, research base, alignment with district and state initiatives, evaluation method, and more. A team of stakeholders then interviewed the service provider. These data informed future decisions about whether a provider could meet district needs. Although the formal process is no longer in place, we continue to consider the criteria when selecting external service providers.

We began working with the National Staff Development Council (now Learning Forward) because the organization offers a comprehensive system of support and tools for a district to build internal capacity. The organization gave not only the research base and evaluation theories, but also practical steps and tools for applying the learning so professional development could be measured in the district. We developed a five-year comprehensive professional development plan together.

We always want to make sure that any service provider carefully aligns the district comprehensive professional development plan with the district strategic plan, the Standards for Professional Learning, and the state department of education protocols. They need to have that knowledge and be clear about that expectation. Communication is key and helps build strong connections.

It's also significant that I feel I can pick up the phone at any time and call to say, "I'm struggling with this. Can you help?" The provider's responsiveness and personal connection are important—it's a relationship.

As additional needs have surfaced in the district, Learning Forward has become our go-to for professional learning expertise. With every service, we regularly assess along the way and use feedback to have conversations with the organization about adjustments.

Some service providers have a more limited focus or specialized service. Although the district builds internal capacity, it is wholly dependent on the provider to continue the service. An analogy is health service. If the goal is wellness, a full-service provider like the Mayo Clinic is preferable. If the goal is care for an immediate short-term health need, a visit to the primary care physician is sufficient.

Leaders in our district are always thinking about how to leverage resources to build internal capacity. Once we understand a need in an area, such as launching a coaching program, then we need that informed voice. That's when we hire an external provider. We look for a gradual release relationship—we are going to partner, but it's not a forever partnership. We want the partner to share knowledge and experience, model for us, watch us do it, and then let us fly.

— Dawn Wilson, director of professional learning
Duval County (Fla.) Public Schools

Reflection
questions

- What circumstances might prompt our district to seek an external assistance provider?

- How do we launch a relationship with a provider? How do we end a relationship?

- What elements distinguish our most effective provider relationships? Which of those would we like to have define all our provider relationships?

- How do we hold our providers accountable for meeting Learning Forward's Standards for Professional Learning?

- How does our work with external assistance providers align with our continuous improvement cycle?

- What checks and balances do we have in place to ensure that our work with external assistance providers fulfills our expectations?

RESOURCES

Crow, T. (2011). Outsiders become key players in making learning sustained and job-embedded. *JSD, 32*(1), 4.

Learning Forward. External partners. Available at http://learningforward.org/external-partners#. U3Dd4F5bTwI

Giouroukakis, V., Cohen, A., Nenchin, J., & Honigsfeld, A. (2011). A second set of eyes and ears. *JSD, 32*(3), 60–63.

Hirsh, S. (2011). Turning to partners doesn't have to create a feeding frenzy. *JSD, 32*(1), 68.

Learning Forward. (2011, February). *JSD: Working with external partners, 32*(1).

Learning Point Associates. (2009). Partnering with external providers. Available at www.centerforcsri.org/sbs/PEP.html.

TOOLS INDEX

TOOL	TITLE	PURPOSE
9.1	External partnerships: What our district values	Define the criteria the district values for effective partnerships.
9.2	Conducting a landscape analysis of current and potential partnerships	Analyze existing and potential partnerships' alignment with district priorities.
9.3	Determining a focus for the external provider partnerships	Clarify the focus of an external partnership.
9.4	Focusing the Request for Proposals process	Generate focused questions to ask external providers during the Request for Proposals process.
9.5	The essentials of external provider agreements	Ensure essential elements are present when negotiating an agreement with an external provider.
9.6	Evaluating the effectiveness of external partnerships using the Standards for Professional Learning	Evaluate district partnerships using the Standards.
9.7	The essentials of writing and reviewing an RFP	Review proposals and select an external provider.

CHAPTER 10

Building
trust

WHERE ARE WE NOW?

Our school leaders and leadership teams are confident that leaders are honest, sincere, benevolent, reliable, and competent.

STRONGLY AGREE   AGREE   NO OPINION   DISAGREE   STRONGLY DISAGREE

Our district leaders take steps to ensure their trustworthiness by intentionally focusing on honesty, sincerity, competence, reliability, and benevolence.

STRONGLY AGREE   AGREE   NO OPINION   DISAGREE   STRONGLY DISAGREE

Our district leaders take seriously the way others view them and recognize how their actions affect themselves and others.

STRONGLY AGREE   AGREE   NO OPINION   DISAGREE   STRONGLY DISAGREE

Our district leaders regularly remind themselves of the coherence of body, language, and emotions.

STRONGLY AGREE   AGREE   NO OPINION   DISAGREE   STRONGLY DISAGREE

Our district leaders make clear declarations, requests, and offers so staff members know what work is expected and can develop effective strategies to achieve those expectations.

STRONGLY AGREE   AGREE   NO OPINION   DISAGREE   STRONGLY DISAGREE

Our district leaders routinely demonstrate the power of presuming positive intentions.

STRONGLY AGREE   AGREE   NO OPINION   DISAGREE   STRONGLY DISAGREE

Although many think of trust as an intangible, effective leaders in learning systems know the importance of taking steps to create the conditions in which trust flourishes. In *The Speed of Trust*, Stephen M. R. Covey and Rebecca R. Merrill state that individuals can take steps to increase others' trust and improve the quality of life of those surrounding them, enhancing the results all are able to achieve (2008).

Leaders in learning systems inspire confidence in those around them. They gain others' trust by acting with sincerity, reliability, and competence. Those who trust the leader believe the leader has their best interest at heart, as well as the organization's mission. They believe the leader is honest and straightforward and believe that they can count on what the leader says.

When trust is broken, relationships falter; people become inauthentic, and their chances of working collaboratively decrease. When trust is strong, mutual respect and interdependence flourish, providing the basis for trusting relationships, and staff are more likely to be honest about their problems and more willing to ask for help when they need it.

Learning system leaders use a variety of strategies to gain people's confidence and inspire them to effectively implement innovations. These concepts help leaders build and sustain trust in an organization:

- Leaders demonstrate coherency. They recognize the effect of the coherence of their body, language, and emotions on their relationships.

- Leaders recognize how their actions affect themselves and others.

- Leaders share similar positive characteristics; they are self-aware, honest, sincere, competent, reliable, and presume others' positive intentions.

"There is one thing that is common to every individual relationship, team, family, organization, nation, economy, and civilization throughout the world—one thing which if removed will destroy the most powerful government, the most successful business, the most thriving economy, the most influential leadership, the greatest friendship, the strongest character, the deepest love. On the other hand, if developed and leveraged, the one thing has the potential to create unparalleled success and prosperity in every dimension of life. Yet it is the least understood, most neglected, and most underestimated possibility of our time. That one thing is trust."

—S. M. R. Covey with R. Merrill, 2008, p. xxvii

Demonstrate coherency

Learning system leaders are consistently vigilant about the coherence of their own body, language, and emotions and work to deepen that awareness. They recognize the effect of that coherence on their relationships.

When the body is not well, leaders pay attention. Effective leaders recognize that when they are ill, they send powerful—if unintended—messages to others. Their attitude may unintentionally dim, and others may perceive these emotions as negativity about how the organization is progressing or about work quality. Some leaders say, "I am really good at hiding my emotions," but science does not support that statement. The majority of what we communicate to others in person is nonverbal. Researchers have gauged anywhere from 60% to 93% of communication is nonverbal.

Leaders understand that the body affects emotions, and the result often is manifested in language. In turn, language affects individuals' bodies as well as emotions. Some scientists report that emotional distress affects the body in the same way as physical traumas. However, many people recognize the effect of language only at an unconscious level and fail to recognize the connections. The English language is full of statements that reflect a deeper understanding of how body and mind are tightly related: "He was paralyzed with fear." "She shouted for joy." "She ripped him to shreds." "Those words pierced him like an arrow." Learning system leaders understand that each of us is a complete system, relying on coherence of body, language, and emotion (Psencik, 2011).

Recognize actions' effects

Integrity and honesty are central to being a learning system leader. An effective leader is who she says she is and does what she says she will do. Those surrounding the leader watch for signs that the leader is honest. Others must believe that the leader is reliable. In today's fast-paced world, many leaders overcommit. When they fail to follow through, their inaction chips away at trust.

Leaders model sincerity and demonstrate personal integrity by remaining consistent in their words and actions. When working with teams,

leaders in learning systems are intensely aware of how their conversations and others' comments may hinder a team member's creativity or learning. When leaders give fake praise or feint telling the truth, others sense the discrepancy. They are sensitive, too, about comments such as, "Well, that is a good idea, but in my experience . . ." or "I understand what you are saying, but we tried that and it never worked!"

Teams unsure of their leader's integrity in words and actions may adopt a "wait and see" attitude. Seeing that the leader's words are congruent with the leader's actions, however, elicits the feeling

> Leaders create trust when others see that the leader's actions are congruent with the leader's words, eliciting the feeling that the leader is sincere and authentic.

that the leader is sincere and authentic. When team members trust that their leader can achieve what she says she can, they don't hesitate in their work.

Develop personal qualities

The best leaders are self-aware, honest, sincere, competent, reliable, and presume positive intentions—and actively work to strengthen these qualities. They spend time thinking about who they are and articulating the principles that guide their actions and attitudes (Psencik, 2011). Dennis Sparks (2007) says we become clearer about who we are by clarifying assumptions in writing and by talking with others about these assumptions.

Leaders understand that how they observe the world causes them to create or close off opportunities for themselves and everyone they lead. They recognize how their own observations affect every interaction, every conversation, and every decision. They guard themselves from limiting opportunities for themselves and others based on their personal perspective or "lens." Effective leaders ask, "Are my observations of the world limiting opportunities and the possibilities of breakthrough thinking?"

The learning system leader understands the power of intentions. Most people wonder, "Does the person I am working with have the best intentions toward me?" Covey and Merrill (2008) term this idea *benevolence* and say leaders should ask themselves, Am I authentically aware of the needs and interests of those around me, and do I value the contributions they make?

Jim Meehan, British psychologist and poet, puts it this way: "Having spent many years trying to define the essentials of trust, I arrived at the position that if two people could say two things to each other and mean them, then there was the basis for real trust. The two things were 'I mean you no harm' and 'I seek your greatest good'" (Covey with Merrill, 2008, p. 80).

Although engaging more people and perspectives may take more time initially, doing so can help ensure an initiative is implemented successfully.

Skilled leaders establish a culture of respect and personal regard for all when they demonstrate respect and regard for each individual in the school, listen intently to others to identify breakdowns, and work to find common ground. They do so by making clear declarations, requests, and offers. They establish conditions of satisfaction so that staff members know what work is expected and are ready to learn effective strategies to achieve those expectations.

Implications for district leaders

Building trust is challenging. Historically, relationships between district officials and school staff have been distrustful. In fact, recently one school-based facilitator planning a session with central office staff reported that her school staff friends joked she was "going over to the dark side."

In addition to following the core principles of trust, in all interactions, leaders

- Act transparently and openly;
- Constantly, purposefully reiterate their vision and expectations;
- Model what it means be purpose driven;
- Seek continuous feedback about the impact of their decisions; and
- Know all principals and teacher leaders personally.

Successful district leaders ensure they discuss potential decisions with those affected before finalizing the decision. This simple principle is a powerful demonstration of the leader's openness. Group decisions that consider each person's observations are often better than those made independently by district leaders. Although engaging more people and perspectives may take more time initially, doing so can help ensure an initiative is implemented successfully.

Learning system leaders are "keepers of the vision" and thread the district's principles, norms, mission, and vision through their conversations with teacher-leaders, principals, parents, and school board members. Each reiteration clarifies the vision and helps those who affect student learning internalize it. With a clear sense of that purpose, leaders are not afraid of feedback and develop systems to gather input from students, parents, community members, and staff. They may host regular community forums for others to share ideas.

Highly successful district leaders see their role as one of service and support. They build relationships with school principals and others so that staff members get to know one another well, support each other, and develop a feeling of community.

A group of principals one of the authors worked with witnessed the concept in a Learning Forward video. The video showed teachers collaborating in a learning team in Ford Middle School in Allen, Texas. The principals' task was to characterize Learning Forward's Standards for Professional Learning embedded in the team's work. One principal observed that underlying the teachers' learning was a great sense of trust.

"These teachers feel free to lead, to set up classroom observations, to share strategies," the principal said. "There is no principal present, but his support is evident in the freedom they feel to do what is best for students. No one said, 'I don't know if we can do that; we better ask our principal first.'"

Implications for school leaders

School leaders face virtually the same issues as district leaders. The added challenge for school leaders in developing trusting relationships is that so many more interactions occur in schools each day—interactions between the principal and parents, principal and teachers, teachers and students, and between teachers—and any of these interactions could break down a culture of trust.

Effective principals form strong relationships with staff, students, parents, and district leaders. Staff members want a trusting relationship with the principal and to feel that the principal has the best intentions for them. School leadership teams want trusting relationships with their peers so that they are able to coordinate actions in ways that focus on everyone's learning. Principals want to create trusting relationships with and among teachers so that teachers develop strong relationships with students and their parents. Parents want to trust the principal, teachers, and other staff so they feel confident the school cares about their children and has their best interests at heart. Students want to know the principal well and to feel that they can count on him or her. Most important, students want to feel safe in their classrooms with their teachers, which is most likely when the relationship is built on high levels of trust.

In a learning system, effective school leaders start to build trust when they take steps to ensure that the school's work aligns with the district's goals and vision. They model respect for all those responsible for meeting the district's goals and achieving that vision. They seek feedback from those they serve to ensure staff members have the confidence to learn. Because they are in a dynamic relationship with the staff, feedback flows freely within the school and with district leaders, ensuring transparency and openness.

Trust serves as the connective tissue that allows teachers to question current practices, take risks, and try new strategies, because they are confident their leader supports and encourages their creativity and innovation as they work to achieve their goals.

Trusted leaders create learning organizations

I had a friend say to me once that after your first seven years as a leader you really have to leave because you've done everything you came to do and everything you know how to do. That's the old paradigm, in which the leader came in as the change agent with specific skills and traits.

Now, leadership is about creating learning organizations. It's about being the lead learner who helps move the organization toward new places even when you're not quite sure where you're going because you don't have that skill set yet. Nevertheless, you work alongside everybody to develop and move forward.

Leaders need some longevity to be able to achieve goals that result in meaningful change. Leading a district to become high performing takes building staff members' trust and their confidence in the leader's integrity. It also requires the leader's coherence. When I look at why I've been able to sustain my work as superintendent for 15 years in my district, it has been because of the relationships I've built. Because of my relationships, when I say to staff, "Trust me on this," they're more likely to do so, and to give me some latitude. If you're not in relationship, then people question your motives.

You have to *demonstrate* competence and character. Staff have to know that you'll hold true to your promises, and leaders need to realize that everything we say to people, in their minds, is a promise. I constantly need to ask myself, "Did I follow through on what I said I would do?"

The little things that a leader does matter a lot. If the little things aren't in line, then the big things won't be in line. Leadership requires taking an interest in people. I know everybody who works here by name, and I usually know their spouses' names. We have 1,600 students and 300 staff, so knowing everybody's name and being pleasant and spending a couple minutes with everybody at some time isn't hard. If I'm in a large, urban environment, I can't do that, but I'll have other people who are able to do that and break the system down into smaller pieces.

Every year, most districts turn over 8% to 12% of staff, and so leaders constantly have to build new relationships. I've taught administrators that when we interview candidates, we have to try to get them all to fall in love with us because we're going to hire some of them and we want them to love us before they start. We have to be humanistic and thought provoking, and convince candidates we're going to feed their personal as well as intellectual needs. When we do our new teacher training, I'm usually teaching them for five days. I want them to see my instructional capabilities so that when I talk about instruction, they know I know what I'm talking about. And it's also about spending time with them. I go into their classrooms before school opens and ask if I can help set up their rooms and if they have everything they need to start the year. Taking that interest in new staff builds relationships.

When we care about each other, we do more for each other. As that old adage goes: "People don't care what you know until they know that you care." That's true in any learning organization.

— Mike Ford, superintendent
Phelps–Clifton Springs (N.Y.)
Central School District

Reflection
questions

- How do members of our district leadership team intentionally focus on and build trusting relationships?

- What strategies or protocols do district leaders use to ensure transparency?

- In what ways do I, as a leader, reflect on how well I am exhibiting the qualities of self-awareness, honesty, sincerity, competence, and reliability?

- Do I keep at the forefront the idea of presuming positive intentions?

- How well do the leaders in our district demonstrate personal integrity?

- What are some examples in our district of someone acting with coherence of body, mind, and spirit?

RESOURCES

Bryk, A. S. & Schneider, B. (2003, March). Trust in schools: A core resource for school reform. *Educational Leadership, 60*(6), 40–45.

Covey, S. M. R. (2006). *The speed of trust.* New York, NY: Free Press.

Jolly, A. (2008). *Team to teach: A facilitator's guide to professional learning teams.* Oxford, OH: National Staff Development Council.

Geisler, J. (2012, May 10). To build the team, build the trust. Available at www.poynter.org/how-tos/leadership-management/what-great-bosses-know/172819/to-build-the-team-build-the-trust-with-these-8-tips.

Psencik, K. (2011). *The coach's craft: Powerful practices to support school leaders.* Oxford, OH: Learning Forward.

Roy, P. (2012, May). Tools: Build collaboration and collegiality and bring structure to classroom observation. *The Leading Teacher, 7*(6), 6–7.

Tschannen-Moran, M. (2004). *Trust matters: Leadership for successful schools.* San Francisco, CA: Jossey-Bass.

TOOLS INDEX

TOOL	TITLE	PURPOSE
10.1	Let's get acquainted!	Build knowledge of one another in order to foster mutual trust.
10.2	Self-assessment: The Covey 4 cores of credibility	Understand the level to which one may be considered trustworthy and reflect on the skills and attributes underpinning that determination.
10.3	Creating a trust pyramid	Develop an ability to strengthen trust in relationships.
10.4	Developing strategies for strengthening trust	Reflect and develop strategies that will strengthen trust among colleagues.
10.5	Trust matters—for educators, parents, and students	Help schools assess and build one-on-one and team relationships over time.
10.6	Using speech acts effectively	Consider the effects of language on relationships that build and sustain trust.
10.7	Effectively coordinating action	Develop conditions of satisfaction that build trust to ensure success.

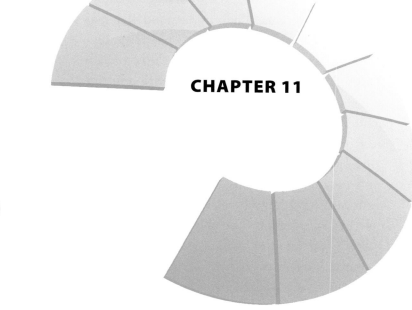

CHAPTER 11

Moving
vision into
action

WHERE ARE WE NOW?

Our leaders clearly articulate the district's vision and engage principals and teacher leaders in a cycle of continuous improvement to achieve it.

| STRONGLY AGREE | AGREE | NO OPINION | DISAGREE | STRONGLY DISAGREE |

Our district and school leaders clearly understand first- and second-order change.

| STRONGLY AGREE | AGREE | NO OPINION | DISAGREE | STRONGLY DISAGREE |

We have developed an authentic theory of change for our organization.

| STRONGLY AGREE | AGREE | NO OPINION | DISAGREE | STRONGLY DISAGREE |

Our district and school leaders carefully monitor progress, share success stories, and shift their strategies or plans of action based on what they learn.

| STRONGLY AGREE | AGREE | NO OPINION | DISAGREE | STRONGLY DISAGREE |

We have allowed adequate time to implement the expected change with fidelity.

| STRONGLY AGREE | AGREE | NO OPINION | DISAGREE | STRONGLY DISAGREE |

Successful district and school leaders are systems thinkers. They understand that passion for work comes from purpose. They recognize the challenges of change and the difficulty of steering many people with multiple perspectives toward the same end. They meet challenges with the conviction and fortitude needed to forge a new approach without diminishing past practices.

In a learning system, leaders have the critical skills needed to develop a shared vision throughout the organization. The ability to develop that vision is an essential skill. A shared vision is a dynamic force in people's hearts and minds, and employees who share a vision *connect* to one another through their common aspiration.

Peter Senge describes common aspiration as "the capacity to hold a shared picture of the future we want to create. When there is a genuine vision (as opposed to the all-too-familiar 'vision statement'), people excel and learn, not because they are told to, but because they want to" (1990, p. 9).

Beyond forging the straightforward vision statement, change leaders develop metaphors that explain the vision and regularly share stories with staff about educators making dynamic shifts in their practices. They inspire others and build shared vision by modeling passion for the work, high energy, and high expectations for all. They recognize that their words and actions set the tone for the entire organization.

In learning systems, the superintendent and leadership team members are mission-driven, other-centered, caring leaders who have a passion for their moral purpose of educating all children to high standards and are committed to see it through. They work to develop collective responsibility for the vision and then to move the vision statement from paper to practice.

Polar explorer Ernest Shackleton headed three British expeditions to the Antarctic around the turn of the 20th century. When Shackleton saw his dream of becoming the first explorer to reach the South Pole lost to another explorer, he set a new goal. He was on a mission to be the first to cross the continent when his ship—*Endurance*—became frozen in the ice. The ship was destroyed and the crew forced to camp on the ice for five months. Shackleton made sure the sailors got the warmest blankets and the officers the less desirable ones. When a crew member lost a glove, Shackleton gave the man one of his own. Facing disaster, the leader continuously reminded his men that his priority was to get every one of them out alive. He reportedly told the survivors, "Ship and stores have gone, so now we'll go home." He then sailed 800 miles over 17 days in a lifeboat across the world's most dangerous seas and then walked continuously for 36 hours to a whaling station to summon help. The crew made it home. (American Museum of Natural History, 1999.)

Leaders who are most successful at creating a shared vision and putting it into action first describe the vision and consider the magnitude of change it reflects, and then commit to success.

Describe the vision

Those who lead organizations driven by moral purpose take steps to develop a compelling shared vision because they know it provides a focus and energy for learning and achieving challenging goals. Learning system leaders understand that a shared vision helps a community accomplish what individuals working independently cannot.

Developing a compelling vision requires significant skill. Leaders base their work on a grounded theory of change and a logic model that clarify how members of the organization will learn. These tools allow district leaders to debate effective strategies, incorporate research findings and others' experiences, and seek feedback from school leadership teams before establishing a learning agenda, designing professional learning, and initiating implementation.

Margaret Wheatley, author and management consultant, says that in order for leaders to put a vision into action they must continuously work to build clarity around the organization's message:

> Creating the field through the dissemination of those ideas is essential. The field must reach all corners of the organization, involve everyone and be available everywhere. Vision statements move off the walls into the corridors, seeking out every employee, every recess of the organization. In the past we may have thought of ourselves as skilled crafters of organizations, assembling the pieces of an organization, exerting our energy on the painstaking creation of links between all those parts. Now, we need to imagine ourselves as broadcasters, tall radio beacons of information, pulsing out messages everywhere. We need all of us out there, stating, clarifying, discussing, modeling, filling all of the space with the messages we care about. (Wheatley, 1992, pp. 65–56)

In other words, leaders articulate the vision's message and then make sure that they continually speak it so that in time, the vision permeates the organization. Wheatley explains that when employees repeatedly "bump up against" the message, they begin to see themselves in that mission. As staff deepen their commitment to the vision, they develop a sense of collective responsibility for achieving it. This is one indicator that a system is truly a learning system. One way successful leaders support the shared vision is to use documents and visuals that reinforce the message.

Consider the magnitude of change

Effective leaders consider the magnitude and implications of changes they expect from those in the organization. They begin by establishing a theory of change that outlines the essential actions required for an innovation to be implemented well. A basic theory of change explains how early and intermediate accomplishments set the stage for long-term results and what further actions will be needed to move the organization toward full implementation with fidelity.

Successful district teams trying to implement any innovation think carefully about what it will take to move the entire organization through first- and second-order change and where any breakdowns might occur in order to add another stepping stone. In first-order change, people's behavior does not vary much, if at all, from past practice. Teams simply become aware of new expectations and engage in professional learning to develop their understanding of how to meet them (Waters, Marzano, & McNulty, 2004). In second-order change, staff make a significant break with current practices.

As people move through first-order change to engage in new practices and experience second-order change, they often become frustrated. They may misunderstand the initiative or find it

Judy Taylor, principal of Iduma Elementary School in Killeen, Texas, led staff through a process of defining not only their purpose, but also the knowledge, attitudes, skills, aspirations, and behaviors educators were expected to evidence in the classroom each day. They created this statement:

Iduma Elementary is a fun-loving, collaborative, focused, enthusiastic, risk-taking, intelligent community of learners with a reputation for excellence:

- *Students* engage in learning what is meaningful to them and make significant progress in achieving state and national standards. They value learning; they respect themselves and others; they share in the responsibility of a democratic school in which all achieve at high levels.

- *Staff members* engage in continuous learning. We use research and data to guide our decisions. We support each other and mentor each other so that all are highly competent. We share the responsibility for all students in the school and acknowledge our power and control to change those aspects of the school that have the greatest impact on student learning. We meaningfully engage students, parents, and community members in understanding the learning process, the expectations for student success, and ways they can powerfully partner with us.

- *Parents and community members* engage as equal partners in ensuring the success of all students. They make positive contributions at school, in their businesses and places of community service, and at home to ensure students are healthy and engaged in learning.

difficult to implement the change. When leaders understand how those in their organization learn best and how adult learners move from first-order to second-order change, the innovation is far more likely to succeed.

Successful leaders clarify the vision and goals by carefully crafting a logic model. Logic models help leaders set a series of expected outcomes over time that allow them to manage the change process. They declare short-, medium-, and long-term goals based on the theory of change, as well as clear outputs and the resources needed for the initiative to succeed. One example demonstrates an approach to implementing a new way of teaching reading (see Figure 11.1).

Strategies to monitor progress build the new vision into the organization's culture. Some leaders use the Concerns-Based Adoption Model (CBAM) (Hord, Rutherford, Huling-Austin, & Hall, 1987) to determine different levels of

Figure 11.1 Theory of change

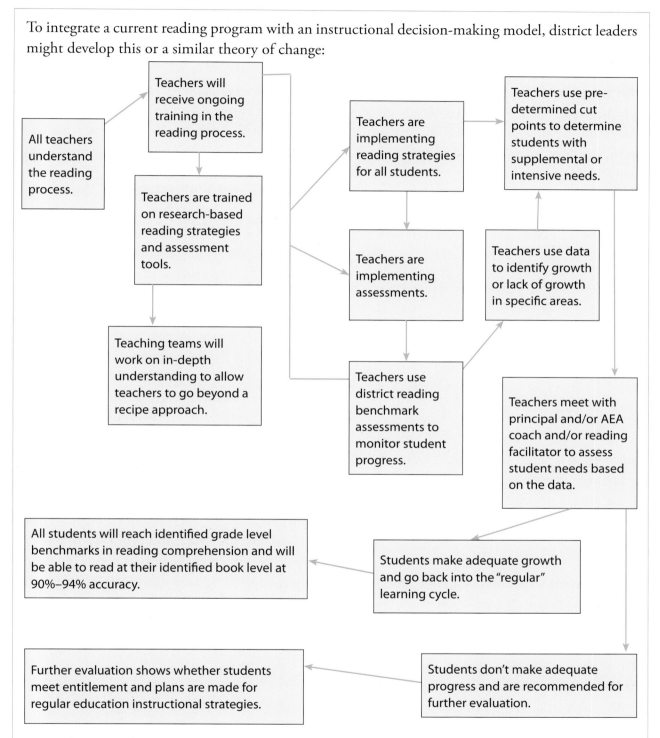

To integrate a current reading program with an instructional decision-making model, district leaders might develop this or a similar theory of change:

As district and school leaders consider what essential steps must be taken for teachers to authentically learn and use new strategies, they also consider what barriers teachers will face and how they will overcome them.

use of a new initiative among staff. CBAM, available through the Southwest Educational Development Laboratory (SEDL), a nonprofit education research, development, and dissemination organization based in Austin, Texas, helps leaders understand staff members' level of understanding of and concerns about any new innovation. Leaders can develop surveys using a specific series of questions to determine to what extent staff members are implementing an initiative—from basic awareness of the change to refining the method. They then are able to use the results to match professional learning with

The best way to lead people into the future is to connect deeply in the present with their passions and their moral purpose for teaching and leading.

staff members' needs as they work to implement the change. The model also asks staff to provide feedback to their principal about how well he or she is leading change.

Commit to success

Building shared vision and designing and initiating innovations is only part of the work involved in increasing all students' academic success. Leaders also make a deep, personal commitment to steering the organization through the change process. They build strong relationships with their boards and district and school leaders in order to lead all in the system to share a powerful, compelling vision and to work together to achieve it.

Research finds that a superintendent's tenure positively affects student achievement (Waters & Marzano, 2006). However, many district and school leaders don't intend to stay in their positions for long, or do not expect to be allowed to stay. Despite the rewards of seeing the effects of new practices on student learning, by the time the organization has moved to second-order change, many superintendents have moved to new districts. According to a report from the Council of the Great City Schools, the average tenure of urban superintendents increased from 2.3 years in 1999 to 3.6 years in 2010, a 56% increase that educators are celebrating. Yet fundamental change in a district requires a seven- to 10-year commitment (CGCS, 2010). District leaders who focus on the right goals, manage change effectively, and remain in their roles long enough to see results have higher-performing students (Waters & Marzano, 2006).

The best way to lead people into the future is to connect deeply in the present with their passions and their moral purpose for teaching and leading. Only shared visions take root, and leaders create shared visions only when they listen closely to others, appreciate others' hopes and attend to others' needs, communicate their own beliefs and vision clearly, and use systems, processes, and protocols to navigate the change process. The best leaders bring people into the future because they engage in the oldest form of research: They observe their team members and connect these members' desires and aspirations to the vision. Then that vision truly becomes shared.

Implications for district leaders

Learning system leaders are cautious about the number and type of innovations they initiate at the district level. When district leaders do not think through the change process, they may adopt too many innovations at once, and staff are not able to internalize the multiple, complex changes involved. The innovations then may not be valued and implemented effectively or with fidelity. Consequently, even sound initiatives are unlikely to result in significant change.

District leaders find that setting goals is a more powerful strategy than enacting programs. They recognize that a moral purpose, compelling vision and mission, and clearly articulated beliefs help move an organization forward. A clearly articulated vision allows district leaders to recognize the complexities of the changes they want others to make and the importance of staying the course for several years to ensure that the district vision is integrated into the culture of all schools.

They also understand that because few schools have exactly the same needs, school leaders must be given the flexibility to implement strategies and modify initiatives based on their own needs and the needs of their students. Flexibility also builds ownership. When district leaders strive to control schools, they may get compliance, but they seldom get commitment.

District leaders next develop strategies to assess progress. They may initiate systematic walk-throughs to spend time in schools observing innovations in action. Effective district leaders then differentiate professional learning strategies and support for schools. Some schools may need

encouragement; others may need coaching for the principal and leadership team; and some may need modeling and consistent support as they work through implementation challenges.

A clearly articulated vision allows district leaders to recognize the complexities of the changes they want others to make and the importance of staying the course for several years to ensure that the district vision is integrated into the culture of all schools.

Implications for school leaders

School leaders spend time with teachers to help them understand the district's vision, the school's expectations for implementing the innovation, and the anticipated student outcomes.

They build collective responsibility for students, first in their school and then in the district as a whole.

School leaders monitor shifts in teacher practices and symbolically connect those shifts to the vision. They give district leaders regular feedback on the progress the staff is making and ask for support when they face challenges. They routinely share accomplishments and celebrate benchmarks with staff, inviting district leaders to recognize progress.

Moral purpose must guide actions

If you're trying to be successful, particularly as an urban district with the diverse needs of your students, you have to center on a moral purpose. That moral purpose has to be an imperative for every person in the district.

A few years ago, I was at a conference and Michael Fullan was presenting. I knew of his work and went to see him. The place was packed, and I had to sit on the floor against the wall to listen. Embedded in that presentation was the whole concept of the triple P's—precision, personalization, and professional learning. What attracted me most was that at the center was the moral purpose, accomplished through the three components. In my view, as a new superintendent, those pieces weren't infused in our district, weren't a way of life. They were in pockets in the district, but not districtwide.

Precision involves more than just recording a grade that a child is given or test score in a grade book. It is taking that information, tearing it apart, figuring out what it says to you, and then changing how you teach. Precision is, I think, of all of the pieces the most complicated and the most threatening because we're asking adults to do things differently, to research and be honest with themselves and others whether they have been successful with any one child.

Precision at the principal level is not only test scores but whether a principal has been precise in terms of classroom visits, knowing the individual teachers and whether they are making the right decisions, and supporting professional learning based on staff needs.

Part of our job, whether it's with the students in our district or with the adults, is to decide what we know about their learning styles. Everybody takes in information differently, everybody processes information differently, and we have to be responsible for figuring out different ways of helping them master the standard. So that's what we believe personalization is about—that you recognize that everyone is not going to learn the same way.

As a result, we have coaches to help grown-ups and interventionists as additional support for students who are not progressing at the same speed as the other kids in the classroom or are progressing more rapidly than the other kids. The coach and the principal are the system of personalized and precise support for teachers, based upon the principal visiting classrooms, looking at the rubric determining what teachers should be doing, and identifying areas of growth that a teacher may have. The principal then assigns the coach work based on those needs.

You can be as philosophical as you want to about a vision and moral purpose, but if people don't see where that ties to their everyday jobs, the accountability isn't going to exist. So we just started off by believing that if you tell people the moral purpose enough times, if people see it enough times, if people have to have it as a part of planning when they are writing their school plans and their department plans, they will absorb it.

The good thing for us was that we had started this work before the pressure came from the state to be more successful, so we simply used that as a rallying cry. We didn't then focus on any particular school, but understood that everyone in the district is responsible for all of us working together on our moral purpose. Having that foundation in place first was necessary for change to take place.

— Wendy Robinson, superintendent
   Fort Wayne (Ind.) Community Schools

Reflection
questions

- What strategies have we used to intentionally build a shared vision in our district or school?

- What actions have we taken as leaders to model the vision?

- What strategies might we use with those we serve to move our organization closer to owning the vision?

- What is our theory of change?

- What stepping stones have we considered that will help to achieve our vision?

- How have we, as leaders, demonstrated a true commitment to change?

RESOURCES

Hord, S. M., Rutherford, W. L., Huling-Austin, L., & Hall, G. E. (1987). *Taking charge of change.* Alexandria, VA: ASCD.

Killion, J. (2002). *Assessing impact.* Oxford, OH: NSDC.

Pascopella, A. (2011, April). Superintendent staying power. *District Administration.* Available at www.districtadministration.com/article/superintendent-staying-power

Perkins, D. N. T. (2000). *Leading at the edge: Leadership lessons from the extraordinary saga of Shackleton's Antarctic expedition.* New York, NY: AMACOM, American Management Association.

Mid-continent Research for Education and Learning. (2012, March). The influence of superintendents on student achievement. Available at www.mcrel.org/about-us/hot-topics/ht-superintendents-on-student-achievement#sthash.VDpxivKR.dpuf

TOOLS INDEX

TOOL	TITLE	PURPOSE
11.1	Assessing the organization's shared vision	Consider the underlying beliefs and assumptions regarding change associated with the Standards for Professional Learning.
11.2	Clearly articulating a vision	Develop a clearly articulated vision that all in the organization comes to share.
11.3	Develop a vision using KASAB	Continue vision work by declaring the roles of those who are to implement the innovation.
11.4	Establishing a theory of change	Define a theory of change and describe a process for developing a theory of change with a team.
11.5	Developing a logic model aligned with the theory of change	Clearly articulate first and second order change in terms of time, outcomes, and essential resources.
11.6	Putting it all together	Form the details of an innovation by articulating foundational pieces, from beliefs and assumptions to a theory of change and the logic model.

CHAPTER 12

Analyzing
student learning

WHERE ARE WE NOW?

Our district ensures that all staff members have the skills needed to analyze student data in order to identify professional learning successes and needs.

STRONGLY AGREE   AGREE   NO OPINION   DISAGREE   STRONGLY DISAGREE

Our district leaders routinely analyze student learning data in order to set districtwide learning goals.

STRONGLY AGREE   AGREE   NO OPINION   DISAGREE   STRONGLY DISAGREE

Our district leaders have developed a thoughtful assessment plan that results in ongoing information about student learning.

STRONGLY AGREE   AGREE   NO OPINION   DISAGREE   STRONGLY DISAGREE

Our district leaders have regular conversations with principals about student achievement, professional learning, and ongoing support.

STRONGLY AGREE   AGREE   NO OPINION   DISAGREE   STRONGLY DISAGREE

School leaders use various assessments of learning and for learning to intervene when students fail to make progress.

STRONGLY AGREE   AGREE   NO OPINION   DISAGREE   STRONGLY DISAGREE

School leaders use data about areas in which students are not learning to guide teachers' professional learning.

STRONGLY AGREE   AGREE   NO OPINION   DISAGREE   STRONGLY DISAGREE

Learning system leaders understand that student learning results depend on professional learning. A 2008 analysis of six studies on the connection between teacher learning and student learning found that as teachers focused on student learning in learning communities, the school culture improved, teachers were empowered, and student achievement improved as measured by test scores over time. In other words, teacher learning that focused intensely on student learning and achievement affected student learning (Viscio, Ross, & Adams, 2008).

When leaders set goals for student outcomes and use data to shift the school's core instructional program, educators take more collective responsibility for every child's success.

When leaders set goals for student outcomes and use data to shift the school's core instructional program, educators take more collective responsibility for every child's success. As adults at the district and school level connect their learning to student needs, they begin to see the power of their own learning.

Knowing that student outcomes will not change without adult behavior shifting, learning system leaders align professional learning with Learning Forward's Standards for Professional Learning to ensure that educators stay focused on building high levels of professional capital.

Learning system leaders pay careful and constant attention to where the district is in relationship to where they want the district to be. Leaders use the Data Standard in planning professional learning to address the gap between the district's vision and what has been achieved, and to provide information that helps set the course to reach districtwide student learning goals.

In a learning system, teachers use those goals along with data from assessments *for* learning to identify the knowledge students need. They then work to develop skills that help them give students precise feedback and involve them in understanding what they know and what they need and want to learn.

Educators determine arrays of assessments that offer valid and reliable data about student and staff learning, establish goals and benchmarks for student and adult learning, regularly analyze data and monitor progress, and then shift practices based on that analysis using strategies such as extending learning time for students, revising units and assessments, celebrating successes, and redesigning professional learning to better align with the needs of students and staff. (See Figure 12.1.)

Determine student and staff learning assessments

In most districts, systemwide considerations *of* student learning are limited to analyzing the results of state standardized exams. Large-scale assessments

Figure 12.1 Improving student learning

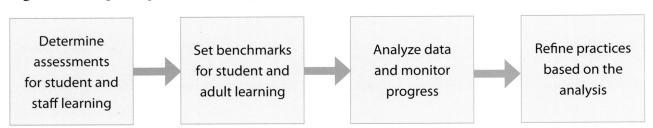

Determine assessments for student and staff learning → Set benchmarks for student and adult learning → Analyze data and monitor progress → Refine practices based on the analysis

can offer districts historical data but provide little information on what students are learning in ways that help staff shift practices. In addition, research on large-scale assessments finds that the data are wrong one-fifth of the time (Mansell, James, & the Assessment Reform Group, 2009). In other words, for every class of 25 students, data from these large-scale assessments are inaccurate for *five of those children.*

Classroom teachers often can more accurately assess overall student learning using running records, observation checklists, daily observation, questioning, and interaction with their students.

Learning system leaders, therefore, carefully consider which assessments will provide the most valuable data. The learning system leadership team is cautious about the impact its choices will have at the district level *and* school level. Leaders ask: Are assessments *of* and *for* learning reliable and valid instruments? What assessments for learning should be given to all students at a specific grade level or in a course of study to measure student growth districtwide? For example, should we give all 3rd-grade students a math problem-solving assessment four or six times a year to examine the growth of all students in all schools? Should we give all 10th-grade students a writing sample several times a year?

Leaders also consider the data: Are the assessment data providing the information needed to allow us to carefully select approaches to learning in our district and schools? What strategies will help teachers learn to use these data?

Learning system leaders select an array of reliable, valid assessment strategies. They are thoughtful about system-level projects that broaden the kinds of assessments used to judge student and staff learning. International Baccalaureate (IB) schools, for example, require students who want an IB diploma not only to pass the IB exams, but also to understand global affairs and engage in a research project. Using multiple measures to determine what students are learning helps districts make better decisions about curriculum and instructional design, understand student progress, and determine staff professional learning needs.

School leadership teams and staff are more concerned about ongoing assessments *for* learning. They understand that assessing students daily and giving them precise feedback is more significant than using summative data. Although they incorporate state standardized testing in their curriculum

> Classroom teachers often can more accurately assess overall student learning using running records, observation checklists, daily observation, questioning, and interaction with their students.

expectations for students and maximize the use of district assessments to guide instruction, they want to intervene regularly before students take standardized tests to ensure students not only perform well on the tests but also are learning.

School leaders also are concerned with the quality of assessments and ensure that teams continually ask themselves the following questions: What do quality classroom assessments look like? What do we look for when we develop assessments? How do we help teachers differentiate between assessments that are culminating demonstrations of learning and summative in nature (assessments *of* learning) from ongoing assessments (assessments *for* learning) in order to determine the effect of their instruction on student progress? How do we gather and monitor assessment data? How can we be the lead learners we aspire to be? What conversations shift the core instructional approach in our school, student groupings, and team learning to increase our effectiveness?

Teachers in Woodburn (Oregon) Public Schools felt that data from quarterly district assessments were not giving them sufficient information to shift their practices quickly enough to affect student learning, and so they set out to develop more effective instruments. They studied how to develop reliable, valid formative assessment strategies and developed more timely assessments for teacher teams to use.

Set benchmarks for student and adult learning

Learning system leaders routinely analyze student learning data in order to set districtwide learning goals. They develop a thoughtful assessment plan that results in ongoing information about student learning.

Learning system leaders use several years of data from multiple sources, not just annual state test results, to determine to what extent a program is affecting student learning. For example, an evaluation of a new approach to teaching writing might include districtwide assessments, student writing samples over time, and annual state writing assessments.

Leaders also look at data on shifts in teacher practices. Current teacher evaluation systems and principal walk-throughs can provide data for understanding teachers' strengths and challenges. By analyzing the connections between data on student achievement and data on teacher effectiveness, district and school leadership teams can begin to develop effective professional learning designs. Tools such as the Concerns-Based Adoption Model's (CBAM) levels of use help school leaders differentiate professional learning and address teachers' concerns (Hall & Hord, 2006). CBAM proposes, for example, that staff survey principals to identify their strengths in leading and facilitating change. Leaders also may develop a district-level walk-through system to gather data on how an initiative is being implemented and then differentiate support to school-level staff.

Once district and school leaders have carefully analyzed trends in student and adult data, they select SMART goals (specific, measurable, attainable, results-based and time-bound) to focus their professional learning on the outcomes—and new skills, attitudes, and behaviors that they want to see in the staff—that they believe will positively affect teacher practice and

The Mineola Union Free School District in Garden City Park, New York, established an array of assessments to gauge learning. The district leadership team broadened its approach to include not only state assessments, but also student surveys, and included as new graduation requirements a student portfolio, performance task, and character self-analysis. All the assessments carried equal weight in measuring student effectiveness.

The Franklin Township (Ind.) Community School Corporation initiated a system to engage students in projects based on topics of interest. Students set learning goals, and because the work was personalized, they became more involved. They shared their new knowledge at a public hearing and flourished academically. Teachers and staff engaged in professional learning around the process of setting effective goals and coaching students through a long-term annual or multiyear project.

student learning. Clearly articulated SMART goals guide the design and evaluation of professional learning.

Analyze data

Learning system leaders model the learning they expect to see. Modeling is a powerful strategy. When system leadership teams model what they expect to see in school teams and systematically and purposefully share their findings, teams and systematically and purposefully share their findings, schools have the best opportunity to learn from them how to use data well.

Learning system leaders use a purposeful, thoughtful cycle of continuous improvement (see Appendix) and become proficient in using all its components to make data-driven decisions not only about instruction but also about professional learning.

They have regular conversations with principals about what students are learning and how

well school leadership teams are supporting teachers in ways that increase student achievement. As system leaders coach principals, principals realize how much their leaders value using data to guide decisions, and they grow in their ability to effectively use data with their staffs.

School leaders use data about areas where students are not learning to guide teachers' professional learning. Teacher teams work collaboratively through a cycle of continuous improvement. As staff members come to better understand the data and shift their practices, student learning accelerates.

The Austin (Texas) Independent School District leadership team developed a walk-through process to give schools feedback about their efforts to implement district innovations and to use the observations to find out how well district leaders were supporting schools. District leaders established teams that included a cross-section of teachers and administrators to conduct the walk-throughs at least twice a year in each building. At the end of each walk-through, district leaders visited with the school's leadership team to share findings and interview them about how they, as district leaders, could better support the school.

Monitor progress

When district and school leadership teams monitor student progress through collaborative analysis of data and student work, they gain crucial information about how well students are doing. Similarly, learning system leaders monitor teacher learning. Learning system leaders evaluate professional learning's effect on teacher practices and student learning. They find or develop tools to measure changes in teacher practices and assess how professional learning caused those changes.

System leaders know that determining the staff's progress in implementing an innovation is essential to discovering whether teacher practice is shifting in ways that can affect student outcomes. Learning Forward's Standards Assessment Inventory (SAI2) is an online survey that captures teachers' perceptions about how well the

> The best way to lead people into the future is to connect deeply in the present with their passions and their moral purpose for teaching and leading.

school is implementing Learning Forward's Standards for Professional Learning. The survey provides baseline data about a staff's progress toward becoming a community of learners. The inventory provides a host of information, including

- District data to help leaders understand teachers' perceptions of professional learning;
- The degree of success or challenge a school or district faces with respect to professional learning practices and their implementation; and
- Data for decision makers on the quality of professional learning as defined by the Standards and alignment of the district's professional learning to the Standards.

Refine practice

As district and school leaders become precise and systematic about the use of data around student and adult learning, they engage meaningfully in a cycle of continuous improvement and consequently are continuously refining their practice.

Implications for district leaders

District-level decision makers continually ask themselves the following questions:

- Do our student programs, instructional frameworks, and adult learning processes have a positive effect on student learning? What evidence do we have to support our conclusions?
  - Do we have a method to select effective, district-level assessments to give the district and school leadership teams information about student learning?
  - Do we have enough information about shifts in adult practices?
  - Do we model and promote a culture of data-driven decisions through a clearly articulated cycle of continuous improvement?
- Do we have a data system that enables staff to analyze student outcomes at the classroom, school, and district levels? Do we use a sufficient array of assessment strategies?
- Do school communities have easy access to student information through an accurate, longitudinal database?
- Do we promote a culture of data-driven decision making to support school goal setting and planning efforts?
- Do we have sufficient professional learning, data tools, technical assistance, and support for principals and school leadership teams

to know how to change instruction to best meet the needs of their students?

- Do we consistently use data to inform resource allocations?

(Hamilton et al., 2009)

When learning system leaders analyze summative data to look at program effectiveness, how resources are allocated, and what support school leaders need, principals better understand how to work with staff to use data effectively.

Implications for school leaders

To improve student achievement, leaders need a laser-focused approach to collecting data and a systematic process for ongoing analysis. They use the array of data flowing through the school daily to clarify goals and establish clear plans. They develop their own and their teachers' skills to analyze the data they have collected.

Principals routinely

- Develop a systematic approach to collecting and analyzing data that positively impact student and staff learning;
- Help school teams develop a culture of collective responsibility for student learning;
- Ensure that school-level professional learning is embedded in a cycle of continuous improvement;

- Coach others to use a variety of data to determine student needs, modify core instructional programs, and identify teacher professional learning needs;
- Develop staff members' skills and proficiency in using assessments *for* learning in order to give students precise feedback;
- Develop staff members' skills and proficiency in designing instruction and in using data to group students; and
- Engage in and facilitate ongoing, strategic professional learning that increases teacher effectiveness in identifying and meeting students' most critical areas of need.

When learning system leaders analyze summative data to look at program effectiveness, how resources are allocated, and what support school leaders need, principals better understand how to work with staff to use data effectively.

As school leaders observe and work with teams in the school, they use ongoing data to give staff and school teams feedback and coach them when they struggle. Coaching becomes an integral part of life for every teacher as all work together to learn.

Teachers use data to create powerful results

Beginning in 2010, the district identified a small group of schools among the system's 51 buildings to begin working with intensively. The five elementary schools—Leading Educational Achievement with Distinction schools—were to be incubators of reform.

As a district, we discussed Michael Fullan's Triple P's—precision, how to look very precisely at data and analyze that data to make sure that what we did actually met student needs; personalization, about personalizing our instruction to fit the needs of those students; and professional learning, that teachers are continuous learners and as they look at data and develop a system for delivering instruction, they also are learning what they need to know to deliver that instruction.

We took apart the standards to determine what we needed to teach. Through data analysis we learned that we needed more frequent assessments for learning and developed assessments that addressed the standards that our students did not understand. We also had to make sure that we were tight in our delivery of instruction, so we developed a district framework for delivery of instruction. We used our data to determine how we were going to address whole and small group instruction and intervention.

Teachers had to articulate and plan what students were going to learn. Every time teachers presented a new lesson or a new unit, they would have small group instruction, interventions, and conversations aligned to the standards that they were teaching.

Then principals were expected to do daily walk-throughs to look for and monitor that alignment and communicate with teachers. Once each semester, principals would visit the classroom to give focused feedback to ensure that the district expectations were being adhered to. Once upon a time, the district school administrators didn't go to the schools very often, but now part of my responsibility is to visit each of my schools several times a year to observe a principal doing a daily snapshot or a focused feedback observation. Or I might observe a teacher collaboration meeting to see whether teachers are analyzing data precisely and using the data to inform their planning.

We taught school teams a simple data conversation protocol teachers can use. The expectation is that they come prepared knowing their data and then the common planning time is used to answer, "What we do next? How do we address this? What do I do in my small groups to address all of my students' needs?" Teachers have to not only know students' data but know where individual students are performing and how to address their learning. They have to commit to planning together to make sure that instruction is tight and aligned in their school.

As a result, teachers have depended less on just the textbook, used student data to inform all units of planning, and begun to understand that collaboration is more than just getting together and meeting. For the first time, we are committed to a system of collaboration where teachers are looking at student work and at student data, professional learning is embedded in the day, and teachers understand the expectation for cohesive learning not only for them through professional learning, but also for students.

We just became much more powerful, more aligned, and more defined—and as a result, we saw improvement in student test scores.

— Get Nichols, director of elementary education
Fort Wayne (Ind.) Community Schools

Reflection
questions

- How well do we use data to set goals in our school or district? How could we improve the way we incorporate data into our planning?

- What knowledge and skills do all staff need in order to support using data to drive and evaluate professional learning?

- Do our data show us shifts in teacher practice? How might we determine what effect professional learning is having?

- What other types of data could we collect that might reflect what our students know and are capable of doing?

- How are we evaluating what teachers need to learn in order to better support students?

- How is our district leadership team working with schools to understand site-level data?

RESOURCES

Bambrick-Santoyo, P. (2010). *Driven by data: A practical guide to improve instruction.* San Francisco, CA: Jossey-Bass.

Boudett, E., City, A., & Murnane, R. J. (Eds.). (2005). *Data wise: A step-by-step guide to using assessment results to improve teaching and learning.* Cambridge, MA: Harvard Education Press.

Davies, A., Herbst, S., & Reynolds, B. P. (2011). *Leading the way to assessment* for *learning: A practical guide.* Bloomington, IN: Solution Tree.

Guskey, T. (2003). How classroom assessments improve learning. *Educational Leadership, 60*(5), 6–11.

Psencik, K. (2009). *Accelerating student and staff learning: Purposeful curriculum collaboration.* Thousand Oaks, CA: Corwin Press.

Sadler, D. R. (1989). Formative assessment and the design of instructional systems. *Instructional Science,* 18, 119–144.

Stiggins, R. J. (2008). *Assessment manifesto: A call for the development of balanced assessment systems.* Portland, OR: ETS Assessment Training Institute.

The Institute from Higher Education Policy. (n.d.). *Using data to improve educational outcomes: A college readiness issue brief.* Washington, DC: Pathways to College Network, the Institute from Higher Education Policy.

TOOLS INDEX

TOOL	TITLE	PURPOSE
12.1	Determining research questions and essential data	Help district leaders establish clear research questions, determine the most effective data for answering the questions, and finalize the recommendation of data to be used at the district level to answer the research questions they established.
12.2	Developing a district-level assessment plan	Work with a district-level assessment team to design a district assessment plan.
12.3	Sample district-level assessment plan	Develop quality district-level assessment strategies.
12.4	Developing a district-level assessment/data calendar	Develop a district assessment calendar based on the district assessment system.
12.5	Developing a school-level assessment calendar	Design a school assessment calendar that incorporates the district assessment calendar.
12.6	Hosting district-level data conversations	Engage district leaders in thoughtful conversations with school principals or leadership teams about data and strategies to increase staff effectiveness and student achievement.
12.7	Hosting school-level data conversations	Engage principals in thoughtful conversations with leadership teams about data and strategies to increase staff effectiveness and student achievement.

CHAPTER 13

Developing an
instructional
framework

WHERE ARE WE NOW?

Our district uses a clearly articulated instructional framework to guide schools to make thoughtful, research-based instructional decisions.

STRONGLY AGREE   AGREE   NO OPINION   DISAGREE   STRONGLY DISAGREE

Our district leaders ensure that schools make curriculum and assessment decisions based on student needs.

STRONGLY AGREE   AGREE   NO OPINION   DISAGREE   STRONGLY DISAGREE

Our district leadership teams conduct regular walk-throughs to engage principals and teaching teams in conversations about student learning.

STRONGLY AGREE   AGREE   NO OPINION   DISAGREE   STRONGLY DISAGREE

Principals facilitate grade-level or course teams' work designing curriculum to guarantee the curriculum aligns with the district's instructional framework and engages students in meaningful instruction.

STRONGLY AGREE   AGREE   NO OPINION   DISAGREE   STRONGLY DISAGREE

School teams continually give school and district leadership teams information about their challenges and the support they need to succeed.

STRONGLY AGREE   AGREE   NO OPINION   DISAGREE   STRONGLY DISAGREE

Teaching teams value curriculum design and spend collaborative time developing common curriculum units, assessments, and high-yield instructional plans.

STRONGLY AGREE   AGREE   NO OPINION   DISAGREE   STRONGLY DISAGREE

An instructional framework is a figurative structure that educators use as a means to examine and understand a set of ideas for how learning in the district is designed. It captures the assumptions, concepts, values, and practices that help those within the organization speak with a common vocabulary. The framework adds value to an organization by giving meaning to what might seem like discrepant practices, policies, and protocols and clearly depicting how the pieces fit together to achieve the organization's moral purpose.

> The framework adds value to an organization by giving meaning to what might seem like discrepant practices, policies, and protocols, and clearly depicting how the pieces fit together to achieve the organization's moral purpose.

For example, one well-known instructional framework is Charlotte Danielson's *Framework for Teaching*, a comprehensive and coherent description of a teacher's responsibilities grounded in empirical studies and theoretical research on improving teaching and learning. The framework helps all see what elements of quality instruction are teachers' responsibilities. Robert Marzano has also developed a research-based framework for quality instruction, as have others.

A framework may be used for many purposes, but its full value is realized when it serves as the foundation for professional conversations among practitioners as they seek to enhance their teaching skills. The framework also may provide the foundation for a school's or district's mentoring, coaching, professional development, and teacher evaluation processes, linking those activities together and helping teachers become more thoughtful practitioners.

An effective instructional framework is *not* a prescribed program, a set of detailed lesson plans, a detailed scope and sequence of curriculum objectives, or a mandate for specific methodologies or programs.

Learning system leaders use frameworks effectively. One of the learning system's greatest challenges is to define district and school leaders' responsibilities for curriculum design, assessment, and instruction. Traditionally, district leaders have had a difficult time relinquishing control of these areas, and school leaders have been reluctant to take responsibility for innovating. Learning system leaders ensure that school leaders understand their responsibilities in creating effective school-based curriculum and make thoughtful decisions in this and other areas based on the unique needs of their students.

When districts give schools a framework or boundaries within which to work while also giving them significant latitude to base decisions on student performance data, student interests, and teacher expertise, they develop a relationship that allows school teams to take collective responsibility for the success of all the students in their school.

Developing an instructional framework requires addressing how the learning system will view curriculum design, assessments, and instructional strategies.

Design curriculum

Learning system leaders view curriculum design as a learning opportunity and develop strategies

What is an instructional framework?

A framework offers

- A clear, research-based vision that includes high-quality professional learning standards and a set of student performance expectations, along with a description of the instructional strategies that will help ensure students meet them;
- The district's stated beliefs and assumptions about student learning expectations aligned with its strategic plan and goals, and a summary of the research that supports those beliefs and assumptions;
- Structures and supports to help school communities develop purposeful, thoughtful curriculum maps, assessments *of* and *for* learning, and inspiring and engaging instructional designs;
- A districtwide assessment plan;
- A collection of reference materials to help school-based teams understand the framework's concepts and assumptions;
- A description of effective instruction and assessment strategies with an analysis of how they address Learning Forward's Standards for Professional Learning;
- A guide for planning professional learning at the district and school levels; and
- A tool to communicate the goals of the Standards to the community.

for all in the organization to deepen their understanding of what the system expects students to learn. Some district leaders may not have expertise in designing curriculum or may not value the process. They may confuse curriculum with textbooks or lengthy documents explaining instructional strategies. Successful district leaders understand that curriculum is the material the district expects students to learn and learn well, material described in clearly articulated and easily understood standards that are the touchstones guiding all work around assessment and instruction (English & Steffy, 2001; Marzano, 2010; Guskey & Jung, 2012).

Districts are challenged to ensure that learning communities at the schools value the curriculum and intentionally use it to guide assessment and instructional design. When school leaders own the work and hold themselves accountable, student learning increases.

Districts are challenged to ensure that learning communities at the schools value the curriculum and intentionally use it to guide assessment and instructional design.

Develop assessments

In learning systems, leaders take seriously the quality of assessments used to judge students and because of the margin of error, never use just one assessment to place a student or hold a student back. Robert Marzano's study of assessments (2010) found that, even with a high level of reliability and validity, scores ranged by 20%.

Brenda West, principal of Adams Elementary in the Fort Wayne (Ind.) Community Schools, was familiar with the district's language arts curriculum; however, when the district adopted a new language arts textbook, teachers became confused about the differences. West decided to focus on the district's learning standards. She designed a system for mapping the standards with particular emphasis on the skills students were not mastering. She let teachers know she expected teams to work together to study the standards, map them for their next unit of study, and then design assessments *of* and *for* learning. They used materials provided by the district to select the most closely aligned instructional approaches. Through weekly assessments, they monitored student growth, standard by standard, and posted data outside their rooms. Teachers had regular conversations with the principal as they continued to study the standards, map them, develop assessments, design instruction, and monitor student progress. By the end of the year, students had demonstrated significant growth. West met regularly with her area superintendent to review her goals and her process, share challenges, solve problems, reflect on student performance data, and plan for next steps.

Assessments can be carelessly developed, not aligned to the district's student learning standards, and as a result, may be inadequate to measure a student's performance and mastery level. Districts may purchase programs that purport to align to state and national standards only to find on closer examination that they are not at all aligned. Yet these programs are used for grading, to determine class placement, and to decide whether a student passes or fails.

In a learning system, leaders are serious about the quality of assessments and carefully analyze any proposed assessment to be sure it aligns with district standards and is appropriate for the district's student population.

District and school leaders value teams' work and provide time for them to develop clearly aligned assessment strategies. Leaders put effective systems in place to monitor quality. Most important, they understand the power of multiple measures and the importance of using ongoing assessments to intervene early if students are not learning. These teams are effective because they take time up front to ensure that students know what they need to learn and what quality work looks like. They may develop standards charts and rubrics with students and share exemplars so that there is no question in the mind of students what their goals are. They help students chart their own growth and set goals for themselves so that they take ownership in their own learning (Stiggins, 2008; Marzano, 2010).

Furthermore, highly effective district and school leaders use assessment *of* and *for* learning as the organizing core of adult learning. For many highly effective district leadership teams, seizing this opportunity to support student learning requires rethinking adult learning in general and using assessment to guide professional learning (Stiggins, 2008; Learning Forward, 2011).

Rather than buying assessments, the Douglas County (Georgia) School System decided to have teachers use their expertise to develop districtwide unit assessments. Administrators formed a teacher leadership team to oversee the effort. This team, facilitated by an external expert, developed a precise system for engaging teachers. Team members created a design plan, developed a rubric to ensure the assessments were high quality, aligned the assessments to the district's learning standards, worked through Webb's Depth of Knowledge Guide to determine the complexity of thinking required of students, and used state samples to guarantee rigor. The team also created a system for all teachers in the district to offer feedback on the assessments.

Identify high-yield instructional strategies

High-quality instruction yields positive results for the learner. In learning systems, teachers engage learners in meaningful ways that are intriguing and inspirational. They understand that unless students are interested and eager to explore, they will not expend the energy required to develop proficiency. Studies of effective teaching show that high-level learning results require

- Creating ambitious, meaningful tasks that reflect how knowledge is used in the field;
- Engaging students in active learning so they apply and test what they know;
- Drawing connections to students' prior knowledge and experiences;
- Diagnosing student understanding in order to scaffold the learning process step by step;
- Continually assessing student learning and adapting teaching to student needs;
- Providing clear standards, constant feedback, and opportunities for work; and
- Encouraging strategic and metacognitive thinking so that students can learn to evaluate and guide their own learning.

(Darling-Hammond, 2008)

In a learning system, school teams' central, long-term work is instructional design; teams increase their effectiveness with all students by exploring strategies and asking themselves the following questions:

- Do these instructional strategies help and inspire students to develop high levels of proficiency?
- Do these strategies help students meet the standards?
- Do they challenge students to think at a high level?
- What do adults need in order to learn together?
- Who are the leaders in this field? What evidence do they have that what they promote works?
- How can we best apply what we are learning?
- What impact are these strategies having on student success?

Implications for district leaders

Leaders of learning systems deepen their understanding of instruction and develop the skills needed to align instruction with challenging, complex learning standards to help students become master readers, writers, thinkers, and questioners across the curriculum by

- Collaborating with school leaders to develop a clearly articulated framework that gives schools direction and support to ensure they engage in effective, collaborative curriculum design;
- Broadening student performance expectations beyond national and state curriculum standards to ensure a rigorous, challenging curriculum so that students become thoughtful, participating citizens;
- Ensuring all principals have the skills to lead the intense instructional work that students need in order to learn at high levels;
- Organizing district leaders to support and coach school leaders;

> When teams work in an environment that values curriculum, assessment, and instructional design and are structured to engage authentically in this work, teachers experience transformational professional learning.

- Working to inspire, facilitate, and coach school leaders to take responsibility for all students' success by engaging leaders in curriculum mapping and in developing assessment strategies and research-based instructional strategies;
- Establishing assessments that give students opportunities to demonstrate their success
- Creating supports that promote risk taking and powerful professional learning, and processes that generate the data needed to redesign curriculum and modify practices;

- Providing adequate resources for curriculum design, professional learning, and assessment development and use;
- Differentiating support for schools based on school data, observations of practices from regular walk-throughs, conversations with principals about teaching teams' progress using the framework and resources, and the effect on student outcomes; and
- Assessing the effect of district curriculum on student success.

Implications for school leaders

School leaders are responsible for developing curriculum expertise and skillfully leading and facilitating instructional design. They model for others how to use assessments *for* learning—to differentiate instruction, group and regroup students, conference one-on-one with students, and redesign curriculum, assessment, and instructional plans to meet the needs of all students. When teams work in an environment that values curriculum, assessment, and instructional design and are structured to engage authentically in this work, teachers experience transformational professional learning.

School leaders build an environment that supports quality curriculum, assessment, and instructional design by taking steps to

- Guide and inspire school teams to embrace their district's student performance standards and use those standards to ensure all students succeed;
- Facilitate teacher teams in developing common curriculum maps to ensure students master the standards, designing common assessments *of* and *for* learning to know which students are mastering what

skills, and designing high-yield instructional strategies that accelerate student learning, motivate students, and lead to mastery;

- Engage teams in continuous professional learning to develop the skills they need to lead students to mastery;
- Analyze data from ongoing common assessments regularly, and consider modifying curriculum plans, regrouping students, and extending learning opportunities as needed;
- Coach and support teams and individual teachers who are struggling; and
- Have regular conversations with district leaders about the school's progress, successes, and challenges.

Careful restructuring transforms teacher, student learning

When I first came to Webster eight years ago, we discovered that the district had great pockets of excellence but not really a consistent thread that wove throughout the whole system. We have 11 buildings, and there were 11 slightly different systems not really woven together as a unit. Teachers were not regularly a part of the instructional decision-making framework, and there was no consistency throughout K–12 in content.

We began talking as an administration about what structure we would need to put in place in order to transform student learning. With 54 administrators, we went through process activities for people to think, report out, develop ideas, give feedback, and then correlate information.

We developed a teacher leadership structure that was fairly applied K–12. Rather than 12 positions that were high school department heads and included release time, guaranteed summer days, and a lesser course load, we reappropriated the resources and created 92 lead teacher positions that had no release time guaranteed but created teacher leadership in every elementary, every middle school, every high school. And then we created the next layer, curriculum directors in K–12 content divisions, and assigned lead teachers to those directors. So lead teachers now had a voice with their building principal and in content curriculum with district personnel.

Teacher leaders' job was to work with the building principal to look at the buildings' instructional data to help create the focus for that building. Then they connected through the curriculum director on content. We also formed an elementary cabinet and a secondary cabinet so that we could work together on leveled curriculum and data.

At the same time, we had teachers connect to professional learning communities by grade level in elementary or department in secondary to give teachers time to really get to the work of curriculum. We gathered data, created common assessments, analyzed the data from our kids, implemented new techniques, and identified the most powerful teaching strategies—and the wheel went around again. The teacher communities now are talking systematically about teacher practice.

Then we developed a comprehensive, credible data set for the board to set its goals. Before, it was more anecdotal conversation, and we couldn't say that the system staff understood or even knew what the board's goals were. We wanted to make that process intentional and connected to the other systems changes. From those goals, the administrative team developed measurable action steps to meet the goals, and then the building principals and curriculum directors took the steps to the content groups and the building instructional teams. And all staff developed SMART goals to respond to the board goals in a very tangible way.

In our original plan, we described a vision of *effective* collaboration. By the end of the process, our union president suggested that we change the wording to *transformational* collaboration, because he said this work has transformed the way we think about teaching and learning. Our system has been transformed by the impact on the curriculum of a K–12 application of leadership for teachers, the way that we look at data, and the instructional decisions that we make now.

— Adele Bovard, superintendent
Webster (N.Y.) Central School District

Reflection
questions

- How would we answer the question: What is your instructional framework?

- How do we we, as district-level leaders, direct and support school-based teams in collaborating around curriculum, assessments, and instruction?

- What district-level systems might hinder school leaders and learning communities from taking responsibility for designing and implementing high-yield curriculum, assessment, and instruction?

- In what ways is our district leadership team skilled in helping principals become instructional leaders?

- How do we support risk taking?

- Which of our school leaders are models for others on how to build collective responsibility for student outcomes, the curriculum, assessments, and intriguing instruction? How might we leverage these role models?

RESOURCES

Cushman, K. (2010). *Fires in the mind: What kids can tell us about motivation and mastery.* San Francisco, CA: Jossey-Bass.

Davies, A., Herbst, S., Reynolds, B. P. (2011). *Leading the way to assessment for learning: A practical guide.* Bloomington, IN: Solution Tree.

Dean, C. B., Hubbel, E. R., Pitler, H., & Stone, B. (2012). *Classroom instruction that works* (2nd ed.). Alexandria, VA: ASCD.

Guskey, T. R. (Ed.). (2009). *The principal as assessment leader.* Bloomington, IN: Solution Tree.

Markham, T. & Larmer, J. (2003). *Project-based learning handbook: A guide to standards-focused project based learning for middle and high school teachers.* Novato, CA: Buck Institute for Education.

Psencik, K. (2009). *Accelerating student and staff learning: Purposeful curriculum collaboration.* Thousand Oaks, CA: Corwin Press.

TOOLS INDEX

TOOL	TITLE	PURPOSE
13.1	Developing an instructional framework	Help district leaders develop a framework to guide the work of school leaders and school learning communities.
13.2	Exploring and establishing our assumptions about learners and learning	Examine assumptions about learning and learners and make visible beliefs to promote greater student success.
13.3	Designing curriculum	Design and implement a system in the community to develop annual work plans or curriculum maps to achieve the vision.
13.4	Designing assessments	Establish and implement an effective system for assessment of learning.
13.5	Designing instruction	Help facilitators work with teaching teams to develop aligned, thoughtful units of study.
13.6	Analyzing a video of an effective instructional team	Develop a critical view of a high-achieving team of teachers learning from each other.

CHAPTER 14

Building a
learning agenda

WHERE ARE WE NOW?

Our district has a clearly articulated professional learning agenda to ensure that every day, everyone is learning.

STRONGLY AGREE   AGREE   NO OPINION   DISAGREE   STRONGLY DISAGREE

Our district and school leaders thoughtfully engage learners using adult learning theories and differentiate learning strategies based on learners' needs.

STRONGLY AGREE   AGREE   NO OPINION   DISAGREE   STRONGLY DISAGREE

Our district and school leaders ensure that professional learning designs are based on the needs of individuals, teams, schools, and the district.

STRONGLY AGREE   AGREE   NO OPINION   DISAGREE   STRONGLY DISAGREE

Our district and school leaders connect professional learning to educator and student performance data.

STRONGLY AGREE   AGREE   NO OPINION   DISAGREE   STRONGLY DISAGREE

Our district and school leaders support adult learners and learning teams as they become competent in and implement new strategies designed to improve their effectiveness and increase student learning.

STRONGLY AGREE   AGREE   NO OPINION   DISAGREE   STRONGLY DISAGREE

Our district and school leaders adhere to the Design and Implementation Standards in their ongoing work.

STRONGLY AGREE   AGREE   NO OPINION   DISAGREE   STRONGLY DISAGREE

A learning agenda is a collection of strategies or designs leaders select in order to ensure that educators can understand and apply practices that improve their own performance and student outcomes. Learning agendas help create a supportive environment that allows individuals and teams to reflect on and learn from their own and others' experiences, and then create action plans to deepen their practice around what they are learning.

Learning agendas help staff envision the future. Learning agendas are built around dreams and aspirations, vision, and moral purpose and help transform a district into a learning system.

Leaders begin to develop a learning agenda by asking open-ended questions that, when educators study and research the answers, strengthen the learning system and enable the district to achieve its compelling moral purpose. Questions can include the following:

- What will it take for everyone in our district to ensure that every student learns at high levels?
- What do we all need to learn in order to lead a district in which everyone thinks in that way?
- What would it look like if we all were on a learning journey together?
- What barriers will we face, and what are the best ways to overcome them?
- What evidence would demonstrate that we are making progress?

To create a learning agenda, effective leaders consider key factors, shift understanding, offer precise feedback, and focus on their district's community of learners. They must then implement the agenda and follow through.

Consider key factors

Designing a learning agenda is challenging work, particularly for large, urban districts. Designers align their plans with intended outcomes and clear expectations to move learners beyond comprehension to mastering the knowledge, skills, dispositions, and practices needed to improve practice. The agenda sets out learning designs that are

- Grounded in an accurate, logical theory of change;
- Demonstrate an understanding of adult learning;
- Connected to adult learning and student outcomes; and
- Assessed for impact.

A theory of change. The traditional approach to professional learning is training, based on the belief that individuals' practices will change when they are trained to use new ones. Educators came to realize that training alone did not significantly change teachers' practice and added coaching for support.

As long as teachers developed a trusting relationship with an effective coach skilled in the new practices and in coaching, learners shifted their practices (Knight, 2007). However, most districts continue to find breakdowns between learning and practice—a knowing-doing gap (Kegan & Lahey, 2009).

Learning system leaders think through the change process and develop a clearly articulated theory of change aimed at closing the knowing-doing gap. To design an effective professional learning agenda, thoughtful leaders use an articulated theory of change along with other tools—such as charts designed to help teachers examine their knowledge, attitudes, skills, aspirations, and behaviors (KASAB); Innovation Configuration maps; and logic models—designed to build understanding and shared vision around the purpose and processes for the learning.

An understanding of adult learning. Jacqueline Kennedy writes (2012) that leaders designing a new system for professional learning should embed adult motivations in their learning designs. Daniel Pink (2011) identifies three drivers that motivate individuals and increase job satisfaction:

- Autonomy. People want control over their work.
- Mastery. People want to get better at what they do.
- Purpose. People want to be part of something bigger than themselves.

Jacqueline Kennedy (2012) suggests giving learners control over their work, using technology to meet their needs, and providing them greater flexibility.

Malcolm Knowles (1973) notes that adult learners

- Value meaningful work;
- Bring experience and expertise to new learning;
- Are goal oriented;
- Participate completely in the learning process and take control over its nature and direction; and
- Like to be respected.

In learning systems, those designing learning agendas take into account the fact that adults learn differently than young people and consider not only adults' levels of understanding, but also their past learning experiences.

A connection to outcomes. Learning agendas connect adult learning to essential student learning. Designers plan adult learning only after identifying student needs. They hold professional learning to high standards so that all students learn what they need to and at high levels.

In a learning system, adults clearly understand the link between their learning and student learning. When professional learning connects educators' performance standards and curriculum, professional learning is more likely to improve student learning (Learning Forward,

2011; Drago-Severson, 2011).

Without that clear understanding, the resources required to support quality professional learning may be difficult to maintain. In the absence of long-term planning and an understanding of professional learning's effects, some systems faced with budget shortfalls have reduced coaching staffs, eliminated collaborative time for teacher team meetings, and reduced other professional learning efforts in order to fund different initiatives.

An assessment of impact. The ultimate goal of all professional learning is improved student learning. The only way to determine whether a learning design is successful is to assess the strategy. In learning systems, designers construct ways to evaluate professional learning as they are planning the learning strategy. Including such measures in the planning stage ensures that data or artifacts needed for evaluation will be collected as learning proceeds rather than having to try to retrieve evidence after the learning occurs.

Evaluators should select an evaluation process that will meet the design goals of the learning agenda, the evaluator's abilities, and available resources (Killion, 2008). Evaluations do not need to scientifically prove that the adult learning resulted in student achievement. As Joellen Killion writes, "Frequently, policymakers want evaluators to prove causality, but it is not frequently the case that they understand the complexity of the design needed to answer questions about causality" (2008, p. 72).

What is most important is the level of evaluation. Thomas Guskey (2000) describes five such levels for evaluating professional learning. At the highest level, he says, evaluators determine the effect of teacher learning on student outcomes by asking questions such as the following:

- Did it affect student performance?
- Is student attendance improving?

- Are fewer students dropping out?
- Did it influence students' physical or emotional well-being?
- Have students become more confident learners?

Guskey says evidence can be gleaned from school and student records, questionnaires, interviews, and teacher portfolios.

Shift understanding

Learning system leaders create a meaningful learning agenda through careful planning, evaluation that helps create a cycle of continuous improvement (see Appendix), and most importantly, providing adequate time for teachers to learn.

Few districts are creating learning agendas that value the time teams need in order to change practices. In a study led by Linda Darling-Hammond and her team on professional learning around the world, researchers found that teachers working in the United States did not have adequate time for professional learning. The study also revealed that although professional learning is most effective when sustained over time, few U.S. teachers experience that kind of professional learning. According to the study (2009, p. 7),

> While teachers typically need substantial professional development in a given area (close to 50 hours) to improve their skills and their students' learning, most professional development opportunities in the United States are much shorter. On the 2003–04 national Schools and Staffing Survey (SASS), a majority of teachers (57%) said they had received no more than 16 hours (two days or less) of professional development during the previous 12 months on the content of the subject(s) they taught. This was the most frequent area in which teachers identified having had professional development opportunities. Fewer than one-quarter

of teachers (23%) reported that they had received at least 33 hours (more than four days) of professional development on the content of the subject(s) they taught.

> (Darling-Hammond, Wei, Andree, Richardson & Arphonos, 2009, p. 7)

Nearly every teacher has participated in short-term conferences or workshops. According to the study, fewer teachers have experienced other forms of traditional professional development, such as university courses related to teaching (36%) or visiting other schools to observe (22%). The percentage of teachers who visited classrooms in other schools dropped from 34% to 22% between 2000 and 2004, the most recent year for which national data are available. Meanwhile, Darling-Hammond and her co-authors note, other nations' learning agendas have resulted in greater teacher success and higher student performance (2009).

Workshops simply do not shift practice. Effective district and school leaders are clear about learning strategies and designs that are powerful enough to create desired change. Effective learning designs allow educators to clarify learning outcomes, including the knowledge, skills, dispositions, and practices expected as a result of program-specific professional learning. Because not all learning strategies serve the same purpose or get the same results, powerful designs use a variety of protocols to engage leader and teacher teams in learning.

Learning system leaders know the power of differentiated and long-term support for adult learners, and they use multiple approaches to learning in their learning design. Book studies, for example, may help teams develop a vision of an innovation, but alone they rarely help close the knowing-doing gap. Action research may give team members deeper understanding of an issue they are experiencing and the best strategies to use to address a concern, but alone they will not shift practice. In a learning system, leaders carefully select a variety of learning strategies to close that knowing-doing gap, strategies that get teams to think differently about their work and their learning. These learning designs help district leaders, principals, and teachers see in new ways, question their current practice, reflect on what they are doing, and consider the effect they are having on student learning.

Offer precise feedback

Eleanor Drago-Severson (2011) says that specific and precise feedback during the learning process supports learners. Learners will make small corrections and build greater strength and competence when peers, coaches, and principals give them regular, precise feedback about what they are doing well.

Leaders of learning systems regularly pause to recognize good work. They understand that celebrating progress toward achieving a goal affects future successes. This is particularly true if the district's leadership team makes a routine of celebrating (Bolman, & Deal, 2013).

As important as feedback is, learners also value the opportunity to set challenging goals for themselves; establish their own learning plans; and gather data, student work, and artifacts to help them reflect on their learning, evaluate its effect, and share relevant observations with others. Learners who experience early "wins" do not give up. When they see that a new approach has a positive effect on student outcomes, they more highly value their own learning.

For district leaders to design effective professional learning that shifts adult practice and increases student learning, they must consider whose learning agenda is central to the work—an individual's or a community's.

Focus on the community of learners

In a learning system, leaders focus not only on individual learners, but also on the broader community of learners to which they belong. Andy Hargreaves and Michael Fullan (2012) state that an organization cannot increase individuals' strengths in isolation. One individual on his or her own cannot learn enough to ensure a student's success. Every effective team or community is a learning laboratory in which each person comes to understand and support the group's goals. Some teams learn better than others, and individuals accelerate their teammates' learning by increasing their own awareness and adapting their behavior as needed. The group's resulting feelings of safety, trust, and intimacy determine how effective it is. Learning systems create communities of learners.

As Andy Hargreaves and Michael Fullan write,, "To sum it up, collaborative cultures build social capital and therefore also professional capital in a school community. They accumulate and circulate knowledge and ideas, as well as assistance and support, that help teachers become more effective, increase their confidence, and encourage them to be more open to and actively engaged in improvement and change" (2012, p. 114).

Implement the agenda and follow through

Professional learning's primary goal is to change educator practice in ways that increase student learning. Quality professional learning is by definition systemic, ongoing, and embedded in teaching teams' daily work. As system and school leaders struggle to design effective professional learning that addresses the system's strategic goals and meets individuals' needs, the greatest challenge may be found less in the design than in implementing it and following through until each practitioner is proficient.

In a learning system, leaders establish agendas that create effective, results-oriented professional learning designs. The best designs integrate theories, research, and models of human learning with an

Selecting a design

Different learning designs require greater amounts of trust and organization. Designs also result in different outcomes. Some are more likely to shift practice, and effective leaders select designs carefully.

CHARACTERISTICS	LEARNING DESIGN
Shifts practice over time Requires high trust Greater complexity	• Lesson study • Analyzing student work • Tuning protocol • Videotaping and analyzing lessons
Medium results in shifting practice Medium level of trust required Medium complexity	• Critical friends groups • Designing lessons, assessments, and curriculum maps together • Analyzing student performance data • Peer observations • Action research
Low yield in shifting practice Low level of trust required Easy to organize	• Book studies • Classroom walk-throughs • Case studies • Online learning (such as webinars)

intense focus on adult and student learning goals, characteristics, comfort with the learning process and one another, familiarity with the content, expected change, educators' work environment, and resources available to support learning. Those who design effective professional learning intentionally connect what adults must learn to what students are expected to know and do well. They continually adapt the learning agenda as the organization strives to "stay the course" to achieve its mission.

As with many professions, education is changing rapidly. For a practitioner to move from unskilled to highly proficient is a long-term process that requires support. Learning system leaders at the district and school levels regularly observe one another's practice and reflect on their own practice to ensure the new strategies are being implemented. They continually remind teams of the district's moral purpose in order to inspire team members to persist through the inevitable difficulties.

As learners develop a sense of community, they initiate their journey of continuous improvement and build collective responsibility for student outcomes. Their moral purpose is strengthened as they build on each other's strengths. They establish challenging goals to inspire them to continue to learn from one another, from the larger community of educators of which they are part, and from their students. As they progress and celebrate successes, they develop confidence, take greater risks, and are never content with the status quo.

Implications for district leaders

In a learning system, leaders play a major role in developing a learning agenda, studying and reflecting on the factors that make a difference to the district achieving its goals and its moral purpose. Specifically, district leaders

- Establish systems to select the right people and build their strengths;
- Ground themselves in the principles of adult learning and change theory;
- Develop knowledge about, skills to facilitate, and expertise to implement varied and appropriate high-quality learning designs;
- Develop others' capacity to clarify learning outcomes, including the knowledge, skills, dispositions, and practices expected as a result of program-specific professional learning;
- Answer these questions:
  - What are the new skills, attitudes, and behaviors we wish to see?
  - How clearly have we articulated what is to be learned and why?
  - How intentionally are we connecting adult learning to student expectations, standards, and goals?
  - What factors are important to consider when selecting learning designs?
  - Which learning designs contribute most to learners' active engagement?
  - What theories and principles about learning guide our selection of learning designs?
  - When and how will we monitor implementation and check for progress?
  - What strategies will help us make course corrections?
  - How often will we do this work?
  - How will we celebrate successes and share stories to make new practices part of the district's culture?
- Have regular conversations with school leadership teams about teams' implementation of new strategies learned through district-level professional development;
- Conduct regular walk-throughs to give principals and school leadership teams precise feedback about progress and to discuss what support schools need to successfully implement new practices; and
- Develop a long-term view of change and help others through first- and second-order change.

Implications for school leaders

School leaders

- Accomplish the tasks listed for district leaders;
- Skillfully develop learning agendas for teams in their buildings based on staff needs and learning styles, and student needs;
- Share what they learn about their staff and the progress staff members make in implementing new practices;
- Effectively monitor how well individuals and teams apply new learning and offer precise feedback; and
- Monitor the effect the new practices have on student learning.

Agenda is built on vision, goals

While districts have boundaries set for us in some regards, such as through state and federal guidelines, and financial and time constraints, every system develops, guides, and facilitates its own path. We have to establish our own attainable and sustainable goals to create opportunities. We have to ask ourselves, "How far can we reach?"

If our vision is for our kids to be 21st-century ready and digital, we need a clear plan of action. So we start by looking at all the data—state assessments, district assessments, attendance, behavior, and enrollment in different types of courses such as dual credit and Advanced Placement. We bring together all the information we possibly can to get a picture of the district. Board members and the superintendent then go on a retreat to examine the data and establish the district's goals.

Our learning agenda is based on those goals. Each department and every campus uses the goals to collaboratively focus on where we are now and where we want to be. Action steps come from that planning. If students are performing well in one area, we analyze what contributed to that achievement so that we can continue such efforts. We also look at the areas in which they're not performing well and for ways to make changes. Whether it's things that we're happy with or things that need improvement, every group's plan for accomplishing their goals includes professional learning.

Learning is the inherent, foundational part of the district's plan for accomplishing our goals. We start with the vision of where we want to go, knowing we need adults who are confident that they're well equipped to get there, in part because they are continuing to grow.

We identify some strategies that are universal to all, but teacher needs look very different. One-size-fits-all learning doesn't work. We can't define for each group what they need in order to move forward because each campus's student needs are different. With guidance, facilitation, and assistance from our specialists in different areas, teachers work in groups to define and implement their plans. It is not a top-down-driven process, but very collective. Teachers grow within the systems of their own groups. As they work collegially, they see the outcomes of their productive learning communities.

Obviously things change and we have to adjust, so our overall district and professional development goals remain dynamic. But we start with a solid vision that focuses on student outcomes. When we start from student data and build collectively on that, everyone has a clear understanding of where we, as a district, are coming from; where we want to go; and how we're going to get there.

— Leigh Wall, superintendent
Santa Fe (Texas)
Independent School District

Reflection
questions

- Is our district's learning agenda grounded in the Standards for Professional Learning?

- How can our district ensure that educators connect adult learning with improved practice and student outcomes?

- What learning designs in our system or school are most effective? Why might these designs be succeeding?

- What would strengthen the learning designs in our district or school? How might we implement these shifts?

- What could I do in my position to ensure that all professional learning is designed in a way that educators achieve the intended results?

RESOURCES

Drago-Severson, E. (2009). *Leading adult learning: Supporting adult development in our schools.* Thousand Oaks, CA: Corwin Press.

Drucker, P. (2008). *Managing oneself.* Boston, MA: Harvard Business.

Easton, L. (Ed.). (2008). *Powerful designs for professional learning.* Oxford, OH: National Staff Development Council.

Goleman, D. (2002). *Primal leadership: Realizing the power of emotional intelligence.* Boston, MA: Harvard Business.

Joyce, B. & Showers, B. (2002). *Designing training and peer coaching: Our needs for learning.* Alexandria, VA: ASCD.

Hirsh, S. & Hord, S. (2012). *A playbook for professional learning: Putting the standards into action.* Oxford, OH: Learning Forward.

Learning Forward. (2012). *Standards into practice: School-based roles Innovation Configuration maps for Standards for Professional Learning.* Oxford, OH: Author.

Rath, T. & Conchie, B. (2009). *Strengths-based leadership.* Washington, DC: Gallup Press.

TOOLS INDEX

TOOL	TITLE	PURPOSE
14.1	Template for designing professional learning	Ensure a thoughtful, research-based approach to designing the learning agenda.
14.2	Stages of Concern survey	Ensure the district and school leaders are aware of the Stages of Concern of those engaging in professional learning to differentiate the experiences based on the concerns.
14.3	Change facilitator style profile	Use the questionnaire and profile to help in setting professional goals that will help ensure change is successful.
14.4	Levels of use	Understand where staff is in using a new strategy or system effectively.
14.5	Developing an Innovation Configuration map	Clarify what the innovation looks like when it is in place, and declare progress along the path to proficiency.
14.6	*A Playbook for Professional Learning* activities	Distinguish the characteristics of professional learning that achieves different levels of impact.
14.7	Data analysis connects staff learning to student performance data	Ensure alignment between adult professional and learning student achievement needs.
14.8	Goal setting system	Help teams decide goals based on the district's and school's learning agenda and decide how to best learn the strategies and systems for achieving those goals.

CHAPTER 15

Shifting
educator practice

WHERE ARE WE NOW?

Our practices are consistent with those called for by the Implementation Standard.

| STRONGLY AGREE | AGREE | NO OPINION | DISAGREE | STRONGLY DISAGREE |

We consistently and thoughtfully monitor how innovations are occurring in our district and schools to make changes as needed.

| STRONGLY AGREE | AGREE | NO OPINION | DISAGREE | STRONGLY DISAGREE |

We consistently and thoughtfully engage in collective inquiry to support schools and school teams.

| STRONGLY AGREE | AGREE | NO OPINION | DISAGREE | STRONGLY DISAGREE |

We understand and anticipate an implementation dip, remaining committed to planned innovations that will bring about improved student learning.

| STRONGLY AGREE | AGREE | NO OPINION | DISAGREE | STRONGLY DISAGREE |

Our leaders are skilled at giving helpful, precise feedback in ways that celebrate successes and shift practices.

| STRONGLY AGREE | AGREE | NO OPINION | DISAGREE | STRONGLY DISAGREE |

We capitalize on each team member's knowledge and provide every individual the support he or she needs to shift his or her practice in a meaningful way.

| STRONGLY AGREE | AGREE | NO OPINION | DISAGREE | STRONGLY DISAGREE |

Effective professional learning changes educator practice in ways that will help improve student learning. Once the district leadership team has developed an instructional framework, members are ready to focus on implementation and look for the shifts in educator practice essential for the district to fulfill its moral purpose and achieve its vision.

Effective district and school leaders recognize that change is personal, a process of shifting practices and beliefs. Change also is challenging, and learning system leaders ensure that they provide adequate support.

"For too long, our education system has viewed professional development as something scheduled once or twice a year, rather than as a cycle of continuous improvement that occurs in schools as a regular part of teachers' workday," writes Stephanie Hirsh (2010). "This mindset about professional

Effective district and school leaders recognize that change is personal, a process of shifting practices and beliefs.

development must change if we are serious about improving our schools and student outcomes."

Those responsible for professional learning apply findings from change research to support long-term change in practice. They recognize that support for implementation of new practices must occur over time in order to embed new learning into practice. They establish a cycle of continuous improvement (see Appendix) that helps everyone achieve the organization's goals. Through this cycle, leaders help develop a culture of collective

inquiry that encourages teams of teachers to learn exponentially.

Effective leaders recognize that change is hard and that making changes often results in a temporary dip in outcomes as teachers take on new practices and struggle to implement them. Understanding that an implementation dip is likely, effective leaders integrate a variety of supports for individuals, teams, and school leaders. They plan carefully for how learning designs are implemented, ensuring that learners have all the support they need. They celebrate short-term wins and honor educators' efforts in order to sustain the momentum.

Learning system leaders integrate conversations, dialogue, constructive feedback, and reflection into their work with educators to support the kind of continuous improvement in practice that allows those educators to move along the continuum from novice to expert. Learners apply their professional learning and adjust their own learning agendas as they monitor the organization's progress.

As educators try out the new practices, leaders focus on continuous improvement, striving to maintain the long-term view and stay the course. Over time, those in the organization who expected an innovation to fade away realize that the district is engaged in powerful change and begin to accept responsibility for their own and others' learning.

Develop a culture of collective inquiry

Learning system leaders intentionally develop a culture of collective inquiry in order to successfully implement innovations. Leaders establish this culture by creating and adhering to structures such as learning communities that enable staff throughout the district to participate in a cycle of continuous improvement.

The cycle begins with district and school leaders defining educator learning goals based on an analysis of student performance data gathered from school walk-throughs and from observing teachers working in their classrooms and collaborating with their peers. Effective district and school leaders then design personalized professional learning agendas that address the needs identified by the data. They ensure that teams of leaders and teachers engage daily in learning strategies and understand that the district's commitment to adult learning is long term. They encourage teams to use evidence-based strategies, such as action research or critical friends groups, in their learning.

As team members examine student work together, they may create or redesign instructional approaches or test new methods for solving problems. Effective district and school leaders ensure success by differentiating support through job-embedded coaching, modeling, working side by side with teams, and providing additional resources and time when needed.

The cycle does not end. It may not be linear, either, as district and school leaders identify data to help adjust professional learning designs. Effective leaders also may seek external support when the learning is complex.

As district and school leaders engage in deep, collective inquiry into the critical questions of leading, teaching, and learning, educators throughout the district become increasingly thoughtful about the process of continuous improvement. They appreciate its value as a search for best practices to help all students and staff learn at high levels and for quality assessment of teaching and learning.

District and school leaders ask these questions to engage educators in a dialogue that fosters the academic focus, collective commitments, and productive professional relationships that enhance learning:

> The cycle begins with district and school leaders defining educator learning goals based on an analysis of student performance data gathered from school walk-throughs and from observing teachers working in their classrooms and collaborating with their peers.

- What do district and school leadership teams need to know in order to improve staff and student learning?
- What are the best strategies to ensure principals are learning?
- How do we connect adult learning to student learning?
- What is the district's role in curriculum design? What is the school's role?
- What are the most effective strategies to teach this content? What is the district's role in ensuring teachers use these strategies? What is the school's role?
- How will we know staff have learned to use these strategies effectively? How will we share and celebrate successes? How will we respond when staff don't learn?

- What can schools learn from each other to enhance staff members' effectiveness?
- How can the district support schools' learning?

By engaging in collective inquiry, educators discover new ideas and create more effective strategies. They commit to research before making decisions. Without collective inquiry, the cycle of continuous improvement may lead teams to the same results they have always gotten, simply because they have not rethought their current practices. Collective inquiry is integral to effective improvement.

Without collective inquiry, the cycle of continuous improvement may lead teams to the same results they have always gotten, simply because they have not rethought their current practices. Collective inquiry is integral to effective improvement.

Anticipate implementation dips

When district and school leaders systematically move through a cycle of continuous improvement, the cycle begins again and the district eventually closes teachers' knowing-doing gap—the gap between teachers' knowledge of best practice and their implementation of those practices in the classroom. However, district and school leaders understand that before teachers reach that high level of practice or proficiency, they are likely to experience an implementation dip as they work through first- and second-order change.

Learning system leaders recognize the difference between first-order and second-order change. First-order change involves learning about an innovation; at this point in the process, those implementing a change are just becoming aware of the expectations and have not yet changed their practices.

Second-order change takes place at the implementation phase. In second-order change, people leave the safe shore and move into uncharted waters. They begin to experiment with the new ideas and try them on. They feel uncomfortable and sometimes ineffective. The tendency for most team members is to return to safe practices.

Michael Fullan describes an implementation dip that occurs as the result of the challenges of second-order change when educators work to change their practice. Fullan writes that "the implementation dip is literally a dip in performance and confidence as one encounters an innovation that requires new skills and new understandings. All innovations worth their salt call upon people to question and in some respects to change their behavior and their beliefs—even in cases where innovations are pursued voluntarily. People feel anxious, fearful, confused, overwhelmed, deskilled, cautious, and—if they have moral purpose—deeply disturbed. Because we are talking about a culture of pell-mell change, there is no shortage of implementation dips or, shall we say, chasms" (Fullan, 2001, p. 40).

Once leaders achieve a culture in which change and learning are the norm, they will find their district reenergized. In fact, a learning school or learning district is always apparent from the energy level that exists within the school.

One way to build on that energy and hopefulness, while alleviating stress for those engaging in the change process, is to celebrate often.

Learning system leaders use early wins to inspire the hard work of second-order change. Early wins lend credibility as participants see that the new idea will have a positive effect on school or district goals.

Effective district and school leaders enhance the likelihood of early wins by designing and implementing an instructional framework that lends itself to identifying them. According to Spiro (2012), early successes must be

- Tangible and observable;
- Achievable;
- Perceived by most as having more benefits than costs;
- Nonthreatening to those who oppose the strategy;
- Symbolic of a shared value;
- Publicized and celebrated; and
- Used to build momentum.

Talk about problems and offer feedback

When district leaders make implementation of new practices a priority, they use a variety of strategies to support educators. Leaders pay attention to and regularly check on what progress is being made. They consider how adults learn, understand what strategies teams need in order to practice what they are learning, and commit to giving teams precise feedback frequently and over time so that team members shift their practices in ways that result in increased student learning (Morris & Hiebert, 2011).

System leaders begin model conversations about what educators are learning. Principals and other district leaders spend much of their time on management issues such as student discipline, teacher evaluations, and traffic flow. However, leaders who work in learning systems realize that if they do not intentionally set aside time to reflect on their own learning, they can

In Douglas County, Georgia, district leaders set professional learning goals that engage teacher teams and principals in regular conversations about their own learning, the progress they are making on shifting their practice, and the effect the changes are having on student learning. At the district level, principal supervisors plan regular meetings with principals to review student performance on the district's common assessments and to discuss the connection between teachers' new practices and the degree of progress they are making in achieving their goals. Most important, they talk about the principals' and district leaders' roles in ensuring teacher effectiveness and what leaders might do to have a greater impact on staff and student learning.

lose focus. Educators' most powerful conversations are about learning.

Reflective dialogue becomes a natural part of leadership team development as leaders ask the following questions:

- What are the best strategies for discussing data with teaching teams?
- How do we best help teachers connect their learning with student learning?
- What is working well for us?
- What do we need to learn together that will strengthen our skills in facilitating learning in our schools?

The learning system's central support team establishes its own learning process to support other teams, using inquiry and reflection to engage with principals, for example, about data in hopes of helping them meet the needs

When leaders have regular, focused conversations, they give each other precise, constructive feedback about their observations. The more precise the feedback, the clearer the issues and the more likely it is that educators will make essential changes in their practices.

of the school staff. The principal leadership team ensures that what is happening in the school aligns with district-level goals and reports on school-level successes and challenges.

When leaders have regular, focused conversations, they give each other precise, constructive feedback about their observations. The more precise the feedback, the clearer the issues and the more likely it is that educators will make essential changes in their practices.

Provide individualized support

In a learning system, district and school leaders understand that working collaboratively is the best way for educators to learn. As Andy Hargreaves and Michael Fullan (2012) state, collaboration builds social capital. Social capital accelerates learning because it capitalizes on each team member's brilliance. When system leaders and support staff work collaboratively and learn

together, they all grow. When adults collaborate to achieve common and compelling goals, learning flourishes.

Often, however, school leaders and school leadership teams need more individualized support. Members of school leadership teams, for example, may need to learn from models working in partner schools. Other individuals may benefit from structures and processes designed to facilitate collaboration. Some struggling leadership teams may need the help of a school-based coach assigned to the school for several years to help teachers establish an effective cycle of continuous improvement.

Ultimately, because the goal is to leave no school behind, district leaders must be flexible in their efforts to provide schools with the individualized support they require in order for implementation to succeed.

Implications for district leaders

Learning system leaders ensure that the district and its schools follow a cycle of continuous improvement to achieve challenging goals and support leaders and learners through first- and second-order change. They establish collective inquiry at the district and school levels and implement processes to honor and recognize early victories.

To be effective, leaders
- Develop their own and others' capacity to apply research findings on change theory to the implementation of professional learning;
- Lead the implementation of professional learning using research findings;
- Monitor implementation;

- Differentiate support;
- Continue support until high-fidelity implementation is achieved;
- Develop their own and others' capacity to give and receive precise, as well as constructive, feedback; and
- Give and receive constructive feedback to accelerate and refine implementation.

Implications for school leaders

In a learning system, school leaders monitor implementation and celebrate early successes to encourage risk taking when change is challenging. They facilitate a school culture that uses data to drive decision making. They ask the following questions:

- What can we do to set expectations and create conditions that support full and faithful implementation of what we are learning?
- How do we as school leaders support teachers as they implement what they are learning within their classrooms?
- When implementation does not occur, what steps do we as school leaders take to reverse the situation?

School leaders maintain the focus on student and educator learning. They leverage time and other resources to support priorities and engage teachers in collective inquiry and cycles of continuous improvement.

Clarity, caring create culture of change

As a first year principal trying to bring change to a school, I really had to hone my focus. I created Teachable Points of View about professional learning and about an approach to staff and students to address the culture in the school.

Wayne High School was a turnaround school. When the principal was replaced, many of the teachers who had followed the principal from a different school remained. Many were really good teachers, and I had to win them over and create trust with them and with students. The school had experienced four principals in just about that many years.

I started by sharing with staff my ideas about what a successful building would look like. I put myself in front of them as a leader who accepts responsibility. I had to make sure that I kept my promises. We also had to work hard to make sure that everyone in the building felt cared for. We tried to show our appreciation for the teachers by doing simple, nice things to show support on a regular basis.

We created a focus on literacy, realizing that while our school improvement plan has five goals, we can't address all of those at once in professional learning. As we asked teachers to change how they work, the administrative team jumped into the work with them. So when we introduced a writing assessment for all 350 of our sophomores that we did three times over the year, about 15 administrators, instructional coaches, and guidance counselors joined with the teachers and each took a stack of student essays to score. We spent time together looking at the rubric so that everyone was comfortable scoring. That helped create a trust among our staff that leadership supports them.

We added two new instructional coaches who have worked on getting into classrooms to support small group instruction to make it easier for teachers to learn the process. And I had regular follow-up conferences with all of the teachers from their evaluations.

I realized we did not have a clear understanding of professional learning. I had initiated the idea of professional learning communities, but recognized halfway through the year that the idea had been introduced too quickly in August and teachers didn't understand it. I also realized we needed to provide time. Teachers had been asked to voluntarily give up their planning period to collaborate around common issues. Their resistance wasn't because they didn't believe in what we were asking them to do; it was because they didn't have the resources to get it done—time and the knowledge of how to do it.

We orchestrated more PLC time and said the time needed to be used to focus on literacy. Then we helped teachers understand the cycle of improvement that includes designing the lesson together, teaching it, then returning to their PLC with samples of student work to score the work together using a rubric.

All the work is starting to make a positive difference in teachers' minds that students can achieve at a higher level. They have more faith in the leadership, more confidence in themselves, and more confidence in the students. We've really changed the culture of the building with our kids and with our staff.

— John Houser, principal
Wayne High School
Fort Wayne (Ind.) Community Schools

Reflection
questions

- What shifts might we make that would strengthen and accelerate our professional learning?

- Are we giving learners the support they need? What barriers exist to their success? How are we assessing their needs?

- If we are not seeing expected changes in teaching and learning, what external assistance would be helpful?

- If we are seeing shifts in practice that reflect our new expectations from the learning, how can we share what we are learning so that everyone is motivated and learning is accelerated?

- What support do we give principals working through second-order change?

- How can we strengthen our system of teacher support and feedback districtwide?

RESOURCES

Knapp, M., Copeland, M., Honig, M., Plecki, M., & Portin, B. (2010, August). *Learning-focused leadership and leadership support: Meaning and practice in urban systems.* New York, NY: The Wallace Foundation.

Munger, L. & von Frank, V. (2010). *Change, lead, succeed.* Oxford, OH: NSDC.

Seashore Louis, K., Leithwood, K., Wahlstrom, K., & Anderson, S. (2010). *Investigating the links to improved student learning: Final report of research findings.* New York, NY: The Wallace Foundation.

Stansbury, M. (2012, February 18). Seven standards for effective professional development. *Eschool News.* Available at www.eschoolnews.com/2012/02/18/seven-standards-for-effective-professional-development/

Spiro, J. (2011). *Leading change step-by-step: Tactics, tools, and tales.* San Francisco: Jossey-Bass.

Von Frank, V. (2009, April). District pulls together in pursuit of excellence: Creating collaboration systemwide requires commitment. *The Learning System, 4*(7), 1, 6–7.

TOOLS INDEX

TOOL	TITLE	PURPOSE
15.1	Early win wonder tool	Consider whether a proposed action meets the characteristics of an effective early win.
15.2	A cycle of continuous improvement	Clearly define a cycle of continuous improvement and commit to leading professional learning and change.
15.3	Logic model monitoring	Establish a system to monitor progress and adjust services and support.
15.4	Scheduled maintenance	Determine ways to follow up on the innovation.
15.5	Success analysis protocol	Celebrate successes as well as analyze the attributes that contributed to the success.

CHAPTER 16

Leveraging
performance
evaluations

WHERE ARE WE NOW?

Our school district has clear policies and procedures for evaluating all educators' performance.

STRONGLY AGREE	AGREE	NO OPINION	DISAGREE	STRONGLY DISAGREE

Our school district uses an instructional framework, teaching and leadership standards, and student standards as the basis for performance evaluations.

STRONGLY AGREE	AGREE	NO OPINION	DISAGREE	STRONGLY DISAGREE

Our school district aligns professional learning with performance evaluations.

STRONGLY AGREE	AGREE	NO OPINION	DISAGREE	STRONGLY DISAGREE

Our school district ensures that all educators have access to appropriate and helpful feedback.

STRONGLY AGREE	AGREE	NO OPINION	DISAGREE	STRONGLY DISAGREE

Our school district supports career advancement and leadership opportunities through its performance evaluation process.

STRONGLY AGREE	AGREE	NO OPINION	DISAGREE	STRONGLY DISAGREE

Leaders of learning systems clearly define and systematically execute performance appraisals. They garner district ownership and collaboratively develop appraisals with input from evaluators and those being evaluated; as a result, they are considered by all parties to be fair, equitable, and helpful in advancing the organization's goals. Effective performance appraisal systems are part of the larger learning agenda focused on ensuring that all educators and students learn and perform at high levels.

Learning system leaders embrace a philosophy of performance appraisals as a means to encourage ongoing educator growth and professional learning rather than as a strict measure only of past performance. They believe that student learning opportunities and performance will improve when the district uses performance appraisals as learning opportunities for educators. Each educator receives ongoing, helpful, specific feedback and so is

> "What we really need is the conception of teacher evaluation as part of a teaching and learning system that supports continuous improvement for individual teachers and the profession. Such a system should enhance teacher learning and skill, while also ensuring that teachers can effectively support student learning throughout their careers."
>
> —Linda Darling-Hammond

supported along a path toward improved practice. To emphasize teacher development, the model must be comprehensive and focus on the teacher's growth in various instructional strategies (Marzano, 2012).

Linda Darling-Hammond and her co-authors state that ". . . What we really need is the conception of teacher evaluation as part of a teaching and learning system that supports continuous improvement for individual teachers and the profession. Such a system should enhance teacher learning and skill, while also ensuring that teachers can effectively support student learning throughout their careers" (2012, p. 1).

The elements of an effective appraisal system are clear policies and procedures, a framework using multiple measures, evaluations aligned with and linked to professional learning, access to feedback, and evaluations used for career advancement.

Create clear policies and procedures

Leaders of learning systems establish policies for employee appraisal systems that address four elements:

> *Philosophy.* What are the foundation and expectations for the employee appraisal process?
>
> *Standards.* What teaching standards provide the foundation for the appraisal, and how are they related to student learning? What is the source of the student standards and teaching standards?
>
> *Multiple measures.* What measures and weights will inform the formative and summative evaluations?
>
> *Role.* What are the roles of supervisors, coaches, team leaders, expert teachers, novice teachers, and individual educators in the evaluation system?

Learning system leaders also establish procedures to support the process. These procedures answer the following critical questions:

Staff preparation and support. How are educators oriented to the district evaluation process? What resources are made available to support them throughout the process?

Timeline and requirements. What are the requirements of the system? What are the critical dates, and what is the overall timeline?

Appraiser qualifications. How are appraisers identified and prepared? What part of the identification and preparation process gives educators confidence in the individuals who collect data, provide feedback, and report on the educators' performance?

Due process. What are the requirements? What recourse do educators have if they feel the district has not treated them fairly?

Data collection. How and what data are collected? How are data accessed? Who has access? How are data used?

Professional learning and other support. How is professional learning integrated into the teacher evaluation system? How does it align with district, school, team, and individual goals? How does professional learning address individual needs? How is it differentiated to support educators' unique needs while also meeting Learning Forward's Standards for Professional Learning?

Detailed performance standards and personalized professional learning are key components of evaluation processes. When a gap exists between a teacher's practices and performance standards, leaders guide the teacher to professional learning to bridge the gap. Professional learning, however, should do more than address an individual teacher's needs; leaders ensure that teachers also learn and improve in ways that help the school and district meet their goals and allow new programs and initiatives to be implemented with fidelity.

Develop a framework using multiple measures

Learning system leaders implement effective appraisal systems for teachers based on research. The Measures of Effective Teaching (MET) project, a three-year study designed to determine how best to promote great teaching, found three measures for identifying effective teachers: classroom

The Measures of Effective Teaching (MET) project, a three-year study designed to determine how best to promote great teaching, found three measures for identifying effective teachers: classroom observations, student perception surveys, and student achievement gains.

observations, student perception surveys, and student achievement gains.

The MET study identified five frameworks with observation protocols as helpful in capturing effective teaching:
- Framework for Teaching
- Classroom Assessment Scoring System (CLASS)
- Mathematic Quality of Instruction (MQI)
- Protocol for Language Arts Teaching Observation (PLATO)
- UTeach Observation Protocol
     (Bill & Melinda Gates Foundation, 2010)
Although many states mandate a specific teaching framework to use for teacher appraisals, districts

benefit from the option of creating a homegrown instrument. Learning systems take time to assess the strengths and weaknesses of a variety of instruments to select or develop one to use.

A second source of data identified as helpful in determining which teachers are most effective is student perception surveys. According to the MET study, students know effective teaching when they experience it. Students in different classes taught by the same teacher are remarkably consistent in their perceptions of the teacher's effectiveness. Classes in which students report positive experiences also demonstrate greater learning gains.

Student perceptions of a teacher's ability to manage student behavior and challenge students with rigorous work are the most predictive of a teacher's effectiveness.

Student perceptions of a teacher's ability to manage student behavior and challenge students with rigorous work are the most predictive of a teacher's effectiveness. Student perceptions also can be a measure of effectiveness for teachers in nontested grades and subjects (Bill & Melinda Gates Foundation, 2010). The information the teacher receives is more specific and actionable than value-added scores or test results alone.

Student achievement gains are a third source of data to identify effective teachers. Learning systems have several options for data to use to document student learning. Some invest in locally developed student learning outcomes to measure student growth. Developing and using ongoing formative assessments and end-of-course and year-end summative assessments represent an investment in professional learning and drive improvements in educator knowledge and practice. Learning systems seek stakeholders' input to determine the relative weight attached to each measure of student learning the system collects.

Align evaluations with professional learning

Carefully developed and thoughtfully implemented teacher and principal evaluations contribute to the learning system's efforts to ensure effective teaching for every student. If professional learning is weak or missing from the evaluation process, the process becomes a perfunctory exercise. On the other hand, when effective professional learning is a core component of evaluation, the process strengthens and refines teaching and improves student learning.

Districts and school leaders define how an educator's participation in professional learning should increase student performance. Leaders then determine whether and to what extent it actually does. Student performance data are among the evidence critical to planning and assessing professional learning. To link student and educator learning, educators collect or access data, whether the results of teacher-designed or standardized tests, observations of student performance, observations of students' classroom interactions, or samples of student work. Learning systems help educators access and understand these data.

In learning systems, performance appraisals are one of several processes used to measure and support individual teacher effectiveness in order to accelerate student growth. However, team and schoolwide professional learning is still needed to help educators examine grade-level, subject area, or schoolwide data and set achievement goals for groups of students.

Link evaluation to professional learning

Learning system leaders promote individual, team, school, district, and program improvement systemwide through the following processes aligned with Learning Forward's definition of and its Standards for Professional Learning (Killion & Hirsh, 2011):

Set student growth goals. The conversation begins, preferably, with peers who share responsibility for the same or similar group of students setting individual and team goals for the year and determining when to assess progress toward those goals: daily, weekly, every six weeks, or at other intervals. Then teachers and supervisors collaboratively examine quantitative and qualitative student achievement data, state assessment results, career- and college-ready standards, and district measures of success.

Set educator performance goals. Educators follow the same process to determine which behaviors they will learn and apply to help meet student growth goals. They analyze observations and evaluations and then articulate goals and identify the support and feedback they want from supervisors and coaches.

Establish educator learning plans. Educators next build individual and team learning plans, guided by Learning Forward's Standards for Professional Learning, particularly the design and implementation standards. They think about how they will gain the skills needed to achieve their performance goals. They develop joint agreements

detailing what the skills will look like in practice, a proposal for gaining feedback, and an outline of needed support.

Gather feedback during classroom implementation. Educators turn to instructional coaches, supervisors, and colleagues for essential information on whether they are implementing the practices needed to improve student performance, at times videotaping their classroom teaching for self-assessment and feedback. Those providing feedback need training to know what they are observing, how to look for fidelity of implementation, and how to ensure their feedback is presented in a manner that will have the intended impact. Information about classroom implementation helps educators and other decision makers see the value of professional learning.

Assess impact and determine next steps. Educators examine student performance data regularly to determine if students are learning. When students achieve their first goals, educators reexamine the data and set new goals. If students have not reached desired levels, educators assess their own practices to determine what learning and support they need in order to help students achieve.

Ensure access to feedback.

Economists Steven G. Rivkin, Eric A. Hanushek, and John F. Kain report that: "There appear to be important gains in teaching quality in the first year of experience and smaller gains over the next few career years. However, there is little evidence that improvements continue after the first three years" (2005, p. 449). Their findings confirm that without ongoing feedback, opportunities to observe and learn from peers, or high-quality professional learning, teachers cannot learn to recognize and improve their practice.

Feedback leading to growth and improvement is data-driven, based on shared definitions and

Teachers receive feedback about their practice directly from a supervisor, nonsupervisory coach, external expert, peer, student, parent, or inanimate sources such as work products, student and educator performance data, student work, photos, and video.

understandings, acts as a foundation for conversation, and includes goals that improve teacher practice by listing strengths and gaps in relation to a clear set of standards, according to Laura Lipton (in Armstrong, 2012).

Effective feedback occurs within systems that have cultures in which
- Observers, coaches, and peers act as growth agents;
- Everyone can move forward to improve practice;
- Feedback conversations establish a baseline; and
- Feedback provides clarity about desired growth and desirable practice.

Feedback is based on preestablished, explicit, and known criteria. It responds to learning

preferences, developmental needs, and context, and requires expert communication skills. Feedback incorporates description, evidence, implications, and next-action thinking.

Teachers receive feedback about their practice directly from a supervisor, nonsupervisory coach, external expert, peer, student, parent, or inanimate sources such as work products, student and educator performance data, student work, photos, and video.

Lipton says evaluators must provide the right quality of feedback and deliver it with psychological and emotional skill. "Without high-quality feedback, people will stagnate—there will be no growth," she says (in Armstrong, 2012). "When people engage in rich conversations, it changes the culture to one of collective efficacy."

Principal observations are essential for promoting teacher growth, according to Jon Saphier, who recommends that principals deepen their abilities to observe the complexities of teaching (in von Frank, 2013a). Valerie von Frank writes, "Principals who pay attention to different measures of teacher effectiveness and hone their abilities to be effective, objective observers provide more meaningful teacher evaluations that promote teacher growth" (2013a, p. 4).

Learning system leaders ensure that principals' feedback is
- Tied to specific teaching standards;
- Immediate (as close to the time data are collected as possible);
- Specific and detailed;
- Focused on data and evidence about the teacher's practice, pedagogical content, efforts to strengthen their practice, and student learning outcomes;
- Constructive, rather than critical; and

- Focused on instructional strategies that address learning needs or practices that promote a positive, engaging classroom environment.

Ultimately, the value of feedback is measured by the changes it prompts. As part of a comprehensive performance appraisal system, effective feedback lays the groundwork for teachers to recognize, accept, and commit to ongoing improvements. Teachers' confidence in their observers and the procedures they use will affect the degree to which teachers embrace feedback as a means to help them improve.

Use evaluation for leadership and career advancement

Educators in learning systems consider the link between teachers' evaluations and their eligibility for additional, formal responsibilities and new roles. Specifically, they address whether teachers in traditional leadership roles should be ranked among the most effective teachers in the school.

Once teachers develop confidence in the evaluations, leaders use the information gathered to determine who serves on school improvement committees, in department and grade-level leader

Ultimately, the value of feedback is measured by the changes it prompts.

roles, as instructional coaches, and as peer reviewers. Leaders consider the following questions:

- What other information will be part of this decision?
- What additional knowledge, skills, and experiences must these teachers demonstrate?
- How can we support teachers so that they can develop the skills they need for leadership positions?

Learning system leaders use the answers to these questions to guide organizational growth, basing their decisions on the system's vision and mission of professional learning. They may add other guiding principles to create a powerful framework that connects formal teacher leadership and career advancement.

District resets the bar on teacher compensation, evaluation

Douglas County (Colo.) School District is one of the first districts in the nation to proactively address the issue of professional compensation for education professionals. Our teachers' pay is based on market value and on an evaluation system that allows teachers to receive pay for better performance.

Rather than using the old step and lane salary schedule, the district takes many factors that make up market value into consideration when determining teachers' salaries to better attract and retain top talent. For example, we know that certain positions are hard to fill. We had to post three times to find a Calculus II and Algebra II teacher. There were not a lot of highly qualified teachers applying for the job. Market-based pay is one component of the pay system. The teacher evaluation is another.

We began a pay-for-performance system in 1993. However, several years ago we recognized that a lot of times our evaluation didn't do what we relied on it to do. With the teachers union and administrators, we redid the evaluation system over a period of four years. Teams went through the evaluation and changed the rubric to reflect the reality of different roles. A nurse's job, for example, looks a lot different than a classroom teacher's. A physical education teacher has different requirements than a classroom teacher.

We talked about what great teachers do and the core philosophy behind each element we included on each evaluation. We considered the state standards. We now have 22 specific job rubrics and an evaluation tool that says exactly what we should be looking for.

We've completely reset the bar. We launched the new evaluation beginning in 2013. Under this model, teacher practice is 50% of the overall evaluation and student performance is the other half. Teachers receive a rating of highly effective, effective, or below effective.

The feedback then is tied to individual development plans that allow individuals to grow through mentoring, feedback, coaching, courses, and so on. Professional development is integrated throughout the system to support teachers at each level of expertise. As teachers continue to develop and grow, they have the potential to earn additional pay.

We have found that approximately 15% of educators are highly effective and most of the rest are effective. These teachers have opportunities for pay increases and bonuses when students meet world-class education targets. Approximately 2% of educators are rated ineffective. These teachers receive feedback, training, and coaching to hone their skills.

Coaching is embedded in all teachers' growth and development. Opportunities for professional development through coaching are available to all so that exemplary teachers can become examples for others. Highly effective teachers have options to pursue different professional pathways. They might mentor other teachers to help them improve or train to become a leader in a different role, from building resource teacher to principal. Each building has a professional learning specialist who can work in the classroom to model, to cover a topic, or even to release teachers to visit other schools.

We are truly trying to reinvent education in our school district. We want to continually innovate and improve. And we want the best teachers in the world—our students deserve that.

— Christian Cutter, assistant superintendent of elementary education
Douglas County (Colo.) School District

Reflection
questions

- What current policies or procedures related to evaluation do we want to review?

- How do our instructional framework, teaching and leadership standards, and student standards influence our current evaluation practices?

- What part does professional learning have in the evaluation process, and how might it be made more integral?

- How well does our performance appraisal process balance individuals' needs with those of the district and its schools?

- How effective is our feedback process? How can feedback be improved?

- How do our leadership and career advancement opportunities align with our appraisal processes?

RESOURCES

Armstrong, A. (2012). The art of feedback. *The Learning System*, *7*(4), 1–7.

Goe, L., Biggers, K., & Croft, A. (2012, May). *Linking teacher evaluation to professional development: Focusing on improving teaching and learning.* Washington, DC: *National Comprehensive Center for Teacher Quality.*

Kennedy, J. (2011). Deconstructing multiple measures of effective teaching. *JSD*, *32*(6), 9–10.

Killion, J. & Hirsh, S. (2011). The elements of effective teaching. *JSD*, *32*(6), 10–16.

Mizell, H. (2011). Integrating individual professional learning into comprehensive learning systems. *JSD*, *32*(6), 53–58.

Psencik, K. & Baldwin, R. (2012). Link data to learning goals. *JSD*, *33*(4), 30–33.

Varlas, L. (2012). Rethinking teacher evaluation. *Education Update*, *54*(12), 1–8.

Von Frank, V. (2011). Learning is the foundation for evaluation. *The Leading Teacher*, *7*(2), 1–4.

TOOLS INDEX

TOOL	TITLE	PURPOSE
16.1	9 principles for designing an effective teacher appraisal system	Build background knowledge of the research on teacher effectiveness and teacher evaluation systems.
16.2	The art of feedback	Learn ways to have data-driven, inquiry-based conversations about improving practice.
16.3	Learning-focused conversations	Use these templates to help shift your culture through conversations about improving practice.
16.4	Evaluations serve as pathways for professional growth	Understand how evaluations can lead to a system of professional growth through professional learning.
16.5	Student surveys	Consider reasons and applications for conducting student surveys.
16.6	Integrating professional learning into comprehensive learning systems	Discover the linkages between teacher evaluations systems and individual professional learning.
16.7	Examining professional learning comprehensively	Clarify how a professional learning system serves individuals, school and team-based and program implementation.

CHAPTER 17

Engaging parents and family members

WHERE ARE WE NOW?

Our district has a clearly articulated philosophy for engaging students' parents and family members.

STRONGLY AGREE   AGREE   NO OPINION   DISAGREE   STRONGLY DISAGREE

Our district has a plan for engaging parents and families, and defines a continuum of opportunities and expectations to help families and parents support their children, their schools, and the district.

STRONGLY AGREE   AGREE   NO OPINION   DISAGREE   STRONGLY DISAGREE

Our district helps family members and parents understand, value, and advocate for educators' professional learning.

STRONGLY AGREE   AGREE   NO OPINION   DISAGREE   STRONGLY DISAGREE

Our district actively helps parents and family members learn so that they can help their children, their schools, and the district.

STRONGLY AGREE   AGREE   NO OPINION   DISAGREE   STRONGLY DISAGREE

Our district applies Learning Forward's Standards for Professional Learning to help family members and parents develop the knowledge and skills they need to effectively advocate for their children and the school district.

STRONGLY AGREE   AGREE   NO OPINION   DISAGREE   STRONGLY DISAGREE

earning systems work to build broad-based community support in order to ensure that all schools in the district are high performing. When all elements of the community support and contribute to schools, students in those schools are able to achieve at higher levels.

Parents and family members play a significant and critical role in school performance. School districts and schools benefit when they define authentic opportunities for parents and family members not only to be active in their children's schools, but also engaged with and able to help make decisions about district innovations and planning. While parent engagement is not a silver bullet that alone can raise student achievement, their involvement is an integral part of the process for ensuring student success.

The best possible academic environment is one in which parents understand their responsibilities as school stakeholders and are involved in decisions that affect their children's education. They then can work in partnership with teachers, school and system leaders, and school boards while respecting professionals' roles in managing the school district. They also play a role in holding schools accountable for student achievement (Henderson, 2011; Warren & Mapp, 2011; Hirsh & Foster, 2013).

Engage families rather than involve them

Stephanie Hirsh and Ann Foster (2013) suggest that parent *involvement* implies that parents perform specific functions at their children's schools when invited to volunteer. Parent *engagement*, on the other hand, implies a different, more active mindset. It suggests that parents play a proactive role in making decisions that affect their children's education.

In some districts, parent involvement is limited to parent/teacher conferences and "fun nights." For example, one elementary school

considered parents to be "very involved." The principal explained that parents regularly showed up to pop popcorn for weekly sales, shelve library books, prepare special staff luncheons, and organize PTA events such as the book fair. When a new parent at the school volunteered to serve as a parent representative on the school improvement committee, the principal agreed but never called the parent about upcoming meetings. The school secretary, however, did phone with a request for supplies for a "new families" dinner.

Research shows that when parents and educators work together to support student learning and achievement, students earn higher grades and test scores, attend school more regularly, take higher-level courses, develop better behavior, and graduate and go on to higher education in larger numbers (Henderson & Mapp, 2002). In schools with authentic parent-school partnerships, all family activities are connected to student learning, parents and teachers discuss and work together on issues, and families are actively involved in making decisions. In school districts with proactive parent engagement, school boards depend on parents to be engaged with the issues, have opinions, give input, and advocate for public education in the community (Hirsh & Foster, 2013; Ferguson, Jordan, & Baldwin, 2010; Henderson & Mapp, 2002).

Leverage engaged families and parents

School districts and individual schools are more successful at addressing organizational issues—such as student performance, funding, graduation requirements, and school closures—when a group of parents partner with schools and the school board. A group of engaged parents, for example, can smooth the way toward necessary changes to graduation requirements or school consolidation. When school district leaders tackle tough issues such as closing schools, merging schools, or changing attendance boundaries, engaged parents are the best friends they can have. But parents have to be part of the process long before such issues arise. They need to learn about and understand funding, demographics, and facilities management not only as it affects their children's schools but also the entire school district. Engaging parents in ongoing learning on school schedules, graduation requirements, and new curriculum allows districts to make needed changes more easily.

Learning systems need a core group of parents who understand the issues and commit to working with the district and their schools to provide quality schools for all children in the community. These parents share the desire to serve all children well. Critics say parents cannot take on this role, but experiences in some school districts suggests otherwise (Epstein, 2007; Ferguson, Jordan, & Baldwin, 2010).

Districts with involved parents have been able to rally support to lobby legislators considering school funding cuts, leverage informed parents to explain to others the need for a school bond, and work with a core group of parents to get the word out about the rationale behind changes to the school schedule to allow teachers time for weekly meetings in professional learning communities, according to Hirsh and Foster (2013).

Hirsh and Foster write (2013) that parents who are more highly educated are likely to understand the advocate's role and to claim it; however, not all parents and family members have had positive experiences with the education system and so may not understand the need for or be willing to do so. Their experiences may make them reluctant to get involved, and they may mistrust district personnel. Some parents may be struggling to get by. Some immigrant parents do not yet speak English fluently. They, as well as others, are intimidated by education jargon and do not understand many of the words that educators use. It is up to district staff to smooth the way for their engagement by ensuring communication is clear and accessible.

Learning system leaders take responsibility for enlisting parents' help and support. Most parents, and in particular low-income parents, make their children's education their first priority. Learning systems call on parents' and caregivers' knowledge to support children's learning (Moll, Amanti, Neff, & Gonzalez, 1992) and to engage them further with the school and school district.

Many districts translate critical communications into other languages when the district's population includes numerous non-English speakers, according to Hirsh and Foster (2013).

Provide professional learning for families

Family members' and parents' comfort level with schools and educators falls along a continuum but can change as their knowledge of and engagement with schools changes. Professional learning can help develop families' understanding and move them to a higher engagement level.

Learning system leaders provide parents with opportunities to engage with the district and schools and help them understand their children's educational process and how to contribute to it. Learning systems give families and parents information about how their children's schools operate, how schools are structured academically, how discipline policies work, and how school districts are governed.

Educators in learning systems carefully prepare family members, parents, and community stakeholders for authentic partnerships. Some sponsor parent leadership academies to engage parents, community members, and educators in collaborative learning. Some offer districtwide leadership programs that invite parents to attend a year-long course on school finance, facilities, accountability, testing, curriculum, school board governance, and other topics.

Most schools recognize the added value of educating parents and family members, and sponsor evening events for them that include math, science, and reading activities. With the advent of new student assessments, teacher evaluation procedures, and revised state standards, these evenings can engage adult participants in the kinds of experiences teachers are committed to providing to children. Educators can take the time to explain to participants the role that parents and other caregivers can play in ensuring children's academic success. In some learning systems, educators may walk the neighborhoods and make home visits, reaching out to families and parents who don't come to the school.

School board members in learning systems join learning events and become part of a learning community with the school and parents as much as possible. School board members work to help parents understand the school board's role and to encourage them to attend school board meetings (Westmoreland, Rosenberg, Lopez, & Weiss, 2009). They offer school board orientation sessions for parents and others interested in learning more about governing boards, as well as those who might be interested in leadership opportunities. The most engaged parents are the most well-informed candidates for school boards and the best advocates for the system.

Engage family members and parents in authentic work

As parents become more engaged with the schools, they develop a keen understanding of the schools' workings and challenges and how their involvement can help their children, their schools, and

their districts. The more parents understand, the more they can hold themselves, their schools, and their school boards accountable for student achievement. Engaged parents recognize their responsibilities toward their schools. They assume a level of responsibility not only for learning about the education being provided to their children, but also for learning about the issues facing public education. They begin to advocate for solutions in the community.

Parents can be engaged at both the district and school levels in strategic planning and in planning professional learning, according to Hirsh and Foster (2013). Family members can take the lead in establishing systems for professional learning for other parents.

Learning system leaders welcome family members and parents as key stakeholders into decision-making groups and value and consider

In the El Paso (Texas) Independent School District, parent leaders host seminars for other parents about how to help children learn to read, how to work effectively with teenagers, and how to help children with homework and keep that assistance positive. They offer non-English-speaking parents language courses. At the school level, parents and family members may take the lead in sharing their expertise through instructional work with students; they may take responsibility for energizing other parents to become engaged and to mentor students.

their input. System leaders organize school councils, site councils, and communication groups. When a major decision is to be made, they make sure that families' voices are heard.

In learning systems, officials consult parents, family members, and other community stakeholders throughout the process of hiring leaders. They seek community members' views on characteristics to seek in a leader. They host forums to discuss the work of leaders in a learning system. A learning system may include parent representatives on principal hiring committees and welcome anyone interested into interviews with superintendent candidate finalists. When parents are partners in the school community, they not only add value through their perspectives but also experience a heightened sense of what is at stake when decisions are made regarding children and schools.

Schools, educators, and school boards can be apprehensive about parents becoming *too* engaged. Their fears may even be justified—especially when parents try to exert influence without understanding educational issues. Learning system leaders manage the expectations of family members, parents, and community stakeholders, recognizing that when parents have the information and knowledge they need and partner with schools for student achievement and continuous improvement, schools benefit (Hoover-Dempsey et al., 2005). When parents are included as valued partners and understand the challenges that teachers and public schools face, they help build a supportive community for public education.

Ask families to support professional learning for educators

Many parents and family members complain when schools release students early or for an entire day for educators' professional learning. They do not understand how the professional learning will benefit their children.

Most schools make little effort to educate parents on the importance of educators' professional learning. In learning systems, leaders provide parents with information about the importance of professional learning, as well as details about how it will benefit their children. Anytime children are released from school so that educators engage in professional learning, parents are told what to expect in classrooms as a result of the district's investment in educators' learning.

In many places, parents are invited into the school to witness firsthand what authentic teacher learning looks like and how it is affecting children's education. The more that families and parents learn about the relationship between teacher learning and student learning, the better positioned those community members are to support professional learning and advocate for it with other parents.

Take responsibility for engaging parents

While families and parents ultimately are responsible for their own children's education and success in life, learning systems help parents recognize the value of parental engagement with the school and school district. Learning systems understand the important role that parents and family members play and proactively include them in making important educational decisions for the district, such as setting priorities within the budget, finding ways to schedule professional learning time, and determining what measures should be put in place to bring about school and districtwide improvement.

Extending opportunities to parents and families to build knowledge and skills and to engage in authentic decision making contributes to a climate of school success. These results, in turn, help create a true learning system. Authentically and appropriately engaged parents can be a powerful force for student achievement and successful schools.

Welcome parents—in all languages

We as educators have to meet the needs of our communities. In Dearborn, an area with one of the largest concentrations of Arabic people outside of Arab countries, we need to be welcoming in our schools for those who are not native English speakers or are unfamiliar with formal education.

We have parent liaisons throughout the district responsible for getting parents involved in the schools. For schools with large immigrant populations, we bring in parents who are bilingual to translate so other parents will feel more comfortable with a person who is part of the community and who can then bring any important information to the principal. Many times we have hired these community members to stay as paraprofessionals. A few years ago, we applied for and received a grant to allow some of those paraprofessionals to continue their education to become certified teachers for the district.

We regularly involve parents in other key roles. All of our principal candidates are interviewed by several committees, including a parent committee to give parents input. Having parents on the selection committee connects them to the decision making. We compile the data from all the committees, and the superintendent considers the ratings to determine the final candidate. Parents also volunteer to be on the school improvement teams at both the district and building levels so they are involved in those major decisions and help create a collaborative environment districtwide. That's a requirement.

We want parents to feel welcome, and so we have to take a service-oriented philosophy. Communication with families and the community is absolutely essential. We have almost all the information we send out translated, mostly in Arabic. In some of our schools, classroom signage is bilingual. We have translated the elementary report card into Arabic. Parents can contact the bilingual department for a translation if the information is not in their own native language.

We get information out through the local media, and all of our principals are required to blog. Notices of new blog postings are emailed to parents' phones automatically. Our superintendent and district leaders are constantly out connecting with the community. One result of that is that we passed an $80 million bond with a 70% majority in the community because of the network of parents and community members we reach, not just around bond time, but all the time.

We also engage parents through parent classes, with social topics, including effective discipline and Parent Talk, to the curriculum with districtwide family math and literacy nights. We have a program called Motor Moms and Dads to bring family members into schools to work with younger kids on their motor skills. We have family members in our classrooms all over the district.

Having parents and families integrated into everything we do is part of our strategic plan. We strongly encourage and almost insist on parent involvement. Support from our families helps our students. When parents are engaged in their children's education and knowledgeable about the curriculum, students will achieve at higher levels.

— Glenn Maleyko, executive director,
staff and student services
Dearborn (Mich.) Public Schools

Reflection
questions

- What are the real and perceived challenges and benefits of family and parent engagement in our school district?

- Do we distinguish between family involvement and engagement? Do we prefer to maintain the distinction between involvement and engagement?

- What do we want all family members and parents to understand and be able to do to support their children and their schools?

- How would we define the current relationship between our district and students' parents and family members?

- What is the learning system's responsibility for educating parents, and how are we measuring up to that responsibility?

RESOURCES

Allen, R. (2005, March). New paradigms for parental involvement: Stronger family role in schools seen as key to achievement. *Education Update, 47*(3).

Epstein, J. L. et al. (2008). *School, family, and community partnerships: Your handbook for action* (3rd ed.). Thousand Oaks, CA: Corwin Press.

Fege, A. F. (2000, April). From fund raising to hell raising: New roles for parents. *Educational Leadership, 57*(7), 39–43.

Houston, P. D., Blankstein, A. M., & Cole, R. W. (2010). *Leadership for family and community involvement.* Thousand Oaks, CA: Corwin Press.

Marzano, R. J. (2003). *What works in schools: Translating research into action.* Chapter 5: Parent and community involvement. Arlington, VA: ASCD.

Von Frank, V. (2012, Spring). Maryland emphasizes the value of family and community involvement. *The Learning System, 7*(3), 3.

Warner, C. & Curry, M. (1997). *Everybody's house—The schoolhouse: Best techniques for connecting home, school, and community.* Thousand Oaks, CA: Corwin Press.

TOOLS INDEX

TOOL	TITLE	PURPOSE
17.1	Why does professional development matter?	Engage family members and other community stakeholders in understanding why professional development is essential to a learning system.
17.2	Understanding the Standards for Professional Learning	Help parents and families understand the significance of the Standards for Professional Learning.
17.3	Research-based practices forge strong family and community partnerships	Become familiar with what research finds are effective parent and family partnerships.
17.4	An inventory of present practices of school, family, and community partnerships	Help a school- or district-level group assess the district's current practices to engage families.
17.5	8 elements for effective family partnerships	Explore types of professional learning that contribute to family and community partnerships.
17.6	Partnering with parents for student achievement	Understand the elements of successful parent/ family partnerships in student achievement.
17.7	Empowered parents partner with schools to meet student needs	Investigate the critical elements of parent empowerment.

CHAPTER 18

Influencing
decision makers

Our district leaders keep policy makers and thought leaders informed about the effects of professional learning.

STRONGLY AGREE   AGREE   NO OPINION   DISAGREE   STRONGLY DISAGREE

Our district leaders are able to give brief summaries of how professional learning can affect student achievement to help persuade others of its value.

STRONGLY AGREE   AGREE   NO OPINION   DISAGREE   STRONGLY DISAGREE

Our district leaders take responsibility for advocating for professional learning to close achievement gaps.

STRONGLY AGREE   AGREE   NO OPINION   DISAGREE   STRONGLY DISAGREE

Our district leaders develop advocates for professional learning among school board members, parents, and community members.

STRONGLY AGREE   AGREE   NO OPINION   DISAGREE   STRONGLY DISAGREE

Our district helps prepare school board members, parents, and community members to advocate for professional learning.

STRONGLY AGREE   AGREE   NO OPINION   DISAGREE   STRONGLY DISAGREE

ecause competing priorities in education can push professional learning to the bottom of the list, key stakeholders must work to keep it in the spotlight. One of Learning Forward's Standards for Professional Learning, the Leadership Standard, calls for every stakeholder in the school district to become an advocate for professional learning. In learning systems, educators at all levels recognize the importance of and work to fulfill this responsibility.

Educators in learning systems are strategic about identifying and educating policymakers and thought leaders. State and local leaders are in positions of authority, have platforms they can use to share their views, and take stands on public policy issues. They are in positions to influence and take actions that advance or inhibit effective professional learning. Thought leaders, according to Learning Forward's Distinguished Senior Fellow Hayes Mizell, are those whose ideas influence many other people's thinking and actions (Mizell, 2010). Figure 18.1 lists some of these roles.

Policy makers and thought leaders use a variety of information sources to help them make decisions and often are influenced by those with whom they have ongoing and trusting relationships. Advocates are most effective when they build relationships with identified leaders, clearly understand the issues and solutions, and meet regularly to plan their advocacy.

Build relationships

In learning systems, all educators take responsibility for identifying decision makers and thought leaders and building strong relationships with those individuals. Educators recognize the lasting influence that decision makers and thought leaders have on professional learning, and so they work to build influence based on long-term, trusting relationships that evolve from a mix of appropriate strategies. Establishing such relationships helps educators ensure that decision makers and thought leaders receive ongoing, relevant, and accurate information about professional learning.

Figure 18.1 Decision makers and thought leaders

STATE LEADERS	LOCAL LEADERS
• Governor	• Mayor/county commissioner
• State legislator	• School board member
• State school board member	• Superintendent
• State superintendent	• Central office deputy
• State teacher/principal/superintendent of the year	• District director of professional learning
• State education organization leader/ executive	• Principal/teacher
• Business organization leader/executive	• Teacher association/union president/ executive
• Foundation executive	• Business organization leader
• Newspaper/TV reporter, columnist, editorial board member	• Foundation executive
• Advocacy organization leader	• Newspaper/TV reporter, columnist, editorial board member
	• Advocacy organization leader

Some strategies to consider when building a relationship with a potential advocate include the following:

- Invite the individual to lunch.
- Invite the decision maker to speak at a locally sponsored event.
- Invite the person to participate on a panel.
- Invite the policymaker to speak with a group of educators at a special meeting.
- Invite the person on a "field trip" to observe exemplary professional learning.
- Establish a regular meeting at least twice a year to discuss the impact of professional learning in the school district.

Engage with policymakers

Individuals who want to become part of the "inner circle" and have an effect on decision makers use common tactics to achieve results. Board members invite legislators to classrooms, schools, and district events. Policymakers like to tell stories and to stay in touch with constituents. These visits give them real examples for speeches and conversations.

Educators can develop lasting relationships with federal and state legislators by first connecting with their staff members responsible for education issues. These staffers are the people who influence the decision maker on the subject. Influencing these individuals' views has an effect on the elected official. Researching and offering a solution for an issue is more useful than just pointing out the problem to the policymaker. Effective advocates then ask to check in on how the effort is progressing—and do so.

Effective advocates are respectful and appreciative of elected officials' service. Few people call on their legislators and staff to thank them for their service. Those in office often remember who recognized their public service—just as educators recall those who acknowledge *their* contributions. Positive interactions are memorable.

Author Stephanie Hirsh, who served on the school board in Richardson, Texas, for three terms, found individuals tended to signal their interest in specific issues and share a point of view by becoming involved in campaigns and elections, making financial contributions, and appearing at meetings where she was speaking. They did not wait for a problem to surface to begin building a relationship.

Similarly, school board members in Richardson made a point of meeting each year with state representatives. Each was assigned to serve as a liaison to a legislator, answering questions and helping connect legislators to the community they were elected to serve. The school board members used the same strategies with the legislators that others were using with them. They understood that waiting to contact a policymaker until there was a problem meant that although the problem would be noted, it would not get the same attention as one raised by an advocate who had previously established credibility.

Build understanding of issues and solutions

Too frequently, decision makers and thought leaders hear about professional learning only when there is a complaint. They need to hear more than the isolated disaster story. They need ongoing information that points to the critical role professional learning plays in advancing a school district agenda.

In a learning system, effective advocates ensure that they build the case that professional learning connects to student achievement, a local and state priority, and use that shared goal as a basis for a compelling argument for learning for all. They

School boards are the bridge between the community and the school district.

focus on time for learning and support for implementation. They work to ensure that resources are not reallocated when someone makes the case for a different priority.

Advocates remind decision makers that all educators need to participate in quality professional learning. They communicate that substantial public funds support professional learning and help policy makers see that educator learning plus its application in schools and classrooms adds up to improved student learning. They provide local examples that demonstrate the validity of that equation.

Position school board members as advocates

Learning system leaders work with school board members to advocate for professional learning. School boards are the bridge between the community and the school district. School board members help the community understand and support public education. Parents have the most personal investment in schools—their children—and the shortest period in which to focus on school quality. For them, time is critical. Many parents are not familiar with the terms *continuous improvement*

and *professional learning*. What they do know is that their children sometimes have days off or are dismissed early from school for teachers' professional learning, creating childcare issues and sometimes resentment toward the school district. Learning system leaders need their school board members to be able to answer parents' questions.

School board members can act as effective advocates for professional learning without having the depth of knowledge of professional educators, Hirsh and Foster write (2013). Ultimately, they say, school board members need a level of knowledge that makes each comfortable answering questions that constituents may ask on the subject. Board members can acquire the basic knowledge they need by becoming familiar with the concept of professional learning, studying Learning Forward's Standards for Professional Learning, and analyzing results of professional learning initiatives put in place in other school districts.

Information about the Standards helps members understand the importance of professional learning in a learning system. School board members benefit from understanding how each standard contributes to continuous improvement that offers the best chance of success for students and teachers. School board members likely will have the greatest interest in the Outcomes Standard; however, familiarity with each standard helps them better understand exactly what they are holding the school system accountable for achieving. With this knowledge, board members then can internalize what professional learning is and how it supports a district's goals and mission.

As parent representatives, school board members have the best opportunities to explain to parents and the community how continuous improvement, school improvement plans, and professional learning standards contribute directly to children's learning. In learning systems, board members share with the community what teachers are doing during professional learning time to advance the system's teaching and learning goals and how professional learning benefits children. Reaching out to families and caregivers with that specific information can increase families' willingness to listen, support, and engage with the system (Hoover-Dempsey et al., 2005).

Parents' levels of understanding of these issues fall along a spectrum. Once some are convinced that professional learning positively affects student learning, they may advocate among all parents (Hoover-Dempsey et al., 2005). As more parents accept the need for professional learning and standards, they may come to demand it, knowing that teachers' learning leads to improved learning for their children.

Plan advocacy

Conversations with decision makers and thought leaders are strengthened by careful planning and skillful execution. Developing a teachable point of view on professional learning prepares individuals for effective advocacy (Sparks, 2007). Professional learning advocates access and use data about outcomes and results to tell stories that have an impact. They develop a professional learning "laser talk"—a short, compelling conversation that identifies a problem and relevant solutions and issues a call for action (Daley-Harris, 1994).

These brief, focused conversations help decision makers reflect on a subject that may not be as relevant to them. It causes them to realize what they do not know, why they need deeper knowledge, how professional learning relates to their

role and responsibilities, and how the advocate can be a valuable source of expertise and information. Advocates never leave a conversation without a specific request that is actionable and within the decision maker's sphere of influence.

Another key to lasting influence is to take time after a meeting with a thought leader or policymaker to reflect and discuss with others what was learned about the individual. The advocate considers what information was gained, assesses how the individual responded to the topic, and reviews commitments to next actions and a timeline.

Other steps may include sending thank-you notes and formally sharing information about the meeting in reports or presentations to larger groups. The ultimate success is having the "target" of influence agree to strategize with the advocate to influence others.

Advocating effectively for professional learning helps stakeholders home in on the message that learning—for students *and* educators—is the core of schools' work. Without a commitment to

Without a commitment to learning for all in the district, improvement stagnates and educators do not get the support they need to develop the knowledge and skills necessary to make decisions that close achievement gaps and advance student learning.

learning for all in the district, improvement stagnates and educators do not get the support they need to develop the knowledge and skills necessary to make decisions that close achievement gaps and advance student learning.

Build value for professional learning, one person at a time

We have focused internally as a district to get the word out about what quality professional learning is. We needed to make visible why professional learning is important, to make that connection for people. To do that, rather than advocate with the community or school board first, we built the value within the staff first, because they are the best advocates if they experience quality professional learning.

We created a Learning and Teaching Advisory Council—a standing committee that provides leadership at the district level and scales to the school level. All principals and teacher leaders from each school are on this council. The council developed a learning community framework that defines the work of teaching and learning, including curriculum, assessments, supports for struggling learners, and enrichment opportunities for students who are being successful. Professional learning is the glue that aligns this work and ensures implementation.

Although we now have two fewer student days each year to allow for staff professional learning and weekly late start days at the high school for teachers to be part of professional learning communities, we haven't had the resistance that we might have faced. Because we knew we were going to get questions, we recognized the need to get the message out and respond to people's concerns.

Change happens one individual at a time, and so we worked with staff to develop Teachable Points of View around the district's purpose and vision. A Teachable Point of View is a succinct response to anyone who asks, What is this about? It is the three to five key points we are able to share in one to two minutes that we want someone to remember, and it always ends with a declarative statement or invitation for further conversation.

We had each school and teacher leader develop a Teachable Point of View and practice with one another at a meeting. Teacher leaders at each school became advocates for professional learning, explaining what quality professional learning is and why it's important. They shared these with other staff, and the ideas then spread quickly throughout the district. In this way, we were able to shift the culture to become a learning system.

People got used to creating TPoVs, and the practice generated a lot of conversation. Using the TPoVs, we were able to scale the message throughout the system, one conversation at a time. We didn't get resistance then to the professional learning. It became a natural part of day-to-day work and the culture of the system.

There is general understanding now around professional learning, and school board members are strong supporters. We present something about professional learning at almost every board meeting in the context of the work we are doing within the system.

The community doesn't question what we are doing with that time. We put a lot online for parents and the community to see so that they know what our professional learning time is about. They can see that it's not just teachers updating grades or getting lectured, that they are spending time learning together and designing work. We are giving a picture of how this learning changes practices.

Now we use Teachable Points of View anytime we are beginning change as a way to get the message across.

— Jeff Ronneberg, superintendent
Spring Lake Park (Minn.) Schools

Reflection
questions

- What is our philosophy about advocating for professional learning?

- Who might we want to influence, and what outcomes do we want from our advocacy strategy?

- Who might we want to develop as advocates, and how would we go about it?

- Which strategies are most effective for keeping policymakers and thought leaders informed about the contributions of effective professional learning?

- What support do our school board members and school district leaders need in order to develop teachable points of view and use strategies such as laser talks to increase or sustain support for professional learning?

RESOURCES

Armstrong, A. (2012). A new game plan. *The Learning System*, *8*(1), 1, 4–5.

Armstrong, A. (2012). Advocacy can be the avenue for change. *The Leading Teacher*, *8*(1), 3–5.

Hirsh, S. (2010). The power of one revisited. *JSD*, *31*(6), 40–45.

Mizell, H. (2010). Thought leaders. *JSD*, *31*(6), 46–51.

Mizell, H. (2012). Who are the advocates in your school. *JSD*, *33*(6), 46–50.

Hirsh, S. (2008). Let stakeholders know what you intend to accomplish. *JSD*, *29*(4), 53–54.

Stoll, L. & Crow, T. (2010). Policy across the pond. *JSD*, *31*(6), 34–39.

TOOLS INDEX

TOOL	TITLE	PURPOSE
18.1	Who are the decision makers?	Experience the thought process needed before trying to influence decision makers around strategic priorities.
18.2	The power of one	Recognize every individual's opportunity to influence learning and clarify reasons to influence policymakers when considering central office transformation.
18.3	Writing a teachable point of view	Write a teachable point of view that helps convey the power of your beliefs and assumptions.
18.4	The tempered radical	Understand how the five attributes of tempered radicals support influencing decision makers.
18.5	What data influence	Investigate possible data sources to influence decision makers.
18.6	Thought leaders	Identify thought leaders, discover how to leverage their influence, and meet with them.
18.7	Delivering a laser talk	Learn to speak succinctly in order to influence decision makers.

CHAPTER 19

Focusing labor/ management work

Our district views collective bargaining negotiations and contract agreements as opportunities to advance the district's vision for learning.

STRONGLY AGREE	AGREE	NO OPINION	DISAGREE	STRONGLY DISAGREE

Our district regularly engages association representatives in work related to professional learning.

STRONGLY AGREE	AGREE	NO OPINION	DISAGREE	STRONGLY DISAGREE

District leaders consider a variety of opportunities to advance professional learning through labor and management collaboration and agreements.

STRONGLY AGREE	AGREE	NO OPINION	DISAGREE	STRONGLY DISAGREE

Labor and management negotiators make educators' professional learning a priority in their discussions.

STRONGLY AGREE	AGREE	NO OPINION	DISAGREE	STRONGLY DISAGREE

Labor and management negotiators are aware of policy areas in which collaboration and negotiation can strengthen professional learning.

STRONGLY AGREE	AGREE	NO OPINION	DISAGREE	STRONGLY DISAGREE

Professional learning can be dramatically enhanced when labor and management collaborate to increase its effect. Through contract negotiations, both sides find ways to make far-reaching, equitable, uniform, and long-lasting improvements.

In a learning system, district and association leaders recognize the potential for leveraging policy and contract language to advance learning opportunities for all educators. Labor representatives are interested in ensuring that association members have the support they need to be able to meet expectations for higher student learning. District and school leaders find that professional learning is more likely to be sustained when supporting language is incorporated into policy and collective bargaining agreements that drive day-to-day operations.

Many district policies and collective bargaining agreements affect educators' professional

Professional learning is infused into a number of policy areas, including standards, schedules, budgets, continuing education requirements, National Board certification, mentoring and induction, individual learning plans, and career pathways.

growth and learning. According to the National Education Association

> Collective bargaining—a mutual exchange of positions followed by agreement— enables a group of employees with a 'community of interest' to negotiate a binding written contract with an employer. It gives workers a voice in their workplace and has become a respected approach, valued by employees and employers in the private sector and throughout various levels of government.
>
> Effective bargaining is based on ideals that resonate with both workers and employers, such as working together to solve problems and treating each other with respect. Parties can exchange the frank views of their constituents as they explore and resolve the issues being bargained. When labor and management can come to agreement on salary and benefits while also improving teaching and learning conditions, everyone benefits (n.d., p. 2).

Leaders of the most effective learning systems work year-round to strengthen their formal and informal agreements between labor and management. They settle on points of agreement long before they reach a negotiation table. Negotiation teams provide continuous input on district priorities and key decisions. District leaders see them as essential to the learning system's success in achieving its goals for employees and students.

In a learning system, school and association leaders collaborate to identify opportunities to ensure all educators engage in quality professional learning that produces better results for students. Professional learning is infused into a number of policy areas, including standards, schedules, budgets, continuing education requirements, National Board certification, mentoring and induction, individual learning plans, and career pathways.

A study by the National Staff Development Council (now Learning Forward), the Council of Chief State School Officers, the National Education Association, the US Department of Education, and the American Federation of Teachers (NSDC, 2010) of how school district policies are linked to professional learning identified at least 12 critical areas for developing collaboratively supported plans for continuous improvement. Among those are adopting standards-based professional learning, making time for professional learning, funding professional learning, supporting advanced learning degrees, mentoring and inducting new teachers, developing individual professional learning plans, creating career paths for teacher leaders, and building a collective bargaining agenda.

Adopt standards-based professional learning

Learning system leaders adopt or adapt standards supported by professional associations, best practice, and research to guide professional learning. They engage all stakeholders in examining potential standards. They discuss the reasons for adopting a set of standards, determine how they expect to benefit from the standards, and specify how they will know if the resulting professional learning achieves its intended goals.

Establishing standards helps create a common understanding and vocabulary around the concept and educate practitioners about quality professional learning. Standards for professional learning identify the essential characteristics of

professional learning, set a level of acceptable practice, and improve the quality of professional learning. The district uses the standards to guide planning and implementation and as the foundation for monitoring and evaluating professional

Establishing standards helps create a common understanding and vocabulary around the concept and educate practitioners about quality professional learning.

learning. Learning system leaders have a responsibility to regularly determine the degree to which district practice meets the standards, and to review and update the standards as needed.

Make time for professional learning

Educators regularly report that they do not have enough time for professional collaboration and learning. Most know they need time for professional learning to ensure all staff and students perform at high levels, and they are committed to collaborating to find that time.

In learning systems, leaders provide adequate time for educators to learn and to practice what they have learned. Labor and management may work together to find ways to redefine state or local requirements to support time for professional learning. For example, they might give local school leadership teams authority to develop schedules that address staff and student needs.

When leaders negotiate additional time, they ensure everyone is on board with how it is to be used. In some cases, school districts extend contracts for groups of teachers and teacher leaders to plan and implement professional learning throughout the year.

Fund professional learning

Effective professional learning requires personnel, time, and materials, each of which carries a cost. Management and labor develop a shared understanding of the purpose, goals, and measures of success of professional learning. They work together over time to ensure the district's budget is helping it meet its professional learning goals, and if it is not, determine appropriate adjustments. Learning systems see professional learning as an investment rather than an expense.

Learning system leaders adequately fund quality professional learning, including personnel (instructional coaches, district professional developers, mentors, etc.), contracted support

> Learning systems see professional learning as an investment rather than an expense.

(external assistance providers, external coaches, etc.); materials and resources (technology, books, memberships, and more); travel (conferences, courses, etc.); and other items (association dues). Some districts establish per educator or per student funding formulas. Others assign a percentage of the operating budget to professional learning. Some set a baseline and allocate additional support depending on need.

Support advanced degrees

Members of any profession continue their learning as they progress in their chosen field. In learning systems, relevant, high-quality professional learning is available to all educators, enabling them to improve teaching and learning for students.

Learning system leaders set expectations for continuing education and advanced licensure. Continuing education requirements offer opportunities for educators to examine their assumptions about ongoing learning and the district's role in and responsibility for supporting it. Teacher associations seek out support for continuing education to help all educators meet standards of excellence. Learning systems align continuing education requirements and incentives with individual, school, and system goals and outcomes.

In learning systems, recognition and compensation for advanced certifications and other degrees may be part of a labor and management agreement. In learning systems, leaders support and value advanced degrees and certifications, such as National Board for Professional Teaching Standards recognition, and may use completion of these to boost salaries, make staff eligible for additional compensation, consider teachers for new responsibilities, or promote an individual to a new position. Districts benefit when teachers participate in such programs because the system develops a more highly qualified and skilled teaching force. Through recognition and compensation, the district attracts and retains accomplished teachers.

Mentor and induct new teachers

Leaders in learning systems adopt policies and negotiate agreements to support consistent, effective, and formalized new teacher induction. Formalized mentor and induction programs best position new teachers for success in the profession by increasing their competency, satisfaction, and retention.

Labor and management leaders collaborate to design and execute a district plan for new teacher induction. They work jointly on articulating the plan's philosophy, underlying beliefs and assumptions, goals, measures of success, and implementation steps. They determine the responsibilities of each individual engaged in the process. They discuss these elements of mentoring and induction programs which contribute to a program's success:

- Mentor qualifications
- Mentor selection
- Mentor preparation
- Mentor support
- Mentor assignments
- Mentor schedules
- Mentor compensation
- Induction requirements
- Induction programming
- Differentiated support for beginning and new teachers
- Personnel evaluation
- Program evaluation

Leaders in learning systems create induction policies that adequately fund mentoring and facilitate mentor and inductee collaboration for extended periods of time. They provide mentor teachers with opportunities for professional learning. Sound induction policies result in programs that help accelerate new teacher competence and satisfaction, ensuring that all students have access to outstanding educators.

Develop individual professional learning plans

Many states and school districts require individual professional learning plans as part of an evaluation and continuous improvement process. Individual professional learning plans give teachers a way to document and address their goals and needs. In learning systems, labor and management collaborate to determine how individual professional learning plans connect to individual as well as team, school, and district goals and needs.

At times, teachers need or seek content or programmatic professional learning beyond what their school or district provides. Personalized professional learning can supplement and complement

> Leaders in learning systems create induction policies that adequately fund mentoring and facilitate mentor and inductee collaboration for extended periods of time. . . . Sound induction policies result in programs that help accelerate new teacher competence and satisfaction, ensuring that all students have access to outstanding educators.

school-based, collaborative professional learning. Learning system leaders establish procedures and processes to support teachers and other educators who seek support for additional learning and development. They use bargaining agreements to spell out support for teacher participation in team and schoolwide learning plans.

Create career paths for teacher leaders

District leaders in learning systems promote continuous growth and career development through leadership opportunities. Management and labor leaders collaborate in learning systems

Build a collective bargaining agenda

While multiple strategies exist for improving teaching and learning, none is as powerful as ensuring that each teacher engages in effective professional learning as a part of his or her daily work.

Learning system and state leaders may leverage their relationships with their educators' professional associations and use the collective bargaining process to increase the quality of professional learning and embed it in educators' workday. To do so, school districts committed to becoming learning systems take these five initial steps:

1. Identify policies, collective bargaining language, and other agreements that address professional learning, and determine whether they are consistent with the district's philosophy, goals, assumptions, beliefs, and Learning Forward's Standards for Professional Learning. Set up a collaborative process to review and, if necessary, revise any relevant materials.

2. Develop and adopt a joint resolution supporting Learning Forward's Standards for Professional Learning. The Standards demonstrate common expectations for quality that strengthen and ensure consistency and equity in professional learning practices. Once the district is using the Standards as a framework, educators can take annual surveys to determine the degree to which professional learning practices adhere to the Standards and how well the district's commitment to the Standards is being met.

3. Develop research-based assessments of professional learning initiatives. Use objective criteria to show which programs meet the Standards and to rate their effectiveness. Evaluations provide data to make improvements and measure impact.

4. Examine investments in professional learning—including time and funding—to ensure that educators have adequate support to meet their professional learning goals. Not every school district has adequate financial and human resources to consistently implement effective professional learning. Management and labor may collaborate to demonstrate need and advocate to local and state policymakers for a larger investment in professional learning.

5. Establish leadership development programs that help educators understand, experience, and appreciate effective professional learning. Leadership development programs also prepare teachers for new leadership responsibilities.

District leaders can take these five steps collectively to accelerate their work toward becoming a learning system. These actions help leaders establish the vision, the culture, the trust, and the agenda that support high levels of learning and success for all.

to develop career continuums for all educators. Many teachers are interested in taking on leadership roles or responsibilities but do not want to become administrators or be required to leave the classroom (MetLife Foundation, 2012). Their leadership options often are limited to roles on committees and teams or as building representatives.

Teachers want more information about formal, hybrid, and informal leadership roles. Formal roles may allow teachers to be released from day-to-day teaching responsibilities to focus instead on supporting colleagues' success by acting as full-time mentors, instructional coaches, and peer evaluators. Teachers who want to split their time between classroom teaching and other responsibilities may be attracted to hybrid roles such as team, grade-level, and department chairs, or association officers. Informal roles may include serving on school improvement committees and other ad hoc task forces.

Through collaborative negotiations, labor and management establish career paths and opportunities for teachers. They create comprehensive plans that address a vision, goals, principles, theory of action, roles and responsibilities. They share the plan and opportunities as well as the requirements

Formal roles may allow teachers to be released from day-to-day teaching responsibilities to focus instead on supporting colleagues' success by acting as full-time mentors, instructional coaches, and peer evaluators.

for qualifying for each opportunity. Each opportunity is accompanied by information about selection, placement, support, evaluation, and compensation. Learning system leaders apply Teacher Leader Model Standards (Teacher Leadership Exploratory Consortium, 2011) to the process.

Labor and management link arms to support learning

When we were threatened with a state take-over, we knew we had to make changes. The district decided to restructure a group of low-performing schools and required all the teachers to reapply for their positions. Labor and management figured out together a way to make it work. The key was communication and the relationship that we had. We worked together to support teachers and help them through all the changes.

We ironed out the nuts and bolts in weekly joint communication meetings and monthly meetings with the superintendent. Having the relationship with the administration and ability to talk about issues and not be afraid was essential. Nothing was forbidden. We could talk about anything and it stayed within that room. We had to say, "We are not each other's enemy. If we don't work together, we are a lost cause as a public school system. We will be gone." We might not have the same philosophies, but we had to come to the best consensus for the good of the cause. That was our mindset, and that's what got us through.

Change is really hard. We all had to compromise. There was a whole new level of re-education for everybody. The superintendent, as a professional learner, and the others trying to figure it out came up with an outline for how the process would work. Everybody knew that for them to grow professionally, they had to embrace new learning. It's all a part of professional responsibility.

Many new situations gave staff the opportunity to grow. We created our own evaluation. The small number of teachers who were identified as not being proficient in certain areas were given support through a coach in the building, a co-worker, visiting another school, reading, being fostered. Our professional development was more one-on-one and fine-tuning.

We had to make sure the professional development overall was differentiated and not just seat time. A lot of teachers saw professional development as just the same material, served a different way. But it's like seeing a movie or reading a book again. There's always something you missed that might be the key to improving.

And we understood we needed a body of time for professional development that was consistent over the entire district. The goal was to have professional development regularly in each building every week. We had to make sure the building principals were using the time consistently and that everyone was on the same page, respecting teachers' time. Teachers were learning a lot in collaborative time, but there are only a certain number of hours in a day, and sometimes we had to work with principals or appeal to the administration to not burn people out. We need to honor and respect people.

The school administration has done a good job helping the board understand its role and authority. And the board has worked hard to know exactly what new things are happening in education. They visit other districts and understand the importance of how change is implemented. That understanding is transferred to teachers.

So even with the complexity of a large urban district, everybody got on the same page about where we were going, how to get there, and what you have to do to be an active participant in the process. People here are committed to this city and this district. They have put their hearts and souls into the district to make it viable.

— Albert Jacquay, former president,
  Fort Wayne Education Association
  Fort Wayne (Ind.) Community Schools

Reflection
questions

- What are some reasons to view professional learning as an opportunity for labor and management to collaborate?

- What views about professional learning do management and labor share?

- How have current policies and collective bargaining agreements advanced individual and system performance?

- How could we strengthen our current policies and collaborative agreements related to professional learning?

- What new areas for collaborative collective bargaining might we address in the future?

RESOURCES

Catone, K. (2013). Teachers unions as partners, not adversaries. *VUE, 36,* 52–59.

Holmes, E. & Maiers, S. (2012). A united commitment to change. *JSD, 33*(2), 40–47.

Killion, J. & Davin, L. (2008). From the statehouse to the school house. *The Learning System, 4*(3), 1–7.

Learning Forward. (2011, June). *JSD: Teacher Leadership, 32*(3).

Raabe, B. (n.d.). Collective bargaining for improved student achievement. Available at www.nea.org/home/10803.htm

Ventello, G. P. (2012). The negotiator: Conditions for successful interest-based bargaining. *Thought and Action, 28,* 40–45.

Von Frank, V. (2013, Winter). Evaluations serve as pathways for professional growth. *The Learning System, 8*(2), 1, 4–5.

TOOLS INDEX

TOOL	TITLE	PURPOSE
19.1	When policy joins practice	Build relations for collaborative work, set the context for building understanding about labor/management, and examine how policy influences practice.
19.2	Key ideas: Labor, management, and professional learning	Understand key ideas from research about collective bargaining and professional learning.
19.3	National study recommendations	Consider recommendations for your own context.
19.4	Barriers to change: Uncovering assumptions	Help individuals within groups with differing agendas uncover their personal values and assumptions so that they can build trust to better work together.
19.5	Reaching consensus	Learn how to arrive at agreement.
19.6	Prioritizing our work	Explore possible professional development pathways to begin labor/management work.

CHAPTER 20

Building
leader pipelines

WHERE ARE WE NOW?

Our district has a clear definition of leadership.

| STRONGLY AGREE | AGREE | NO OPINION | DISAGREE | STRONGLY DISAGREE |

Our district has adopted standards that describe the key elements of effective principal and teacher leader practice.

| STRONGLY AGREE | AGREE | NO OPINION | DISAGREE | STRONGLY DISAGREE |

Principals and teacher leaders begin their positions with a clear understanding of what the job entails.

| STRONGLY AGREE | AGREE | NO OPINION | DISAGREE | STRONGLY DISAGREE |

Our district leaders routinely identify future leaders.

| STRONGLY AGREE | AGREE | NO OPINION | DISAGREE | STRONGLY DISAGREE |

Our district has specific procedures for how new principals and teacher leaders are identified, recruited, hired, inducted, and supported.

| STRONGLY AGREE | AGREE | NO OPINION | DISAGREE | STRONGLY DISAGREE |

Our district supports new leaders.

| STRONGLY AGREE | AGREE | NO OPINION | DISAGREE | STRONGLY DISAGREE |

Developing leaders is a necessary function of a learning system and critical to outcomes. Learning systems do not leave any aspect to chance. Leaders in learning systems do not wait to see who applies for leadership positions and hope for the best. They seek out potential leaders, actively ensuring that aspiring leaders receive high-quality training and on-the-job professional learning and support. District leaders in learning systems identify, prepare, and support all leaders in the organization.

Leadership is an essential component of a quality learning system. According to research, school leadership is second only to classroom teaching in terms of its effect on learning. There are virtually no documented cases of a successful school turnaround without the presence of an effective leader (Leithwood et al., 2004).

Researchers at McREL, a private, nonprofit, nonpartisan education research and development corporation, studied the skills of education leaders, and identified 21 key responsibilities that affect student achievement (Waters, Marzano, & McNulty, 2004). The research is significant because it points

"Mapping career pathways helps ambitious staff understand what positions will help them to grow and what potential jobs they might have."

—Jennifer Abrams and Valerie von Frank

to the link between leadership and student learning, noting that quality leaders and leadership are an integral part of the learning system.

A comprehensive leadership development strategy signals the system's commitment to support employees considering a leadership position in the future. It helps staff members know that the system will focus on developing people's knowledge, skills, and readiness to move into key positions. It demonstrates the district's commitment to tapping talent within the system rather than looking outside. According to Jennifer Abrams and Valerie von Frank, "Mapping career pathways helps ambitious staff understand what positions will help them to grow and what potential jobs they might have" (2013, p. ?). They write that

- Planning for future leadership helps retain staff;
- Investing in future leaders can add to staff members' satisfaction and loyalty to the organization;
- Planning helps avoid emergencies;
- Succession planning helps ensure cultural norms continue; and
- Making sure traditions and tacit knowledge remain intact helps continue the flow of good performance.

(Abrams & von Frank, 2013)

To create a system of strong, successive leadership, learning system leaders create a pipeline, define and leverage standards for leadership, select leaders carefully, induct them, and provide solid support.

Create a pipeline

In a learning system, leaders are always looking for future leaders. Traditional school districts may cast a wide net to seek leaders, attending local or even national job fairs in search of highly qualified candidates. While this strategy isn't necessarily flawed, effective district leaders identify potential leaders from within the organization. The best leaders sometimes are those who did not seek leadership but are afforded opportunities that may lead to moving into such positions.

A 2012 National College for School Leadership report highlighted the importance of identifying leadership talent: "Leaders should be identifying candidates who may have leadership potential as indicated through evidence of leadership ability, resilience, and ambition for the school, not just themselves. Heads (principals) should also look out for emerging leaders in their organizations at all levels, including teaching assistants" (p. 8).

As future leaders are identified, learning systems provide ways for them to connect with one another and with current leaders, both electronically and in person, for formal and informal learning. As the report states, "It is important to encourage people to see themselves as leaders by getting them into networks where they will start to identify with other leaders and identify leadership qualities in themselves, as well as providing opportunities for them to learn how to manage difficult issues" (2012, p. 8).

Learning system leaders engage potential leaders in professional learning to hone their skills and to observe them at work long before hiring them as administrators. Since the potential leaders are employees in the district, they already share the district's moral purpose and understand its goals and values. As more people are engaged in learning about effective leadership and take on additional responsibilities, shared leadership becomes a common practice.

Define and leverage standards for leadership

Learning system leaders set clear standards for practice and use the standards to ensure everyone is aware of what they are expected to know and be able to do.

The Interstate School Leader Licensure Consortium offers school leader and teacher leader model standards in a set of broadly stated expectations (domains) that define the critical dimensions of leadership and performance indicators that define actions or expectations related to each domain. Presenting the information in this way allows educators to understand and begin to define the skills leaders need, to measure whether leaders are fulfilling leadership roles, and to begin to learn the skills needed to take on such roles. Another resource is Learning Forward's Innovation Configuration maps, which complement its

> Learning system leaders engage potential leaders in professional learning to hone their skills and to observe them at work long before hiring them as administrators.

Standards for Professional Learning. These maps identify highly effective practices that leaders in various roles use to meet the Standards.

Other organizations have established leadership standards as frameworks for comprehensive leadership development programs. The Australian Institute for Teaching and School Leadership developed leadership standards that overlap with the ISLLC standards. Another set of leadership standards for school leaders was developed by the National College of School Leadership. Vanderbilt University and the University of Pennsylvania developed the Vanderbilt Assessment of Leadership in Education (VAL-Ed), an assessment tool aligned to the ISLLC standards that is designed to measure principal effectiveness. The sum of these standards and research on

Standards for leaders

The Interstate School Leader Licensure Consortium (ISLLC) Teacher Leader Model Standards uses seven domains to describe the dimensions of **teacher leadership**:

- **Domain I:** Fostering a collaborative culture to support educator development and student learning.

- **Domain II:** Accessing and using research to improve practice and student achievement.

- **Domain III:** Promoting professional learning for continuous improvement.

- **Domain IV:** Facilitating improvements in instruction and student learning.

- **Domain V:** Using assessments and data for school and district improvements.

- **Domain VI:** Improving outreach to and collaboration with families and community.

- **Domain VII:** Advocating for student learning and the profession.

(CCSSO, 2008)

In learning systems, **school leaders** use Learning Forward's Standards for Professional Learning to determine actions that are most likely to result in increased student achievement. School leaders who follow the Standards

- Shape a vision of academic success for all students, based on high standards (*Outcomes Standard*);

- Create a safe, cooperative climate with other foundations of positive interaction (*Learning Communities Standard*);

- Cultivate leadership in others so that teachers and other adults play a role in realizing the school vision (*Leadership Standard*);

- Improve instruction to enable teachers and students to fulfill their potential (*Outcomes and Learning Designs Standards*); and

- Manage people, data, and processes to foster school improvement (*Resources, Data, and Implementation Standards*).

principals' leadership has led to a greater understanding of principals' practice.

After studying and exploring these resources and tools, district leaders begin to define leadership for their own district, help all administrators and aspiring school leaders clearly understand the responsibilities associated with various leadership roles, and set the expectation that all professional learning for leaders will focus on developing skills and competencies in essential areas.

Because professional learning aligned to the Standards is job embedded, often structured with educators assuming collective responsibility for desired results, and based on a cycle of continuous improvement (see Appendix), it's more likely to change educators' knowledge, skills, and dispositions—and student results.

Select leaders carefully

Systems that clearly communicate what they expect from leaders may mitigate the problem of turnover. A RAND study found that more than one-fifth of new principals are likely to leave their jobs within two years, and those placed in schools that failed to meet Adequate Yearly Progress under the No Child Left Behind Act left at even higher rates (Burkhauser, Gates, Hamilton, & Ikemoto, 2012, p. 14). While the report highlights numerous predictors of turnover, including working conditions and principals' prior experiences in other jobs, aspiring principals' lack of understanding of what the position entails also may contribute.

With clear standards in place, leaders of learning systems pay careful attention to hiring to make sure those who move into leadership positions not only have the required knowledge, skills, and dispositions for the job, but also are a good fit for the team or school they will support.

District leaders develop a system or process to use to determine how they will find the best candidate, the criteria for the position, and the list of specific skills they are seeking. They use interviews and observations that allow many to be involved in the decision. They may use questionnaires or surveys to discover and assess potential leaders' motivations, attitudes toward struggling students, alignment with the district's moral purpose, and commitment to professional learning.

Prince George's County (Md.) Public Schools uses a three-stage hiring procedure for new principals (Mendels, 2010). First, candidates complete an assessment designed to measure their leadership potential. Those who score well watch a video of a teacher teaching and write a memo critiquing the lesson. The feedback must align with the district's goals for what principals need to focus on while observing instruction. Those who score well on this task interview with three to four principal supervisors who rate the candidates. Finally, top candidates are matched with schools based on detailed specifications from school representatives.

Partner with other institutions

District and school leaders in learning systems recognize the importance of induction and mentoring programs for new leaders and of continuous professional learning for existing leaders.

One way to establish focused, long-term, sustainable learning for administrators is to form relationships with local institutions of higher education. A large, urban district or a network of smaller districts may establish a partnership with a university or college, agreeing on the kind of training school officials want their leaders and potential leaders to experience. Blending what higher education providers know about

Pamela Mendels (2012) offers several examples in which a district took the lead in developing a learning program for leaders and local partners responded:

- A New York City school district has a relationship with the non-profit New York City Leadership Academy that provides the district with several dozen new principals each year. The district set expectations for the kind of training it wants its aspiring leaders to receive, and the academy delivers the training.

- Charlotte-Mecklenburg (N.C.) Schools partners with Winthrop University and Queens University.

- Denver Public Schools has created the Ritchie Program for School Leaders, a model of district-university collaboration, with the University of Denver.

leadership from research with what schools know from practice strengthens leaders' preservice experience by aligning their learning with the realities of the position.

In most states in the United States, aspiring school principals must take courses at an accredited university in order to receive a license or certificate to become a school principal. By establishing a relationship with a preservice institution, the district makes it more likely that graduates will begin their jobs ready to meet the district's expectations.

Universities and nonprofits across the country are just beginning to partner with school districts to offer training programs specifically for aspiring teacher leaders. In 2011, Ohio instituted a program culminating in a teacher leader endorsement through a partnership between the state and Ohio Dominican University in Columbus, Ohio.

Support new leaders

The support leaders receive when they are hired is critical. Often new principals are placed in some of the most challenging schools, and many mentors focus on helping the new leader with management. The most critical challenges these new principals face, however, are rarely around how to move students through the cafeteria. They are hired to turn around student performance, and longstanding cultural issues may block their success. Thoughtful district leaders recognize that effective professional learning and coaching is necessary to ensure the success of their newest principals.

Professional learning for leaders takes multiple forms. A model program from Ontario, for example, requires that districts "must offer training and resources to new leaders, provide mentoring and informal support from retirees or those who were promoted, and evaluate their processes for supporting instructional leaders. Experienced

Hillsborough County (Fla.) School District prepares principals through an additional series of district-led training experiences. Six months after graduating from the district's initial program, aspiring leaders can apply to the Assistant Principal Induction Program. After serving three years as an assistant principal, they enter the district's two-year Preparing New Principals Program (Turnbull, Riley, Arcaira, Anderson, & MacFarlane, 2013). Thus, principals in Hillsborough spend at least five years in district-developed learning before moving into a school leader position.

leaders' learning opportunities are set through learning networks, self-assessments, and other learning opportunities. Performance appraisals based on the leadership profiles are integral to leaders' professional learning" (Abrams & von Frank, 2013, p. 120).

The district's evaluation process influences professional learning needs. Evaluation alone will not change practice. However, principals and teacher leaders who work with their supervisors to develop individual learning plans that address growth areas noted in their evaluations are more likely to change their practices.

Learning system leaders ensure that aspiring, new, and veteran leaders continuously engage in long-term, sustained professional learning to develop their skills, competencies, attitudes, and aspirations so that they in turn can support teacher and student success.

To help students, build leaders

Gwinnett County Public Schools seeks to become a system of world-class schools rather than a system with individual franchises or pockets of excellences, and we know that to do so, to become a learning system, requires highly effective leaders. Developing leaders has become one of Gwinnett's long-term strategic initiatives.

Early in the process, we created a logic model. Our logic model clearly reveals the reason we develop leaders is to have a positive impact on kids. It is within our human resources that we find our greatest points of leverage for moving student performance. The research is clear that if you want to make the biggest difference with kids, you hire the most effective teacher you can find, and if you want to make a difference in a school, in its culture, with teachers, you hire the strongest, most effective leaders you can find.

In 2005–2006, we forecast a significant turnover in our leadership, driven by Baby Boomer retirements and by continued growth as a district. We had to ask: "Where will these future leaders come from?" "Can we simply rely on our ability to recruit or attract talent, or should we be more thoughtful about that pipeline?" We studied as many leadership development programs as we could identify and pulled together an adaptation of those effective practices to launch our first aspiring principal program. A few years later we began to focus on our assistant principals and developed a similar program for them. Now, we also have a program for district administrators.

For aspiring principals, the first three days of instruction are led by the superintendent to build the foundation of leadership and clarify expectations. The associate superintendent for human resources and talent management teaches for two days on teacher effectiveness, leader effectiveness, and teacher evaluation and hiring. Our chief financial officer teaches about solid fiscal management. They hear from veteran principals and practitioners. We also engage our school board members so that our future principals know them, what they believe in, and that they value leadership. Finally, every aspiring principal enters a six-month residency under the tutelage of a carefully selected veteran mentor principal. They shadow the principal and practice being a school leader.

The benefit of leadership development is that we know who is coming through this pipeline of future talent, their particular skills and the talents that they may have, and how we can work with them to develop and support them well in advance of placing them in a principal position. Of our 132 principals now, 93 are graduates of the program. We've conducted research through our internal research department, and we know our program completers have a statistically proven impact on student achievement.

Still, we continue to monitor and adjust our leadership program. We do a comprehensive external evaluation each year to examine the residency, the curriculum, and adaptations. Our superintendent and our board have a strong belief that we as educators should always be thinking about improving. They understand that our teachers and our leaders are an investment we have to make, that when you look at great and effective organizations, you *always* find that leadership matters—always.

— Glenn Pethel, assistant superintendent of
  leadership development
  Gwinnett County (Ga.) Public Schools

Reflection
questions

- How does a leader pipeline in a learning system look different from one in a traditional school district?

- How can our district improve the way leaders are identified? How they are inducted?

- What gaps do we have in how we support leaders?

- What resources do we need in order to improve our professional learning for leaders? How do learning systems provide that support?

- How does our district ensure that our leaders clearly understand what is expected of them as leaders in a learning system?

- How does adopting a set of standards or expected behaviors affect the actions and learning of leaders?

RESOURCES

Corcoran, S., Schwartz, A. E., & Weinstein, M. (2011). *An evaluation of the NYC Aspiring Principals Program, update through 2008–09.* New York, NY: New York University, Institute for Education and Social Policy. Available at www.wallacefoundation.org/knowledge-center/school-leadership/principal-training/Pages/New-York-City-Aspiring-Principals-Program.aspx.

Johnson, M. (May/June 2010). Fit for principalship: Identifying, training, and clearing the path for potential school leaders. *Principal, 89*(9), 12.

Darling-Hammond, L., LaPointe, M., Meyerson, D., Orr, M. T., & Cohen, C. (2007). *Preparing school leaders for a changing world: Lessons from exemplary leadership development programs.* Stanford, CA: Stanford University, Educational Leadership Institute. Available at www.wallacefoundation.org/knowledge-center/school-leadership/key-research/Pages/Preparing-School-Leaders.aspx.

Seashore Louis, K., Leithwood, K., Wahlstrom, K., & Anderson, S. (2010). *Investigating the links to improved student learning: Final report of research findings.* New York, NY: The Wallace Foundation.

Von Frank, V. (2009, September). Framework for improvement: Effective school leadership translates into increased student learning. *The Learning Principal, 5*(1), 1, 6–7.

Young, D. A. (2013, May/June). From teacher to principals—5 effective tools. Available at www.naesp.org/principal-mayjune-2013-achievement-gap/teacher-principal-five-effective-tools

TOOLS INDEX

TOOL	TITLE	PURPOSE
20.1	Establish leadership expectations	Help district leadership teams establish clear expectations for school- and district-level administrators and focus their professional learning.
20.2	Teacher leadership: A bold move forward	Help teachers understand the role of teacher leaders so that they can make intentional decisions about developing new skills to effectively serve their schools.
20.3	Identifying potential to lead	Provide opportunities for conversations about recognizing potential leaders.

Networking to accelerate learning

WHERE ARE WE NOW?

My district or school has developed structures or resources that support formal learning networks.

| STRONGLY AGREE | AGREE | NO OPINION | DISAGREE | STRONGLY DISAGREE |

Our district encourages and supports my participation in a formal, structured learning network.

| STRONGLY AGREE | AGREE | NO OPINION | DISAGREE | STRONGLY DISAGREE |

I know where to find learning networks and how to gain access to them.

| STRONGLY AGREE | AGREE | NO OPINION | DISAGREE | STRONGLY DISAGREE |

My learning network consists of leaders who support, coach, and share powerful ideas with me.

| STRONGLY AGREE | AGREE | NO OPINION | DISAGREE | STRONGLY DISAGREE |

A learning network has positively affected professional learning in my district or school.

| STRONGLY AGREE | AGREE | NO OPINION | DISAGREE | STRONGLY DISAGREE |

Changing an entrenched institution, such as a school district with longstanding patterns of behavior, requires the power of many minds engaged together. Through networks, district and school leaders can continually engage in dialogue with others facing the same issues. Superintendents, district administrators, and school leaders pool their experiences, knowledge, wisdom, and motivation to improve the learning of the children in their charge.

Yet district and school leaders central to any change effort often work in isolation, removed from what takes place in schools and from what educators are learning through their practices. Bringing leaders together in a strong network allows them to "deisolate" themselves and put aside day-to-day distractions to focus on the strategies and skills necessary to lead high-achieving schools.

Networks provide educators an opportunity to accelerate their learning by learning from others in their network. A network strengthens and enhances a learning system as educators learn from their coworkers and also from knowledge-

> Through networks, district and school leaders can continually engage in dialogue with others facing the same issues.

able people around the nation and the world. Leadership teams, principals, and superintendents who join a network improve their opportunities to learn exponentially, accelerate their learning, and increase their opportunities to dramatically improve children's lives.

A powerful network is one in which learning drives the agenda and in which members set concrete goals as they discuss their needs and clarify issues. Members in a leadership network seek opportunities to develop new skills and strategies in order to lead differently. They may directly observe the work of local colleagues or use videos for long-distance observations. They may share scenarios, asking others to generate ideas and solutions that shed light on an issue. They also may work together on a problem of practice, using action research to test new practices at their schools. All these allow educators to continue their learning.

Support and sustain networks for learning

Learning system leaders recognize that effective networks require ongoing, planned support. Although informal networks make a difference in members' lives, planning and structure give participants the best opportunity to capitalize on the resources of people from around the globe who are working on similar issues. The people in a network structure the network themselves to optimize the ability to learn from each other.

Successful learning networks begin with a clear and compelling vision of their purpose. Members structure the learning to ensure that participants explore the implications of research on leadership and set goals that challenge participants to learn and grow. They use inquiry- and problem-based strategies to engage learners. They create collaborative communities that develop innovative solutions to problems in members' districts and schools and come up with creative ideas to move schools toward a new level of success.

For example, the stated mission of the non-profit School Leaders Network, which includes approximately 400 principals in six locations across the country, is to expand educational opportunities for all students by transforming leadership practices (http://www.connectleadsucceed.org/). Its school leaders meet monthly to share best practices, challenges, and issues that foster or inhibit their individual leadership. Leaders engage in study and support each other as they work through the challenges of changing their practices and developing their skills.

Build relationships, structures, and dialogue

Formal relationships are essential to facilitating network participants' learning and changing their behavior. Although informal networks have and always will be valuable to school leaders, structured networks give individuals more opportunities to develop trusting relationships and engage in more challenging conversations about their districts and schools.

Formal structures require facilitation. In a structured network, a skilled facilitator asks strategic, challenging questions that inspire shifts in participants' skills, attitudes, and behaviors. In addition, because the network sustains its structure over time, participants challenge each other and coach each other, building a sense of collective responsibility within the network.

Networks keep leaders from being isolated and open their eyes to new ways of being, thinking, and doing. Effective networks bring diversity of thought and ideas into the learning system, opening up possibilities for new ideas to flourish and be put into action by the community.

Judge the effect

Leaders in learning systems understand that the value of networks can, indeed, be measured and take steps to do so. The University of California, Los Angeles Educational Evaluation Group studied School Leaders Network principals from across the country and found the network's principals were more confident than their peers in their ability to make cultural changes, change classroom practices, and improve student outcomes. In fact, according to the study, schools led by network principals in New York, Massachusetts, and San Antonio, Texas, outperformed peer schools, with those in Massachusetts reporting higher graduation rates and those in San Antonio increasing math proficiency compared with their local, non-network schools (Marland, 2010).

In addition, "New York City network principals, on average, led schools to higher than the city average scores across all culture indicators, including expectations, communication, engagement, and safety" (Neale & Cone, 2013, p. 5).

Networks take many forms

- The **Learning Forward Academy** is based on the concept of deepening understanding around professional learning as participants address a problem of practice in their own districts. The Academy provides an extended and profound learning experience that immerses members in a model of inquiry- and problem-based learning. Academy members work collaboratively to gain knowledge to solve significant student learning problems in their schools, districts, or organizations. What emerges are networks in which cohorts of participants continue to support and encourage one another long after graduation.

- Learning Forward's **Learning School Alliance** creates networks of school teams each year that take on their schools' toughest challenges and share their successes using online tools, including webinars, facilitated discussion forums, and group chats. Although team members develop customized professional learning plans based on and designed to solve their schools' most pressing problems, the most important work they engage in through their network is learning from each other.

- The **Aspen Institute Urban Superintendent's Network** brings together 10 to 15 superintendents from large districts in the United States for semiannual seminars that use data and case studies to allow leaders to discuss their own issues as they develop cross-district solutions in structured conversations. Several of the network meetings involve daylong visits by "critical friends" to a host district on the day before each seminar in which skilled facilitators engage the district leadership team in identifying an issue or initiative the district is struggling with. Aspen advisers and system leaders then spend a day studying the problem, talking with members of focus groups, and giving feedback and advice. These critical friends visits have become a vital part of the program and help the host district's leadership teams test hypotheses and assumptions they have been working under, surface new ideas and ways of looking at the issues, and ground the network's advisers in the concrete challenges and constraints facing participating districts.

- The **Twin Tiers Principals Coalition** in Corning, New York, formed a regional network in response to the need for continual professional learning opportunities for principals. Many school districts in upstate New York are small, and the only support available to principals

Chapter 21: Networking to accelerate learning

came from the Boards of Cooperative Educational Services, colleges that certify administrators in the state, and local chapters of ASCD. None of these provided long-term, sustained professional learning. Area superintendents, the Corning Inc. Foundation for Learning, and Learning Forward designed, facilitated, and implemented a network of principals who learn from each other, call on each other for problem solving and support, and coach each other on everything from applying for superintendent positions to working with the Common Core State Standards. Participants set goals for themselves, engage in research and study, use action research to achieve their goals and reflect on their progress, and support each other through the process. They meet in each other's schools, conduct walk-throughs, observe each other facilitating and working with staff, and give each other feedback. In a study conducted over several years, principals who fully participated raised student achievement as measured by standardized tests while building a community of learners engaged in a cycle of continuous improvement (see Appendix) and a collective commitment to all children (Munger, 2006).

- Autumn Sadovnik, director of professional development for the **Center for Jewish Education** in Baltimore, Maryland, has developed a relationship with local Jewish Congregational school leaders to strengthen professional learning in schools. For several years, under the Leadership, Excellence, Advocacy and Development (LEAD) program, Sadovnik has brought congregational school leaders together to learn from and support each other. LEAD helps congregational school principals use visioning and goal-setting strategies, work collaboratively, and ensure positive growth in their school programs. Through their time together, they have been successful in increasing effective professional learning strategies in all of their schools. By collaborating around Learning Forward's definition of and Standards for Professional Learning, participating principals have discovered and shared ways to embed professional learning in staff members' day-to-day schedules and personalize learning to meet their individual needs. This network of loosely connected school leaders has developed strong relationships in the several years of its existence, and principals now work together closely to help others understand the value of congregational schools as dynamic environments for high-quality Jewish learning, vibrant synagogue life, and meaningful connections to the larger Jewish community. School leaders have shared stories about the network's success with the Baltimore Center for Jewish Education board to ensure its ongoing financial commitment.

Shared learning breaks down silos

As educators, we have to leverage opportunities to understand each other's work so we're not reinventing wheels. We need to break down the wall between districts and schools, and between districts. If we do not, we miss an opportunity to come together and leverage our understanding, our brainpower, and our manpower, to get better at what we do, to become stronger as a province and as an education system.

Within the province of Ontario, we are sectioned off into regions and meet for sharing sessions—for example, around literacy, student engagement, mathematics. That builds a capacity among senior leaders. Virtually every week, someone is out of the office attending a regional session and making sure we're breaking away the silos.

Because of our proximity to the United States, we're starting to build a relationship with the states. We've had delegations come from the Cleveland, Ohio, area, and from Michigan. We really learn from each other; inevitably in these meetings, someone says, "Isn't *that* interesting?"

As a learning system, we've made huge progress by relinquishing control from a system level. We collect data on the system level and make that transparent, then allocate time for schools for professional learning. They design what that learning looks like. Teacher leaders and administrators choose what the work is and plan what it looks like, when it happens, how it happens, for whom it happens. We provide support on a system level based on their requests and needs, and then we bring them together at different times to share their learning following protocols.

We make space and time available for administrator learning teams based on an area of focus rather than a network based around geography. This is inconvenient on a system level. It's harder to facilitate, but it's the right work. The principals have the liberty to meet as professionals and to problem solve based on their issue, whether instructional, around change, or motivating people, for example. The principals work in trios or sometimes in groups of four and develop capacity and own their learning. They meet at one another's sites and use protocols to have a conversation.

We help them create a space where there's no judgment for them to learn. We offer mentorship if they would like central office support—special education, staff, program and curriculum. We will come out and help as a critical friend. For example, some principals asked for someone to come from the curriculum department to watch them in conversation about their questioning techniques to determine whether they were getting to the root of the problem.

When you build a level of advocacy amongst professionals to own the work, it changes how they do the work. It's about changing attitudes, aspirations, and behavior. It's better to connect with others rather than work in isolation. You develop an appreciation for the profession and how we can make a difference. It's invigorating. It lifts the roof off the schoolhouse, and it changes what happens for kids.

— Clara Howitt, superintendent of education
Greater Essex County (Ontario, Canada)
District School Board

Reflection questions

- What value and benefits do we see in engaging with a network of peers? What are some possible pitfalls?

- What skills, knowledge, attitudes, or behavior might we seek to develop by joining a learning network?

- What kinds of networks might benefit our district leaders' learning?

- Where would we begin to seek out an existing network to join?

- What kinds of networks might our district leaders develop together?

RESOURCES

Learning Forward. Information on the Learning Forward Academy is available at http://learningforward. org/learning-opportunities/academy#.U3JEmT5zl6s

Learning Forward. Information on Learning Forward's School Alliance Network is available at http:// learningforward.org/learning-opportunities/learning-school-alliance#.U3JEyz5zl6s

Riggins Newby, C. (2004). *Principals networking to enhance instruction.* Providence, RI: Northeast & Islands Regional Educational Laboratory and Alexandria, VA: NAESP.

George Lucas Foundation. *Edutopia*: Schools that work. Available at www.edutopia.org/schools-that-work

Nussbaum-Beach, S. & Ritter Hall, L. (2011). *The connected educator: Learning and leading in a digital age.* Indianapolis, IN: Solution Tree.

Hirsh, S. (2009). Foreword. In *The Power of Teacher Networks,* by Ellen Meyers with Peter A. Paul, David E. Kirkland, & Nancy Fichtman. Thousand Oaks, CA: Corwin Press.

Hirsh, S. (2013, February). Q & A with Carina Wong. *JSD, 34*(1), 20–25.

TOOLS INDEX

TOOL	TITLE	PURPOSE
21.1	Deep impact	Understand the effect of networking on school change and student success.
21.2	Build relationships in online communities	Learn to build online networks to expand learning.
21.3	Consider a consortium	Review the work of the Western States Benchmarking Consortium to consider potential regional networks.

CHAPTER 22

Coaching for
improvement

WHERE ARE WE NOW?

Our district leaders view their own learning as central to improving the skills, attitudes, and dispositions of teachers, who in turn directly affect student learning.

STRONGLY AGREE · AGREE · NO OPINION · DISAGREE · STRONGLY DISAGREE

Our district trains, nurtures, and supports leaders at all levels.

STRONGLY AGREE · AGREE · NO OPINION · DISAGREE · STRONGLY DISAGREE

In our district, leaders' learning is part of a coherent curriculum that is purposeful and results oriented.

STRONGLY AGREE · AGREE · NO OPINION · DISAGREE · STRONGLY DISAGREE

Our district's learning for leaders results in intentional shifts in practices around the system's expectations.

STRONGLY AGREE · AGREE · NO OPINION · DISAGREE · STRONGLY DISAGREE

Our district includes coaching as a significant component of leaders' learning.

STRONGLY AGREE · AGREE · NO OPINION · DISAGREE · STRONGLY DISAGREE

Our district has clear expectations of the coach's role and has communicated those expectations to all involved.

STRONGLY AGREE · AGREE · NO OPINION · DISAGREE · STRONGLY DISAGREE

Developing district and school leaders' skills is both a social process and a very personal one. While leaders learn many skills through their day-to-day work, learning systems enhance leaders' effectiveness by allowing them to explore strategies in one-on-one conversations with others through coaching.

Coaching is a customized learning process that focuses on empowering individuals to achieve exceptional results by aligning their purpose, choices, and actions. When coaches help education leaders increase their focus, see in new ways, improve relationships, and augment their ability to make effective choices and changes, coaches support leaders in powerful learning that also inspires the people around them to learn with passion.

Learning system leaders understand that coaching can have a significant effect on changing practices and behaviors. They consider administrators' and school principals' professional learning a priority and the means to ensuring their effectiveness. They know that when leaders experience good coaching, the whole organization benefits, and so they integrate coaching into the overall strategy for leaders' learning, succession planning, and performance management.

Establish coaching for continuous improvement

Administrators traditionally have developed their leadership skills through training, mentoring, and on-the-job learning—strategies designed to acquaint new members of the organization with the district's policies and practices and help them meet district expectations. For example, leaders may be trained in how to facilitate school leadership team meetings or how to conduct walkthroughs. Some district leaders believe serving on district task forces or as members of school improvement teams is a form of professional learning, and it may be—if those groups involve collaborative conversations, study and reflection, and goal setting.

In most districts, however, leaders' learning is not a part of a coherent curriculum that leads to intentional shifts in practices around the system's expectations for leaders and their effect on student learning. Districts often are not clear about which leadership skills are essential for all administrators in the district and do not ensure that leaders develop those skills. And while many school leaders get good ideas from training programs, they often do not receive any follow-up support designed to help them transfer that learning to their real-life situations. In most instances, they have minimal or no accountability for using the strategies they experienced in professional learning.

Although most leaders are evaluated annually, the evaluation often does not create the expectation that they will learn new skills, nor does it provide for ongoing monitoring of their progress. In reality, few school districts institute a regular, results-oriented, long-term, continuous learning process for leaders.

District leaders in learning systems work to ensure that all leaders in the organization are skilled and successful so that all students succeed. They see leaders' learning as central to improving the skills, attitude, and dispositions of the teaching corps, who directly affect student learning. They work to ensure all leaders develop deep understanding of Learning Forward's Standards for Professional Learning and the principles of professional learning in order to support district- or school-level innovations or initiatives, such as the Common Core State Standards or project-based learning. They develop in-depth institutes around district innovations to ensure leaders have a deep understanding of initiatives. They work with teams of leaders to be sure that leaders have peer support as they move through change processes. They design all district-level administrative and principal meetings as professional learning experiences that deepen leaders' proficiency levels in essential skills and behaviors. They have regular, intentional follow-up to help with implementation, share ideas, and redirect efforts.

Coaching is an essential aspect of that learning process and supports leaders in a cycle of continuous learning (see Figure 22.1).

Define the coaching program

To create a districtwide coaching program, leaders in a learning system follow a series of steps:

1. Establish an approach to coaching.

Learning systems leaders are sincere about coaching district and school leaders and spend significant time studying executive coaching: its structure, its value, and its place in a comprehensive professional learning system for administrators.

Coaching systems vary greatly, from highly structured approaches such as ontological coaching—coaching that focuses on the coherence of the body, language, emotions and how the coachee sees the world—to coaching approaches that are more facilitative or like mentoring. Some focus on the work only; others also focus on the coachee and his or her relationships with others. District leaders who establish effective approaches have spent significant time studying coaching and develop a clear vision of coaching for the district.

Figure 22.1 District leadership teams ensure everybody learns

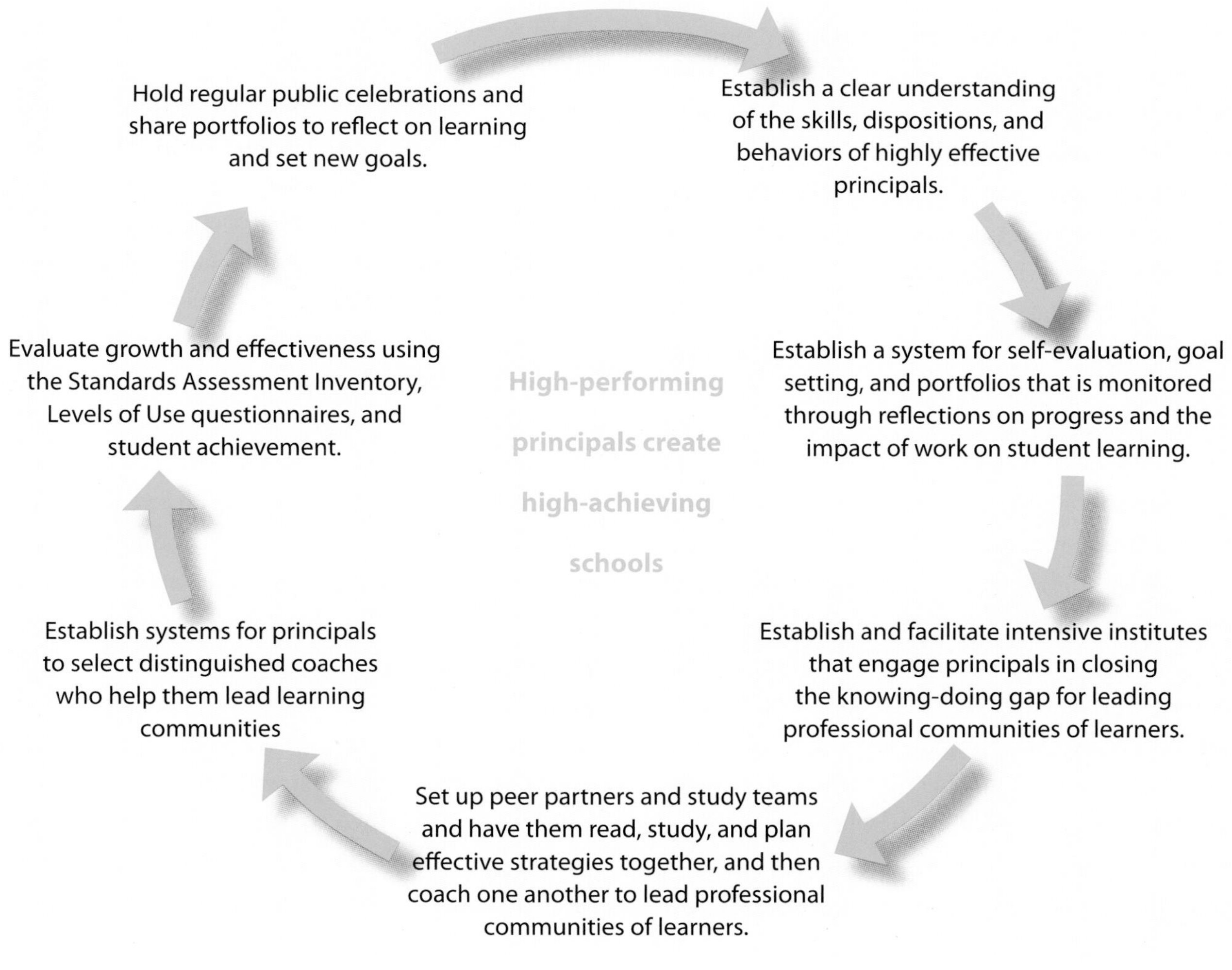

Hold regular public celebrations and share portfolios to reflect on learning and set new goals.

Establish a clear understanding of the skills, dispositions, and behaviors of highly effective principals.

Evaluate growth and effectiveness using the Standards Assessment Inventory, Levels of Use questionnaires, and student achievement.

High-performing

principals create

high-achieving

schools

Establish a system for self-evaluation, goal setting, and portfolios that is monitored through reflections on progress and the impact of work on student learning.

Establish systems for principals to select distinguished coaches who help them lead learning communities

Establish and facilitate intensive institutes that engage principals in closing the knowing-doing gap for leading professional communities of learners.

Set up peer partners and study teams and have them read, study, and plan effective strategies together, and then coach one another to lead professional communities of learners.

2. Develop a theory of change and logic model to ensure success.

Just as important, district leaders think about how coaching will be implemented in the district. As leaders deepen their understanding of coaching, they begin to create a pathway or theory of change to achieve their desired goals for coaching. They will thoughtfully consider a number of questions:

- What are the purpose and expected outcomes of the coaching?
- How will the district select coaches? How will administrators be matched to the coaches?
- Will administrators have a choice about being coached?
- Will they be able to select their coaches?
- To whom will coaches report? What protocols will ensure that the relationship between coach and coachee is based on confidentiality?
- Will coaches be compensated for their work?
- Will coaches coach full time?

District leaders establish a contract for coaches that answers these questions. They outline a plan that describes critical attributes of the district's coaching approach, the qualifications for coaches, and the agreements and expectations of coaches.

3. Hire the right people to coach.

District leaders in effective learning systems hire and develop highly competent coaches. Coaches have a unique attitude. They are other-centered. They have high levels of interpersonal skills and emotional maturity.

District leaders carefully outline selection criteria for coaches in order to make wise hiring decisions. The district plays a major role in ensuring that the coaches it hires are confident, sincere, trusting individuals who are other-centered. Coaching others is not only a skill; it also embodies an attitude of service to others. Leaders in a learning system seek coaches who are sincere

in all their interactions and reliable—coaches who demonstrate that they can be counted on.

4. Match the coach and coachee.

Most challenging for district leaders is connecting coaches to coachees. Coaching is only effective if there is a high level of trust between the coach and coachee, and district leaders are careful in making matches. Highly skilled coaches work on trust at the beginning of the relationship so that the coachee is comfortable being coached.

Sometimes, district leaders may allow administrators to choose whether they want a coach and to select a coach from the district's cadre. Others may differentiate support for leaders or assign a coach.

5. Regularly assess coaching's effect.

Most district leaders are responsible for assessing coaching's effect on leaders, including determining whether leaders develop the skills, attitudes, and behaviors they need in order to lead high-performing schools. Since coaching conversations are confidential, leaders observe coachees working with staff and community members, talk with groups of students and staff, survey teachers, walk through buildings, and use systems such as Learning Forward's Standards Assessment Inventory to assess the effects of the program and determine whether coachees are exhibiting new and essential behaviors.

Leaders in a learning system ensure that all are clear that the coach's role is to ask questions in a way that fosters leaders' self-awareness and awareness of others; helps them practice astute listening; encourages their observations of the world; enables possibility thinking, thoughtful planning, and decision making; champions opportunities and potential; fosters stretch thinking; inspires them to achieve their goals; challenges their perceived limitations in order to illuminate new possibilities; and supports them in creating alternative ways of thinking.

Develop coaches' skills

Effective coaches exhibit high-level skills in listening, observing, and questioning that help their coachees become more thoughtful and reflective. They skillfully guide coachees through a process of understanding the problems they encounter and help them see options to achieve their goals. Successful coaches develop precise skills, including the ability to lead adults to learn, use targeted questioning to help coachees overcome learning barriers, and employ effective strategies that get them to commit to new skills and behaviors. Most important, coaches are skilled in helping coachees set their own goals, determine conditions of satisfaction, learn new skills to help them achieve those goals, and commit to follow through (Psencik, 2011).

The district leaders who hire and develop a cadre of skilled coaches ensure that the coaches have adequate and ongoing support to develop and maintain their skills. Coaches need to belong to and meet regularly in their own learning community, just as all others in the organization meet in learning teams. Effective coaches practice coaching, share issues they are facing, and try new coaching strategies with each other. They may review tapes of coaching sessions so all can reflect on each other's work and offer feedback. As coaches learn from each other, simulate coaching sessions, and share their struggles, they further develop their skills and practice, which in turn helps the district leaders they are coaching grow.

Districts also may want to ensure that coaches are certified by the International Coach Federation

(ICF). This organization has established standards coaches must meet in order to receive the organization's endorsement and certification. Although using certified organizations to train coaches can be expensive, it is not as expensive as a failed program. The ICF has approved several training organizations, including Coaching For Results Global, founded by Karen Anderson and

> Successful coaches develop precise skills, including the ability to lead adults to learn, use targeted questioning to help coachees overcome learning barriers, and employ effective strategies that get them to commit to new skills and behaviors.

Kathy Kee, and the Newfield Network, founded by Julio Olalla. These two organizations are fully certified and can provide intensive training and support for those who wish to coach. Both have websites that can help district leaders make wise decisions about whether to use an external resource. Learning Forward Center for Results also prepares and supports coaches who work predominantly with teachers and teacher leaders. Some districts may choose to send two or three aspiring coaches through these training programs to become fully certified so they then can assist in leading and facilitating professional learning for other coaches.

When a district focuses on professional learning and supports coaches, its coaching program is more likely to be successful and lead to satisfying results.

Coaching instills confidence to create stronger leaders

In 2009, when I took over at Abbett, I'd never been a principal or an assistant principal, and it was scary. The school was last in the state for 4th grade achievement, and just 21.7% of 3rd, 4th, and 5th graders passed both sections of the state standardized exam. We were in a spot where the school could have been closed. I hated that kids were running down the hallways yelling. I hated that when I said good morning, nobody even looked at me—the kids just walked by with their heads down or kept talking.

District central office administrators asked me, "What can we put in place to help this school?" One of the things they did was to assign coaches to me and other principals in each of the district's low-performing schools. I didn't really know what difference coaching would make—if it would be just one more thing I'd have to fit on my calendar or if it would help me turn the school around.

When the coach came, her attitude was, "What can I do to support you?" She helped me get down on paper my vision of what the school would look like in six weeks, in six months, and in a year, and what I would need to put in place to get there.

It wasn't about a coach telling me what I needed to do and saying, "This is how I perceive your problems." We spoke about what I saw, and she helped me form a plan and a system for reflecting on that plan. Later, she checked to see how I was doing. From the start, she made me feel confident in my abilities and in the idea that my staff and I could get there.

We planned staff training together to make sure that staff were on board. We tag-teamed off each other when we led meetings so everyone knew it wasn't about someone coming in to take charge but was a team effort. The intricacy of the planning stages with a coach helps you see the steps you need to take to get somewhere and gives you the freedom to make the changes as you go along because you can visualize the end prize.

Having the district provide me a coach gave me the confidence to feel good about what I was doing. My confidence, in turn, instilled confidence in those working for me because I was seen as someone who had a vision and plan for how to get there, which led to increased buy in from all the stakeholders.

After the first year, 45% of our children passed both math and language arts on the state standardized exam. In three years, we tripled the percentage of students passing. We cut discipline referrals the first year by 250%, not because we weren't writing them, but because behavior was that much better. I attribute the changes to the confidence the staff got from each other, from me, and from my coach. Having a coach made me a better leader.

— Robin Peterman
Abbett Elementary School principal
Fort Wayne (Ind.) Community Schools

Reflection
questions

- What do our district leaders do to ensure that they and the district's principals are skilled and successful so that all students achieve?

- Have we clearly defined the leadership skills we believe are essential for all our district administrators? Is our list based on research?

- What actions would we need to take to support all leaders with coaches?

- How can we strengthen our approach to long-term, systemic, professional learning for leaders?

- In what ways does the district support coaches' continuous professional learning and growth?

- Do we have a clear and effective process for hiring and assigning coaches?

RESOURCES

Beslin, R. & Reddin, C. (2006, January). Trust in your organization's future. *Communication World, 23*(1), 29.

Gorham, M., Finn-Stevenson, M., & Lapin, B. (2008). *Enriching school leadership development through coaching: Research and practice issue brief.* New Haven, CT: Yale University. Available at www.yale.edu/21C

Killion, J., Harrison, C., Bryan, C., & Clifton, H. (2012). *Coaching matters.* Oxford, OH: Learning Forward.

Killion, J. & Harrison, C. (2006). *Taking the lead: New roles for teachers and school-based coaches.* Oxford, OH: NSDC.

Leadership Innovations Team. (n.d.). *Leadership training and executive coaching: Ensuring new principal support is effective, consistent, and research based.* Available at www.slideshare.net/ptl/leadership-trainingand-executive-coaching-ensuring-new-principal-support-is-effective-consistent-and-researchbased

Mazzeo, V. (2003). *Issue Brief: Improving teaching and learning by improving school leadership.* Washington, DC: NGA Center for Best Practices.

Psencik, K. (2011). *The coach's craft: Powerful practices to support school leaders.* Oxford, OH: Learning Forward.

www.newfieldnetwork.com

www.coachingforresultsglobal.com

TOOLS INDEX

TOOL	TITLE	PURPOSE
22.1	Setting powerful goals	Deepen district and school leaders' understanding of the power of purposeful goals.
22.2	Listening as an essential tool for coaching	Help leaders listen more deeply as they coach by using an organizer for taking notes.
22.3	Observing the body	Note the coachee's coherence in body, language, and emotion.
22.4	Establishing a clearly articulated plan of action	Clearly articulate a plan with actions that the coachee commits to doing.
22.5	Strengthening coaching skills	Deepen your skills as a coach.

CHAPTER 23

Celebrating
progress

WHERE ARE WE NOW?

We purposefully celebrate successes in meaningful ways to honor work, energize teams, and build confidence.

| STRONGLY AGREE | AGREE | NO OPINION | DISAGREE | STRONGLY DISAGREE |

We value celebrations as essential components in the change process.

| STRONGLY AGREE | AGREE | NO OPINION | DISAGREE | STRONGLY DISAGREE |

All staff members feel their contributions are recognized, valued, honored, and celebrated.

| STRONGLY AGREE | AGREE | NO OPINION | DISAGREE | STRONGLY DISAGREE |

We set meaningful goals that allow us to celebrate milestones reached.

| STRONGLY AGREE | AGREE | NO OPINION | DISAGREE | STRONGLY DISAGREE |

Celebrations are authentic and meaningful to those involved.

| STRONGLY AGREE | AGREE | NO OPINION | DISAGREE | STRONGLY DISAGREE |

District leaders frequently feel an urgent need for change, and that feeling is regularly transmitted throughout the district to staff. A sense of urgency can inspire action, but without pauses, staff grow weary and frustrated with the change process and what they view as excessive work. They begin to feel insignificant in the decision-making process and feel their toil and effort is unappreciated.

In contrast, leaders of learning systems regularly pause to recognize good work in a meaningful way. Effective leaders understand that celebrating progress toward achieving a goal can have a major effect on future successes. This is particularly true if the district leadership team makes a routine of celebrating (Bolman & Deal, 2011).

Celebrations reignite the human spirit and propel staff toward even greater accomplishments. Celebrations can touch hearts and fire imaginations, bonding people together and connecting them to the organization's goals, vision, and values. Work takes on a new sense of meaning and joy. Staff members have a sense that leaders care about them and notice what they are going through. They can say with conviction, "We count!"

> Celebrations can touch hearts and fire imaginations, bonding people together and connecting them to the organization's goals, vision, and values. Work takes on a new sense of meaning and joy.

Richard DuFour and Robert Eaker (1998) suggest several reasons celebrations are important:
- Recipients feel noticed and appreciated.
- Celebrations signal what the organization views as important.

- Celebrations are "living examples of the values of the school in action" and model for others values they may want to express.
- Celebrations fuel momentum.
- Celebrations can infuse passion and commitment into the organization.

Research on motivation confirms that respect, encouragement, emotional support, affiliation, and recognition are the primary factors in improving motivation and creating a culture in which staff are sustained in their work to achieve key goals (Herzberg, 1966; McGregor, 1960). The progress principle (Amabile & Kramer, 2011) suggests that staff spirits are boosted when workers feel they are making progress, and that setting clear goals, providing the time and resources necessary to do the work, and recognizing small wins are the keys to sustaining motivation.

Educators in learning systems feel that they are making a difference. When they see that district leaders reward and celebrate progress, they are reenergized and recommit to the work.

Choose what to celebrate

To celebrate progress, district leaders must know what progress district and school teams have made. Effective district leaders partner with school principals and leadership teams to ensure that schools and teams have set clear goals and milestones grounded in a thoughtful theory of change, and that they are clear about what evidence will demonstrate that teachers are learning and changing their instruction. If teams have a clearly articulated goal and vision and a thoughtful plan of action, they will have clear milestones. Teams may even include celebrations in their action plans to ensure that they do not forget the commitment to recognize and honor members for achieving goals and implementing change efforts.

District leaders in a learning system routinely meet with individual principals and school leadership teams to discuss progress and the artifacts the school is using as evidence the school is achieving its goals. They are in schools regularly, visiting classrooms and talking to students. They talk to parents. They know the school culture and work with the leadership team to solve problems, question staff members' assumptions that are holding back the school, meet the school team's needs with resources, and help school leaders partner with others in the district who are succeeding at what the school is striving to accomplish.

The Twin Tiers Principals Coalition in Corning, New York, makes celebration a priority. Each year, participants in three of the coalition's active cohorts prepare and present short summaries, based on portfolio materials and other artifacts, of what they learned over the year. Area superintendents, community members who financially support the coalition, board members, and future participants attend the celebration. Diverse groups sit at round tables as participants share their work. Members of the year's graduating class wear T-shirts displaying the coalition logo and are recognized and honored.

When district leaders are closely connected to the schools, they are able to find reasons to celebrate in order to add meaning to staff endeavors.

Ritualizing symbols and creating a regular expectation for celebrations provide staff with outward markers of progress, just as holidays mark our calendars.

They may highlight the schools' work at the district level, sharing information in staff meetings and on websites. They may create symbolic celebrations that can help develop a district's or school's culture and link its past and future. Just as the gold watch at retirement used to be a standard form of recognition, the golden apple or bell award, when used consistently, can become a meaningful symbol of educational success. Ritualizing symbols and creating a regular expectation for celebrations provide staff with outward markers of progress, just as holidays mark our calendars.

Learning system leaders understand what Lee Bolman and Terrence Deal explain, that "symbolic forms and activities are the basic building blocks of culture, accumulated over time to shape an organization's unique identity and character. . . . Rituals and ceremonies provide scripts for celebrating success and facing calamity" (2008, pp. 277–278).

Make celebrations personal

Laughter, cheering, and storytelling solidify a culture of learning, change, and honor. In Watertown, Massachusetts, for example, after the bombing at the 2013 Boston marathon, people lined the streets cheering on police officers for their service in capturing the second bomber. Those service personnel were doing their jobs, but they needed and deserved the celebration of their work.

In learning systems, leadership teams know school leaders personally and let both leaders and other staff know how much they appreciate their efforts and progress.

They create celebrations that people authentically enjoy. Doing so may require involving others in designing the celebrations. What some believe are authentic celebrations can seem shallow to others. Having a collaborative team determine and design celebrations distributes leadership and helps leaders create forms of recognition that more participants will value. When people feel ownership, the recognition will be more meaningful and authentic.

In addition, involving more people's perspectives lessens the likelihood of something—or someone—being overlooked. In one school, for example, the leader took sole responsibility for starting a tradition of recognizing years of service. She was proud to hand out her award pins and announce each name, calling the individuals up and shaking their hands in front of all the staff members. In the end, though, she created more resentment than celebration in the room. She joyfully recognized every full-time and even part-time staff member, down to those who had worked in the school for just a year. But she overlooked the contributions of the contracted workers who had dutifully and faithfully served the school behind

Successful district leaders continually find reasons to celebrate and create celebrations that people authentically enjoy.

the scenes in the kitchen for decades, and who had been invited to sit in the meeting room for the awards celebration before punch was served.

Learning Forward staff members have an internal award and recognition system. Everyone shares "nice notes" that are accumulated into an annual PowerPoint presentation to share with the Board of Trustees. Staff members award each other ABCD certificates for going Above and Beyond the Call of Duty in service to another colleague. These are accompanied by a small gift certificate. Directors award staff members coveted Director Awards for finding ways to improve efficiency and effectiveness of Learning Forward operations and services. Each staff meeting includes celebrations of colleagues and their work.

Make celebrations authentic

Learning system leaders make celebrations meaningful and sincere. They understand that celebrations do not have to be elaborate. Celebrations may be simple, regular recognitions of good work and changes. A personal note, a certificate, a plaque, time away from lunch duty, public recognition, a small gift card, an allocation to offset the cost of attending a state or national association meeting, the opportunity to share in decision making, support for an idea, a potluck supper, an announcement to parents in the school or district newsletter, a pat on the back on the district website, a bulletin

Fort Wayne (Ind.) Community Schools elementary principals spent three years of intensive work to get every school to meet state expectations. At the beginning of a summer leadership institute, district leaders shared the data on student achievement and gave all an opportunity to tell what it was about their work that contributed to the district's success. The principals celebrated progress with toasting glasses filled with sparkling water. Everyone had an opportunity to enjoy the moment before the teams began new work.

board recognition, a media release—all are forms of recognition.

Bolman and Deal explain that celebrations recognize, but also add meaning to, an endeavor. They write (2008) that symbols give meaning to work, energize people, and weave together stories, rituals, heroes and heroines, and organizational myths that help people find the meaning and purpose of their work.

In contrast, a veiled attempt to encourage people to work harder by feinting a celebration defeats the purpose. Staff will see through a celebration with an underlying message that says, in effect, "We've made good progress, but it is time to redouble our efforts," and the negative impact on morale can affect productivity.

Learning system leaders let people know they are appreciated for their efforts and the progress they have made. If there has been no progress, there is no celebration. Ensuring that celebrations are authentic transmits the message to all that celebrating is valued and not a waste of time.

Reinvigorate staff by recognizing milestones

The Center for Advancement of Jewish Education in Miami is a system of autonomous schools. Each school's curriculum, approach, philosophy of Jewish learning is its own, yet we are the communal education agency responsible for high-quality educational leadership and service. About 10 years ago, we realized the key to changing the system is changing the quality of teaching in order to improve the quality of learning. Now we do not do anything without incorporating a professional learning piece into it.

We began a systematic approach with a learning academy for school leadership teams, bringing them together monthly to plan school improvement, determine student goals and achievement outcomes, and understand how to impact teacher outcomes.

We mentored school leaders, teachers to be teacher leaders, and coaches and started to change the culture of the whole system to develop a common language and common understanding. Everyone began to collaborate. We developed a shared understanding of what excellent teaching looks like. While the curriculum of each school may be different, the language of teaching outcomes and learning experience outcomes are a shared linkage.

Every time we came together, we worked through a piece of the specific school plan and celebrated incremental completions of achievement of each school's various goals by having that time and space to work together. To be valued as a professional, to learn from others, and to share your expertise is really affirming and validating. The opportunity to gather together in the middle of a workweek away from the hubbub reenergizes people and is a morale boost. We also use an online community platform where people shared stories of success.

Celebrations bring energy to the organization. They inspire others to share progress toward achieving goals. They help renew the shared vision and the passion for the work. The culmination of the academy experience was the Project Day School Excellence Celebration of Learning. We asked each leadership team to think over the past year's work and identify anecdotes or artifacts from key moments. Each of them prepared a journey map including the learning goal and rationale, key steps to develop shared vision around it, what they learned, their hopes, and artifacts that reflected progress.

They look at where they started and data collected over the year, and they put it together in a visual way. For example, at our last session, some school teams created a video of what was happening at their schools; others created a science board presentation. One school came up with an umbrella design and in each section of the umbrella put different ways in which the school progressed—the idea was it's raining professional learning at our school.

All the teams then share information through a gallery walk or in small groups and consider a set of questions:

- What was similar to your work?
- What was different from your work?
- What is one good idea you saw that might help your school as you move forward?
- What other schools might you be able to collaborate with?

We have learned that if you value and invest in staff and tie professional learning to student learning, it imparts value to the learning. When teachers feel that their talents are acknowledged and that their professional learning will help them solve or face challenges, they feel validated and motivated.

— Julie Lambert, director of professional learning initiatives, and
Valerie Mitrani, director of day school strategy and initiatives
CAJE, Miami

Reflection
questions

- How can we, as district leaders, strengthen celebration in our district?

- How do we model celebrations for schools?

- What celebrations may not seem authentic? In what ways can they be changed so honorees value them more?

- What are some simple, inexpensive ways to celebrate?

- How will we know that staff members feel recognized, honored, and valued?

RESOURCES

Ayres, R. (n.d.). *Celebrate this week.* Available at www.ruthayreswrites.com/p/celebrate-this-week.html

Deal, T. E. & Peterson, K. D. (1999). *Shaping school culture: The heart of leadership.* San Francisco, CA: Jossey-Bass.

Glasser, W. (2001). *Every student can succeed.* Chatsworth, CA: William Glasser, Inc.

Hodges, D. (2004). *Looking forward to Monday morning.* Thousand Oaks, CA: Corwin Press.

Hodges, D. (2007). *Looking forward to more Monday mornings.* Thousand Oaks, CA: Corwin Press.

Hodges, D. (2010). *Season it with fun: A year of recognition, fun and celebration.* Thousand Oaks, CA: Corwin Press.

Peterson, K. D. & Deal, T. (1998, September). How leaders influence the culture of schools. *Educational Leadership, 56*(1), 28–30.

TOOLS INDEX

TOOL	TITLE	PURPOSE
23.1	Celebration of learning	Use this structure to host thoughtful conversations about goals and what staff has accomplished.
23.2	A dozen reasons to celebrate	Reflect on accomplishments from the first few months of school.
23.3	Celebration brainstorming	Learn about and discuss the rationale for having regular celebrations.
23.4	What's your celebration IQ?	Consider how often you recognize staff members' efforts using this rating scale.
23.5	Celebration chart	Plan together how to improve your culture with regular celebrations.

CHAPTER 24

Innovations in adult learning

WHERE ARE WE NOW?

Our district and school communities nurture innovation and creativity in staff and students to positively impact student learning.

STRONGLY AGREE AGREE NO OPINION DISAGREE STRONGLY DISAGREE

We have redesigned the curriculum to meet the needs of tomorrow's students.

STRONGLY AGREE AGREE NO OPINION DISAGREE STRONGLY DISAGREE

Our instructional design for students and adults is based on inquiry and real-world problem solving.

STRONGLY AGREE AGREE NO OPINION DISAGREE STRONGLY DISAGREE

Our district and school communities maximize technology to strengthen our district as a learning system.

STRONGLY AGREE AGREE NO OPINION DISAGREE STRONGLY DISAGREE

We are in regular contact with educators in other districts in the nation and abroad to continuously learn about practices that may help us improve.

STRONGLY AGREE AGREE NO OPINION DISAGREE STRONGLY DISAGREE

Our school district staff members are energized and eager to learn.

STRONGLY AGREE AGREE NO OPINION DISAGREE STRONGLY DISAGREE

In the last few decades, mandates—mandated hours of instruction, mandated testing and evaluation systems, and prescribed textbooks—have driven driven what teachers and students experience in the classroom. These efforts, implemented in good faith to raise standards and expectations for all students, generally have been no more effective than strategies used previously. Data suggest that students, parents, and staff are less satisfied with education. More students are dropping out of school in some states, and student learning has not increased significantly (Rampey, Dion, & Donahue, 2008; Chapman, Laird, Ifill, & Kewal, 2011; Grady & Bielick, 2010).

On the other hand, creativity, flexibility, innovation, respect, and resilience can open doors for educators to a different, more democratic way of engaging students and inspiring them to learn. Student learning drives what educators must learn, and so any innovation must begin with instruction and instructional practices. Educators are faced with the task of creating an environment that can harness students' wisdom, creativity, and intellect. New approaches to educating students demand that teachers work and learn together in community. Collaboratively, in a learning system, they must rethink curriculum design, understand and use inquiry as an instructional approach, build smart teams, strengthen their own professional learning through technology, share ideas with districts across the nation and around the world, and come to implement innovative learning systems.

Rethink curriculum design

Rather than taking an approach to student and educator learning that is based on programs and reading series, what if educators explored different strategies that engaged students in purposeful, intriguing inquiry? What if student communities worked in the school *and* the community with experts to solve problems by applying skills they learned?

The 21st Century Partnership has called for new approaches to teaching and learning, supported by researchers including Linda Darling-Hammond (2008), and Neal Finkelstein, Thomas Hanson, Chun-Wei Huang, Becca Hirschman, and Min Huang (2010). They propose problem-based, project-based instruction that requires an integrated curriculum based on real-world applications. These researchers paint a compelling picture of the future in which students explore authentic issues and become assertive, inquisitive learners. One online study unit asks students to collaborate with same-age peers in other countries to examine the relationship between food and culture. Food, a common factor in socialization and community building for thousands of years, is an entry point for learning and developing a global perspective. Younger students focus on nature, gardening, cooking, and nutrition and fitness—along with cultural studies—to develop multiple literacies (financial, media-related, and ecological). Older students also explore media literacy, as well as topics such as the evolution of the supermarket, health issues, hunger, cultural similarities and differences, traditions, economics, agriculture, food production, law, environmental studies, cookbooks, literature, and celebrations of life and death.

How would a vastly different approach to curriculum design affect learning? When students no longer studied separate subject classes and Carnegie units of study, educator learning would look very different.

Understand and use inquiry as an instructional approach

A student-centered approach to curriculum develops young people's natural curiosity and passion to explore. By structuring learning around authentic tasks, questions, and problems, students have opportunities for greater intellectual engagement.

However, to make the engagement productive, the connection between the topic or task and the intended learning goals must be clear. Simply developing authentic learning opportunities is not enough to guarantee that students will successfully meet the standards (Darling-Hammond, 2008).

Inquiry-based learning is not a new technique—it goes back at least as far as education philosopher John Dewey—but it represents a stark contrast to the structured, curriculum-centered framework used in most schools. Grant Wiggins and Jay McTighe have worked to lead the field to concept-based approaches to learning, helping educators develop enduring understandings and essential questions that promote authentic inquiry. Both educators and students become more active, engaged learners when they explore together the essential questions derived from educators' deepening understanding of what students need to know (Wiggins & McTighe, 2005).

Develop smart teams

Perhaps the most innovative strategy for developing inquiry-based learning is for districts to focus on developing team intelligence. Creating schools and districts built around effective, collaborative teams that harness their members' combined talents results in innovations and solutions to current challenges.

Forming teams is not enough, however. Developing group intelligence requires deliberate actions. Collaborative teams begin their work by developing clear goals and expectations, and then set norms, define the different roles group members can play, clarify the group's decision-making authority, and create focused agendas (Garmston with von Frank, 2012). Higher-performing groups take these actions:

- Ensure that group members carefully consider information from one another as potentially useful.

- Allow equal input from every member.
- Engage in dialogue in the form of a free flow of ideas that build on one another's thoughts.
- Allow constructive critiques that offer concrete ideas to improve a process or idea, never about or judging an individual.

(Garmston with von Frank, 2012)

Improved communication is one element of developing a team's collective intelligence, says Anita Woolley, assistant professor of organizational behavior and theory at Carnegie Mellon University. "Two people can be saying the same thing, but if one person is communicating more effectively, it's actually going to have more of a benefit for the group. . . . There are some groups where people are saying smart things, but it's not finding its way into the group's work" (von Frank, 2013, p. 1).

Collective intelligence is important to "the group's ability to engage in complex cognitive work that results in improved outcomes," write Robert Garmston and Valerie von Frank. "Groups, particularly groups that develop their collective intelligence, are a tremendous force both for change at the individual level and in the ability to affect organizational issues" (2012, p. 5).

Strengthen professional learning through technology

Today's technology provides powerful opportunities for interaction and sharing. Videotaped lessons are one way to initiate professional learning conversations about lesson design and effect. Teaching Channel, for example, enables teachers and teacher leaders to work together through its private collaboration platform. Teachers can add to and customize their learning using a library of high-quality videos to help understand new instructional strategies, test the strategies in their own classrooms, and reflect on their practice in a safe, secure environment, all with the goal of improving student learning. Teaching Channel has partnered with the

Chicago-based Academy of Urban School Leadership to use video to increase teacher effectiveness and to pair teachers across the district. Teachers not only have access to Teaching Channel videos, they also upload and annotate their own videos. Teacher mentors and coaches reflect on the videotaped lessons, sharing ideas across the district. Teachers value the opportunity to observe their own teaching and appreciate partnering with colleagues across the district to share ideas.

Technology also provides multiple opportunities to build relationships with others not close geographically. Establishing sustainable, online learning communities of school boards, administrators, teachers, and leadership teams strengthens professional learning. Social networks allow learning communities to form around concerns and special interests or more general needs.

Share ideas with districts across the nation and around the world

Another hopeful opportunity for districts is to develop "sister districts" in order to learn from each other, share strategies, and benchmark against partners.

In 2005, Specialist Schools and Academies Trust in the United Kingdom approached Andy Hargreaves and Dennis Shirley to establish a network of underperforming schools. The network included 300 schools in a project named Raising Achievement and Transforming Learning. A key transformational element involved connecting the schools through conferences, programs, and interventions. The organization used Web portals to link adults and students from across the schools to exchange study strategies. Another key element was mentoring schools and school leaders. Mentor schools presented at conferences, and participants had opportunities to network with them, set up visits, and learn from exemplars.

When educators learn together and support each other, they exchange strategies and implement innovations. Sharing with each other helps all become smarter.

Implement innovative learning systems

Over the past 50 years, the Pentagon's Defense Advanced Research Projects Agency (DARPA) has been responsible for the most consistent record of radical inventions in history, including the Internet, global positioning satellites (GPS), stealth technology, unmanned aerial vehicles (drones), and micro-electromechanical systems now used in everything from air bags to ink jet printers to video games such as the Wii (Dugan & Gabriel, 2013).

DARPA has autonomy in selecting, planning, and running projects. Such independence allows the organization to move fast and take bold risks. The agency's projects are designed to harness science and engineering advances to solve real-world problems and create new opportunities. The problems must be sufficiently challenging that they cannot be solved without catalyzing the science.

Most of those leading the projects hold Ph.D.s, have five to 10 years of experience, and have made important contributions such as delivering a product to market, successfully leading a university research center, or starting a company. These midcareer leaders must have the confidence to recruit people who are older and more accomplished. The organization brings together world-class experts from industry and academia to work on projects. The projects' intensity, sharp focus, and finite time frame make them attractive to the highest-caliber talent, and the challenges involved inspire unusual levels of collaboration. This proves true even when a project's scope is narrow and its budget modest.

Planning is nimble and flexible. Leaders assess progress by tracking iterations to see whether they are converging on goals, revealing dead ends, and uncovering new applications. Business degrees, which focus on mastering specific skill sets and writing and faithfully executing business plans, are not helpful. These expert leaders of innovation focus instead on managing constant flux, changing tactics, and moving talent in and out.

Many in the public and private sectors have tried to replicate DARPA's processes, with little success. According to Regina Dugan and Kaigham Gabriel (2013), the efforts failed because the critical and mutually reinforcing elements of the DARPA model were not understood and, as a result, were not adopted. The DARPA model is ambitious, sets compelling goals, employs project teams, and offers an independent approach to problem solving.

Hope for the future

Innovative learning leaders challenge the status quo. They are not satisfied with "good enough" and instead benchmark their work against that of the best models of innovation in the world. They see no limits to the possibilities of educating children, and they continuously look for and create innovative solutions to learning barriers that keep an organization stuck.

The greatest innovation for a school district's future is for leaders to embrace and implement an authentic learning system. When leaders own the vision of becoming a high-quality learning system, ground all their actions in the beliefs and assumptions that undergird that vision, and use Learning Forward's Standards for Professional Learning as a guide, they can dramatically increase the learning of all staff and students.

Learning system leaders agree on how to assess proposed changes or innovations. They get everyone to the table to discuss opportunities. When educators know that decisions are made using agreed-upon criteria rather than individual authority, they are more willing to invest in the conversation. Shared decision making and leadership are essential to moving from blocking change to championing change.

Learning system leaders give teams the freedom to innovate, move away from training educators to simply use existing materials and toward deepening their understanding of how children and adults learn, and design systems that allow "special forces" in schools to address real issues. They develop leaders who deeply understand learning and the systems that nurture it.

For too long, educators have failed to value innovation or inspire creativity. In a fast-paced, complex world, everything we thought we knew is being challenged. To succeed, we must embrace change and adopt practices that help all students learn rather than focusing on whatever program or initiative is new this year. Instead of obstructing student learning, we must facilitate new ways of engaging students in their own learning.

Becoming a learning system means giving every adult working in a school the opportunity to live the dream of being part of a compelling, mission-driven community that establishes a norm of learning for all. It means authentically partnering with everyone in the school community—board members, the superintendent, principals, school leadership team members, faculty, staff, students, and parents—in strong relationships that value learning, ensuring that the necessary resources are available and capitalizing on the skills and talents of everyone in the organization.

The best hope with the greatest promise for the future is that we fully embrace the concept of the learning system and act regularly and with fidelity on its principles, vision, and standards.

Hard work, expectations take students to new heights

BASIS Tucson North is a 5th–12th grade school that is part of a national network of 16 schools. We are one of the most diverse schools, with about 50% white, approximately 25% Hispanic, 20% Asian, and 5% other. We do not collect socio-economic data, but anecdotally, one-third of the graduating class of 2013 qualified for an SAT fee waiver, and based on the zip codes in which our students live, about four in 10 may have median household incomes of less than $30,000.

In the 2011 pilot trial of the OECD Test for Schools (based on PISA), Tucson North outscored Shanghai, Finland, Singapore, and Korea in math, reading, and science. The school has been recognized by *Newsweek, U.S. News and World Report,* and *The Washington Post* for the quality of our education.

Our lower school curriculum includes courses in classics, Latin, physics, chemistry, biology, algebra, U.S. and world history, English, martial arts, and fine arts. To graduate high school, each student must take and pass at least six Advanced Placement exams, including at least one each in English, social science, hard science, and math. Across the board, we have heightened expectations for students.

As a charter school in Arizona, we look for teachers who have degrees in the content area of what they're teaching and then train them in pedagogy. BASIS has a weeklong summer institute for all new teachers run by experienced teachers from our schools who have come through the system. For example, I was an English teacher and now regularly give a seminar on teaching critical thinking skills. All our new teachers also read Doug Lemov's *Teach Like A Champion: 49 Techniques that Put Students on the Path to College* for basic classroom strategies.

We have experienced teachers mentor teachers in each school, either formally or informally. More experienced teachers may observe in the classroom and give feedback to another teacher or to the head of school.

With our curriculum, our teachers are resources and collaborate to develop the minimum requirements for each grade and subject. After all, some of them have Ph.D.s in the subject area they are teaching.

At Tucson North, our high school teachers and lower school teachers share with one another in department meetings. Rather than having an all-school faculty meeting each week, we alternate with having department meetings run by different teachers each time.

A lot of natural vertical teaming occurs for teachers' learning. Even the person who teaches 5th grade English is well aware of what the necessary skills are for kids when they take AP English Language or AP English Literature, so they are really thinking about when those skills should be planted, when they should be reviewed, and when they should be reinforced. They are always thinking beyond their own grade level. And we're always hiring smart people who come in with new ideas for how things could be even better.

In addition, teachers who are interested in thinking BASISwide about the curriculum become subject advisers. Mentoring then happens across the schools. Usually that occurs through email, and we are developing a web portal for teachers to share materials and resources.

Our culture at Tucson North is very collaborative. With 50 faculty members, we are small enough and the background of the people we hire is similar enough that we organically have become a close community.

— Julia Toews, head of school
    BASIS Tucson North

Reflection
questions

- Where are pockets of innovation in our district and school communities? In what ways are we nurturing creative approaches?

- In what ways can we, as members of a leadership team, inspire innovation and creativity in our district and school community?

- How do we work to understand which skills our kindergarteners may need when they graduate and adjust to meet their needs?

- What first steps do we need to take to enable our community to engage in more authentic learning?

- How can we connect closely and immediately with educators in districts around the nation and the world to increase our mutual learning and understanding?

RESOURCES

Bellanca, J. A. & Brandt, R. (Eds.). (2010). *21st-century skills: Rethinking how students learn.* Bloomington, IN: Solution Tree.

Hargreaves, A. & Shirley, D. (2009). *The fourth way: The inspiring future for educational change.* Thousand Oaks, CA: Corwin Press.

Neal, D., Ringler, M. C., Lysol, D. B. (Fall, 2009). Skeptics to partners: University teams with district to improve ELL instruction. *JSD, 30*(4), 52–55.

November, A. (2012). *Who owns the learning? Preparing students for success in the Digital Age.* Bloomington, IN: Solution Tree.

Sizer, T. R. (2013). *The new American high school.* San Francisco, CA: Jossey-Bass.

TOOLS INDEX

TOOL	TITLE	PURPOSE
24.1	Envisioning the future and skills students need to know	Develop a clear vision of the world so participants understand the challenges graduates will face as they leave school and enter the work world.
24.2	Mind mapping	Generate ideas and make connections to the organization's current design to ensure new ideas are successful.
24.3	Scenario planning	Encourage departments, schools, and district teams to pose and respond to provocative questions that generate new ideas.
24.4	Encouraging innovation through exchange program	Establish exchange programs in which teachers and students work in industry in their field and business employees share their expertise with students; all create new and innovative ideas for ensuring all students are successful.

Learning Forward's
Seven-Step Cycle of Continuous Improvement

The Learning Communities Standard has three major aspects:

1. The community develops collective responsibility for student learning.
2. The community is results oriented.
3. Community members are judicious about aligning adult learning goals with student learning goals and holding one another accountable.

As the community engages in a cycle of continuous improvement, these aspects become fully developed. Moving through the cycle, learning community members persistently engage in inquiry, take part in action research, analyze data, plan, implement their learning, reflect, and evaluate results to ensure that what they want to accomplish—their goals, driven by data and focused on student learning—is central to all their work.

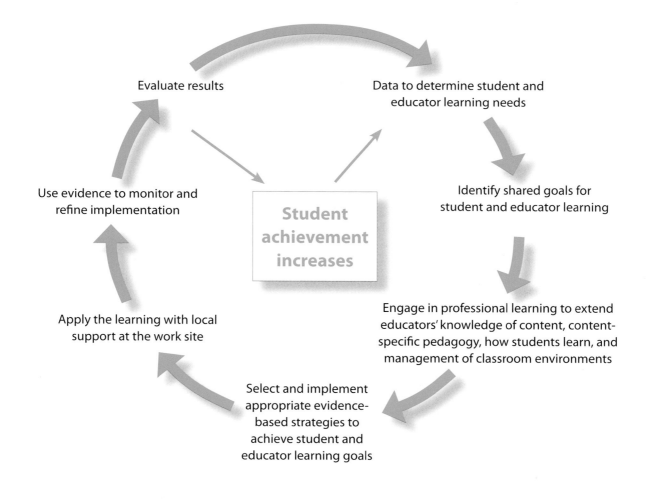

Evaluate results

Data to determine student and educator learning needs

Use evidence to monitor and refine implementation

Student achievement increases

Identify shared goals for student and educator learning

Apply the learning with local support at the work site

Engage in professional learning to extend educators' knowledge of content, content-specific pedagogy, how students learn, and management of classroom environments

Select and implement appropriate evidence-based strategies to achieve student and educator learning goals

References

Abrams, J. & von Frank, V. (2013). *The multigenerational workplace: Communicate, collaborate, and create community.* Thousand Oaks, CA: Corwin Press.

Ammabile, T. & Kramer, S. (2011). *The progress principle: Using small wins to ignite joy, engagement and creativity at work.* Boston, MA: Harvard Business Review Press.

American Museum of Natural History. (1999). *Shackleton: The expedition.* Available at www.amnh. org/exhibitions/past-exhibitions/shackleton

Armstrong, A. (2012, Summer). The art of feedback: Support observers with a system that ensures learning-focused conversations. *The Learning System, 7*(4), 1–7.

Bill & Melinda Gates Foundation. (2010). *Learning about teaching: Initial findings from the measures of effective teaching project.* Seattle, WA: Author. Available at www.metproject.org/downloads/Preliminary_Finding-Policy_Brief.pdf

Bolman, L. G. & Deal, T. E. (2008). *Reframing organizations: Artistry, choice, & leadership* (4th ed.). San Francisco, CA: Jossey-Bass.

Bolman, L. G. & Deal, T. E. (2011). *Leading with soul: An uncommon journey of spirit* (3rd ed.). San Francisco, CA: Jossey-Bass.

Bolman, L. G. & Deal, T. E. (2013). *Reframing organizations: Artistry, choice, & leadership* (5th ed.). San Francisco, CA: Jossey-Bass.

Bottoms, G. & Schmidt-Davis, J. (2010). *The three essentials: Improving schools requires district vision, district and state support, and principal leadership.* Atlanta, GA: SREB.

Burkhauser, S., Gates, S. M., Hamilton, L. S., & Ikemoto, G. S. (2012). *First-year principals in urban school districts: How actions and working conditions relate to outcomes* (p. 14). Washington, DC: RAND Corp.

Center for Educational Leadership & Honig, M. I. (2013). *Central office transformation toolkit.* Seattle, WA: University of Washington, Department of Education.

Council of the Great City Schools. (2010, Fall). Urban school superintendents: Characteristics, tenure, and salary. Seventh survey and report. *Urban Indicator,* pp. 1-12.

Chapman, C., Laird, J., Ifill, N., & KewalRamani, A. (2011). *Trends in high school dropout and completion rates in the United States: 1972–2009* (NCES 2012-006). Washington, DC: National Center for Education Statistics, Institute of Education Services, US Department of Education. Available at www. nces.ed.gov/pubs2012/2012006.pdf

Collins, J. (2001). *Good to great: Why some companies make the leap and others don't.* New York, NY: Harper Business.

Council of Chief State School Officers. (2008). *Educational leadership policy standards: ISLLC 2008.* Washington, DC: Author. Available at www.wallacefoundation.org/knowledge-center/school-leadership/principal-evaluation/Pages/Educational-Leadership-Policy-Standards-ISLLC-2008.aspx

Council of the Great City Schools. (2010, Fall). *Urban school superintendents: Characteristics, tenure, and salary.* Washington, DC: Author. Available at www.cgcs.org/cms/lib/DC00001581/Centricity/Domain/4/Supt_Survey2010.pdf

Covey, S. (1990). *The 7 habits of highly effective people.* New York, NY: Free Press.

Covey, S. (1992). *Principle-centered leadership.* New York, NY: Free Press.

Covey, S. M. R. with Merrill, R. R. (2008). *The speed of trust.* New York, NY: Free Press.

Crow, T. (2009, Fall). Q&A: Chris Steinhauser. *JSD, 30*(4), 56–60.

Daley-Harris, S. (1994). *Reclaiming democracy.* Philadelphia, PA: Camino Books.

Darling-Hammond, L. (2008). *Powerful learning: What we know about teaching for understanding.* San Francisco, CA: Jossey-Bass.

Darling-Hammond, L. (2012, November). The right start: Creating a strong foundation for the teaching career. *Phi Delta Kappan, 94*(3), 8–13.

Darling-Hammond, L., Wei, R. C., Andree, A., Richardson, L., & Arphonos, S. (2009). *Professional learning in the learning profession: A status report on teacher development in the United States and abroad.* Oxford, OH: NSDC.

Drago-Severson, E. (2011, October). How adults learn forms the foundation of the learning designs standard. *JSD, 32*(5), 10–12.

DuFour, R. & Eaker, R. (1998). *Professional learning communities at work: Best practices for enhancing student achievement.* Bloomington, IN: Solution Tree.

DuFour, R. & Marzano, R. J. (2011). *Leaders of learning: How district, school, and classroom leaders improve student achievement.* Bloomington, IN: Solution Tree.

Dugan, R. E. & Gabriel, K. J. (2013, October). "Special Forces" innovation: How DARPA attacks problems. *Harvard Business Review, 91*(10).

English, F. & Steffy, B. (2001). *Deep curriculum alignment: Creating a level playing field for all children on high-stakes tests of educational accountability.* Lanham, MD: Scarecrow Press.

Epstein, J. L. (2007, October). Connections count: Improving family and community involvement in secondary schools. *Principal Leadership, 8*(2), 16–22.

Ferguson, C., Jordan, C., & Baldwin, M. (2010). *Working systemically in action: Engaging family & community.* Austin, TX: SEDL. Available at www.sedl.org/ws/ws-fam-comm.pdf

Ferguson, C. with Ramos, M., Rudo, Z., & Wood, L. (2008). *The school-family connection: Looking at the larger picture.* Austin, TX: SEDL. Available at www.sedl.org/connections/resources/sfclitrev.pdf

Fink, S., Markholt, A., & Bransford, J. (2011). *Leading for instructional improvement: How successful leaders develop teaching and learning expertise.* San Francisco, CA: Jossey-Bass.

Finkelstein, N., Hanson, T., Huang, C. W., Hirschman, B., & Huang, M. (2010). *Effects of problem based economics on high school economics instruction.* (NCEE 2010-4002). Washington, DC: National Center for Education Evaluation and Regional Assistance, Institute of Education Sciences, US Department of Education. Available at www.ies.ed.gov/ncee/edlabs/regions/west/pdf/REL_20104012.pdf

Fritz, R. (1989). *The path of least resistance: Learning to become the creative force in your own life.* New York, NY: Ballantine Books.

Fullan, M. (2001). *Leading in a culture of change.* San Francisco, CA: Jossey-Bass.

Garmston, R. J. with von Frank, V. (2012). *Unlocking group potential to improve schools.* Thousand Oaks, CA: Corwin Press.

Grady, S. & Bielick, S. (2010). *Trends in the use of school choice: 1993 to 2007* (NCES 2010-004). Washington, DC: National Center for Education Statistics, Institute of Education Sciences, US Department of Education. Available at www.nces.ed.gov/pubs2010/2010004.pdf

Guskey, T. R. (2000). *Evaluating professional development.* Thousand Oaks, CA: Corwin Press.

Guskey, T. & Jung, L. A. (2012). *Answers to essential questions about standards, assessments, grading, and reporting.* Thousand Oaks, CA: Corwin Press.

Hall, G. & Hord, S. M. (2006). *Concerns-based adoption model.* Austin, Texas: SEDL.

Hord, S. M., Rutherford, W. L., Huling-Austin, L., & Hall, G. E. (1987). *Taking charge of change.* Alexandria, VA: ASCD.

Hamilton, L., Halverson, R., Jackson, S., Mandinach, E., Supovitz, J., & Wayman, J. (2009). *Using student achievement data to support instructional decision making* (NCEE 2009-4067). Washington, DC: National Center for Education Evaluation and Regional Assistance, Institute of Education Sciences, US Department of Education. Available at www.ies.ed.gov/ncee/wwc/pdf/practiceguides/ dddm_pg_092909.pdf

Hargreaves, A. & Fullan, M. (2012). *Professional capital: Transforming teaching in every school.* New York, NY: Teachers College Press.

Henderson, A. T. (2011). *Family–school–community partnerships 2.0: Collaborative strategies to advance student learning.* Washington, DC: National Education Association.

Henderson, A. T. & Mapp, K. L. (2002). *A new wave of evidence: The impact of school, family, and community connections on student achievement.* Austin, TX: SEDL. Available at www.sedl.org/connections/resources/evidence.pdf

Herzberg, F. (1966). *Work and the nature of man.* Cleveland, OH: World Publishing.

Hirsh, S. (2010). MetLife survey validates need to focus on continuous improvement of teachers (press release). Available at http://learningforward.org/who-we-are/announcements/press-releases/2010/02/23/metlife-survey-validates-need-to-focus-on-continuous-improvement-of-teachers#. U2ZOlV74QQQ

Hirsh, S. & Foster, A. W. (2013). *A school board guide to leading successful schools: Focusing on learning.* Thousand Oaks, CA: Corwin Press.

Hirsh, S. & Killion, J. (2007). *The learning educator: A new era for professional learning.* Oxford, OH: NSDC.

Honig, M. I. & Copland, M. (2008, September). *Reinventing district central offices to expand student learning* (*Issue Brief*). Available at http://eric.ed.gov/?q=Reinventing+district+central+offices+to+expand+student+learning&id=ED502905

Honig, M. I., Copland, M. A., Rainey, L., Lorton, J. A., & Newton, M. (2010). *Central office transformation for districtwide teaching and learning improvement.* Seattle, WA: Center for the Study of Teaching and Policy, University of Washington. Available at www.wallacefoundation.org/knowledge-center/school-leadership/district-policy-and-practice/Documents/Central-Office-Transformation-District-Wide-Teaching-and-Learning.pdf

Hoover-Dempsey, K. V., Walker, J. M. T., Sandler, H. M., Whetsel, D., Green, C. L., Wilkins, A. S., & Closson, K. (2005, November). Why do parents become involved? Research findings and implications. *The Elementary School Journal, 106*(2), 105–130.

Hord, S. M. (1997). *Professional learning communities: Communities of continuous inquiry and improvement.* Austin, TX: SEDL.

Hord, S. M., Rutherford, W. L., Huling-Austin, L., & Hall, G. E. (1987). *Taking charge of change.* Alexandria, VA: ASCD.

Horwitz, J., Hoy, L., & Bradley, J. (2011, February). Identity crisis: External coaches struggle to clarify roles and maintain focus on student learning. *JSD, 32*(1), 30–32.

Kagan, R. & Lahey, L. L. (2009). *Immunity to change: How to overcome it and unlock the potential in yourself and your organization.* Boston, MA: Harvard Business Press.

Kennedy, J. (2012, May). Design learning that drives satisfaction. *The Leading Teacher, 7*(6), 2.

Killion, J. (2008). *Assessing impact: Evaluating staff development* (2nd ed.). Thousand Oaks, CA: Corwin Press.

Killion, J. (2013). New education initiatives demand a new engine to drive them forward. *Education Week* blog. Available at http://blogs.edweek.org/edweek/learning_forwards_pd_watch/2013/09/new_education_initiatives_demand_a_new_engine_to_drive_them_forward.html

Killion, J. & Hirsh, S. (2011, December). The elements of effective teaching. *JSD, 32*(6), 10–16.

Killion, J. & Roy, P. (2008). *Becoming a learning school.* Oxford, OH: NSDC.

KIPP. (n.d.). *KIPP: School leadership programs.* Available at www.kippsa.org/join/teacherandslrecruiting/KIPP%20School%20Leadership%20Program%202010-11.pdf

Knight, J. (2007). *Instructional coaching: A partnership approach to improving instruction.* Thousand Oaks, CA: Corwin Press.

Knowles, M. S. (1973). *The adult learner: A neglected species.* Houston, TX: Gulf Publishing.

Koch, S. & Borg, T. (2011, February). Real-time learning, real-world teaching: University teams with school district to improve curriculum and instruction. *JSD, 32*(1), 26–29.

Lachman, A. & Wlodarczyk, S. (2011, February). Partners at every level: From the classroom to the boardroom, consultants work toward district's goals. *JSD, 32*(1), 16–19.

Learning Forward. (2011). *Standards for Professional Learning* (2nd ed.). Oxford, OH: Learning Forward.

Learning Forward. (2012). *Standards into practice: School-based roles.* Oxford, OH: Learning Forward.

Learning Forward. (2013). *Comprehensive professional learning system: A workbook for states and districts.* Oxford, OH: Learning Forward.

Leithwood, K., Seashore Louis, K., Anderson, S., & Wahlstrom, K. (2004). *How leadership influences student learning.* New York, NY: The Wallace Foundation.

Loehr, J. & Schwartz, T. (2005). *The power of full engagement: Managing energy, not time, is the key to high performance and personal renewal.* New York, NY: Free Press.

Loucks-Horsley, S., Hewson, P., Love, N., & Stiles, K. E. (1998). *Designing professional development for teachers of science and mathematics.* Thousand Oaks, CA: Corwin Press.

Luebchow, L. (2009). *Equitable resources in low-income schools.* Washington, DC: New America Foundation. Available at www.newamerica.net/publications/policy/equitable_resources_low_income_schools

McGregor, D. (1960). *The human side of enterprise.* New York, NY: McGraw-Hill.

Mansell, W., James, M., & the Assessment Reform Group. (2009). *Assessment in schools. Fit for purpose? A commentary by the Teaching and Learning Research Programme.* London, UK: Economic and Social Research Council, Teaching and Learning Research Programme.

Marland, J. (2010). *Student achievement gains for school leader network cluster regions.* New York, NY: School Leaders Network.

Marzano, R. J. (2010). *Formative assessment & standards-based grading: Classroom strategies that work.* Bloomington, IN: Solution Tree.

Marzano, R. J. (2012, November). The two purposes of teacher evaluation. *Educational Leadership, 70*(3), 14-19.

Marzano, R. J. & Waters, T. (2009). *District leadership that works: Striking the right balance.* Bloomington, IN: Solution Tree.

Marzano, R. J., Waters, T., & McNulty, B. A. (2005). *School leadership that works: From research to results.* Alexandria, VA: ASCD.

Mendels, P. (2012, June). Principals in the pipeline: Districts construct a framework to develop school leaders. *JSD, 33*(3), 48–52.

MetLife Foundation. (2012). *MetLife survey of the American teacher: Challenges for school leadership.* New York, NY: Author. Available at www.metlife.com/metlife-foundation/about/survey-american-teacher.html?WT.mc_id=vu1101

Mizell, H. M. (2008, November). Superintendent's leadership needed to turn battleship of district's vision. *The Learning System, 4*(3), 2.

Mizell, H. M. (2010, December). Thought leaders: Who they are, why they matter, and how to reach them. *JSD, 31*(6), 46-51.

Mizell, H. M. (2011, Winter). Develop a clear and unified vision of professional learning's purpose. *The Learning System, 6*(2), 2.

Moll, L. C., Amanti, C., Neff, D., & Gonzalez, N. (1992, Spring). Funds of knowledge for teaching: Using a qualitative approach to connect homes and classrooms. *Theory Into Practice, 31*(2), 132–141.

Morris, A. K. & Hiebert, J. (2011, January/February). Creating shared instructional products: An alternative approach to improving teaching. *Educational Researcher, 40*(1), 5–14.

Munger, L. (2006). Evaluation of the Twin Tiers Principals Coalition, New York. (Study commissioned by the National Staff Development Council). Unpublished raw data.

National Association of Secondary School Principals. (2007). *NASSP board position statement: Highly effective principals.* Alexandria, VA: Author. Available at www.nassp.org/Content.aspx?topic=55879

National College for School Leadership. (November 27-28, 2012). School leadership for a self-improving system: Seminar report. Nottingham, UK: Author.

National Education Association. (n.d.). *Collective bargaining: What it is and how it works* (pp. 1–3). Available at www.nea.org/assets/docs/120701-CBWhatisitandHow-itWorks-3page.pdf

National School Boards Association. (n.d.) The key work of school boards. Available at www.nsba.org/services/school-board-leadership-services/key-work-school-boards

National Staff Development Council. (2010). *Advancing high-quality professional learning through collective bargaining and state policy: An initial review and recommendations to support student learning.* Oxford, OH: Author.

Neale, E. & Cone, M. (2013, Spring). Strong principal networks influence school culture. *The Learning Principal, 8*(3), 1, 4–5.

Odden, A. (2011, August). Resources. *JSD, 32*(4), 26–27, 29–32.

Peterson, K. D. & Cosner, S. (2005, Spring). Teaching your principal: Top tips for the professional development of the school's chief. *JSD, 26*(2), 28–32.

Peterson, K. D. & Deal, T. E. (1998). How leaders influence the culture of schools, *Educational Leadership, 56*(1), 28–30.

Pink, D. H. (2011). *Drive: The surprising truth about what motivates us.* New York, NY: Riverhead Books.

Psencik, K. (2009). *Accelerating student and staff learning: Purposeful curriculum collaboration.* Thousand Oaks, CA: Corwin Press.

Psencik, K. (2011). *The coach's craft: Powerful practices to support school leaders.* Oxford, OH: Learning Forward.

Rampey, B. D., Dion, G. S., & Donahue, P. L. (2009). *The nation's report card: Trends in academic progress in reading and mathematics 2008.* Available at http://nces.ed.gov/nationsreportcard/pubs/main2008/2009479.asp

Rasmussen, C. T. & Karschney, K. (2012, June). A tapestry of inquiry and action: Cycle of learning weaves its way through Washington district. *JSD, 33*(3), 10–14.

Rivkin, S. G., Hanushek, E. A., & Kain, J. F. (2005, March). Teachers, schools, and academic achievement. *Econometrica, 73*(2), 417–458.

Rowan, C. (2013, August 1). *The value of setting clear expectations.* Available at www.tac-focus.com/article/value-setting-clear-expectations#.U2mF0xaGmwI

Salim, K. (2012, October). With a focus on standards, coherence, and outcomes, we can realize ambitious and necessary goals. *JSD, 33*(5), 69.

Schmoker, M. (1999). *Results: The key to continuous school improvement* (2nd ed.). Alexandria, VA: ASCD.

Seashore Louis, K., Leithwood, K., Wahlstrom, K., & Anderson, S. E. (2010). *Investigating the links to improved student learning: Final report of research findings.* Minneapolis, MN: University of Minnesota.

Senge, P. (1990). *The fifth discipline.* New York, NY: Doubleday.

Southern Regional Education Board. (2010). *The three essentials: Improving schools requires district vision, district and state support, and principal leadership.* Atlanta, GA: SREB/The Wallace Foundation. Available at www.publications.sreb.org/2010/10V16_Three_Essentials.pdf

Spanneut, G. & Ford, M. (2008, Spring). Guiding hand of the superintendent helps principals flourish. *JSD, 29*(2), 28–32.

Sparks, D. (2003, Winter). Transformational learning. *Journal of Staff Development, 24*(1), 29.

Sparks, D. (2007). *Leading for results: Transforming teaching, learning, and relationships in schools* (2nd ed.). Thousand Oaks, CA: Corwin Press.

Spiro, J. (2012, April). Winning strategy: Set benchmarks of early success to build momentum for the long term. *JSD, 33*(2), 10–16.

Stiggins, R. (2008). *A call for the development of balanced assessments.* Portland, OR: Educational Testing Service.

Stover, D. (2012, April 20). Board and superintendent evaluations key to improvement. *School Board News Today.* Available at www.schoolboardnews.nsba.org/2012/04/board-and-superintendent-evaluations-key-to-improvement/

Tallerico, M. (2011). *Leading curriculum improvement: Fundamentals for school principals.* Lanham, MD: R&L Education.

Teacher Leadership Exploratory Consortium. (2011). *Teacher leader model standards.* Available at www.teacherleaderstandards.org

Tobia, E., Chauvin, R., Lewis, D., & Hammel, P. (2011, February). The light bulb clicks on: Consultants help teachers, administrators, and coaches see the value of learning in teams. *JSD, 32*(1), 22–25, 29.

Turnbull, B. J., Riley, D. L., Arcaira, E. R., Anderson, L. M., & MacFarlane, J. R. (2013). *Building a stronger principalship: Six districts begin the principal pipeline initiative* (p. 18). Washington, DC: Policy Studies Associates.

Viscio, V., Ross, D., & Adams, A. (2008, January). A review of research on the impact of professional learning communities on teaching practice and student learning. *Teaching and Teacher Education, 24*(1), 80–91.

Von Frank, V. (2011, August). The budget speaks volumes about priorities. *JSD, 32*(4), 28.

Von Frank, V. (2013a, Winter). Evaluations serve as pathways for professional growth: Teacher-led teams help build evaluation system that promotes learning. *The Learning System, 8*(2), 1, 4–5.

Von Frank, V. (2013b, Winter). The power of observation: 5 ways to ensure teacher evaluations lead to teacher growth. *The Learning Principal, 8*(2), 1, 4–5.

The Wallace Foundation. (2012). *The school principal as leader: Guiding schools to better teaching and learning.* New York, NY: Author.

Wang, Y. L., Frechtling, J. A., & Sanders, W. L. (1999, April). *Exploring linkages between professional development and student learning: A pilot study.* Paper presented at the annual meeting of the American Educational Research Association, Montreal.

Warren, M. R. & Mapp, K. L. (2011). *A match on dry grass: Community organizing as a catalyst for school reform.* New York, NY: Oxford University Press.

Waters, J. T. & Marzano, R. J. (2006). *School district leadership that works: The effect of superintendent leadership on student achievement.* Denver, CO: Mid-continent Research for Education and Learning.

Waters, J. T., Marzano, R. J. & McNulty, T. (2004, Winter). McREL's balanced leadership framework: Developing the science of educational leadership. *ERS Spectrum, 22*(1), 4–13.

Westmoreland, H., Rosenberg, H. M., Lopez, E., & Weiss, H. (2009). *Seeing is believing: Promising practices for how school districts promote family engagement.* Washington, DC: PTA and Harvard Family Research Project.

Wheatley, M. (1992). *Leadership and the new science: Learning about organization from an orderly universe.* San Francisco, CA: Berrett-Koehler.

Wheatley, M. J. (2009). *Turning to one another: Simple conversations to restore hope to the future* (expanded 2nd ed.). San Francisco, CA: Berrett-Koehler.

Wiggins, G. & McTighe, J. (2005). *Understanding by design* (2nd ed.). Upper Saddle River, NJ: Pearson.

Wiseman, L. with McKeown, G. (2010). *Multipliers: How the best leaders make everyone smarter.* New York, NY: Harper Collins Publishers.

Yoon, K. S., Duncan, T., Lee, S. W. Y., Scarloss, B., & Shapley, K. (2007). *Reviewing the evidence on how teacher professional development affects student achievement* (Issues & Answers Report, REL 2007– No. 033). Washington, DC: U.S. Department of Education, Institute of Education Sciences, National Center for Education Evaluation and Regional Assistance, Regional Educational Laboratory Southwest. Retrieved from http://ies.ed.gov/ncee/edlabs

About the Authors

Stephanie Hirsh is executive director of Learning Forward. Learning Forward is an international association of more than 12,000 learning educators committed to one purpose in K–12 education: Every educator engages in effective professional learning every day so every student achieves.

Hirsh presents, publishes, and consults on Learning Forward's behalf across North America. Her books include *A Playbook for Professional Learning: Putting the Standards Into Action,* co-authored with Shirley Hord (Learning Forward, 2012); *The Learning Educator: A New Era for Professional Learning,* co-authored with Joellen Killion (NSDC, 2007); and *Transforming Schools Through Powerful Planning,* co-authored with Kay Psencik, (NSDC, 2004). Hirsh writes a regular column for *JSD,* Learning Forward's bimonthly magazine. She also has written articles for *Educational Leadership, Phi Delta Kappan, The Record, The School Administrator, American School Board Journal, The High School Magazine,* and *Education Week.*

Hirsh serves on advisory boards for Learning First Alliance, Region IX (Arizona) Equity Assistance Center, Chalkboard (Oregon) Project

CLASS Program; the University of Texas College of Education Advisory Council; and The Teaching Channel. She has been recognized by the Texas Staff Development Council with a Lifetime Achievement Award, by the University of North Texas as a Distinguished Alumna, and by the Texas Association of School Boards as Master Trustee and member of an Honor Board.

Prior to joining Learning Forward, Hirsh completed 15 years of district and school-based leadership. In 2005, she completed three terms as a school board trustee in the Richardson Independent School District. She has been married to Mike for more than 35 years. They have one son and a daughter who is an elementary school teacher.

Kay Psencik is a senior consultant for Learning Forward, specializing in facilitating strategic planning, helping schools develop professional learning communities, and supporting teams of teachers developing standards-driven curriculum, assessment, and instructional plans. She also coaches

teachers, principals, and district leaders in schools throughout the United States and around the world.

Psencik served more than a decade in strategic leadership positions in the Austin, Temple, and Belton Independent School Districts in Texas. In assistant, associate, and deputy superintendent positions, she honed her deep knowledge of curriculum and instruction and of leadership development. She began her career as a high school English teacher and spent nearly 15 years in the classroom, twice being recognized as Teacher of the Year. She has received numerous other awards, including Excellence in Leadership from Baylor University. She has taught graduate-level leadership development and curriculum design courses at the University of Texas at Austin and Texas A & M University.

Psencik has her doctorate in educational administration from Baylor, her master's in educational administration from Southwest Texas State University, and a bachelor's degree from the University of Mary Hardin-Baylor.

She is the author of *The Coach's Craft: Powerful Practices to Support School Leaders* (2011, Learning Forward), *Accelerating Student and*

Staff Learning: Purposeful Curriculum Collaboration (Corwin Press, 2009), *Transforming Schools Through Powerful Planning,* co-authored with Stephanie Hirsh (NSDC, 2004), and has published numerous articles in *JSD, Educational Leadership, The School Administrator,* and other education publications.

Frederick Brown is Learning Forward's director of strategy and development. Prior to joining Learning Forward, he served as senior program officer for The Wallace Foundation, where he guided the work of several major grantees, including the Southern Regional Education Board, the Institute for Learning at the University of Pittsburgh, and the states of Ohio, Iowa, Wisconsin, Oregon, Kansas, and New Jersey.

Prior to joining The Wallace Foundation, Brown was director of the Leadership Academy and Urban Network for Chicago (LAUNCH), an organization whose mission was to identify, train, and support principals for the Chicago Public Schools. In 2005, LAUNCH was highlighted by the US Department of Education as an innovative pathway to the principalship.

Brown's expertise is grounded in real-world experience. He has been an elementary school

teacher and principal, as well as a middle school assistant principal. He also served as a founding member of the mathematics and equity teams for Ohio's Project Discovery, a statewide initiative to improve mathematics and science instruction.

Over the past 15 years, Brown has been a leader in designing and facilitating cutting-edge learning experiences for school and district administrators on topics such as cultural competence, leadership, and professional learning communities.